# Learning and Work and the Politics of Working Life

Large-scale changes in work and education are a key feature of contemporary global transformations, with a pervasive politics that affects people's experiences of workplaces and learning spaces.

This thought provoking book uses empirical research to question prevailing debates surrounding compliance at work, education and lifelong learning, and emphasises the importance of debate and dissent within the current terms and conditions of work. Examining a number of types of work, including teaching, nursing and social work, through a transnational research space, the contributors investigate how disturbances in work both constrain and enable collective identities in practical politics.

Structured around three main themes, the book covers:

- disturbed work: with cases of occupational reform in nursing and vocational teaching in Finland and re-regulating work in Australia;
- disturbing work: examining contested occupational knowledge in German school-to-work transitions, paraprofessional healthwork in the UK, social work in Finland, and mobilising professional expertise in US community college faculty and Australian adult literacy; and
- transforming politics: negotiating an ageing workforce in Germany, young adults moving through identities and careers, and building a politics of 'we' through a global book project.

An enlightening collection of international contributions, this book will appeal to all postgraduate students, researchers and policy makers in education, work and lifelong learning.

**Terri Seddon** is Professor of Education at Monash University, Australia, and Director for Work and Learning Studies.

**Lea Henriksson** is Docent in Social Policy and an Academy of Finland Research Fellow at the University of Tampere, Finland.

**Beatrix Niemeyer** is Docent (PD) in Educational Science and Senior Researcher at the Institute of Vocational Education, University of Flensburg, Germany.

# Learning and Work and the Politics of Working Life

## Global transformations and collective identities in teaching, nursing and social work

Edited by Terri Seddon,
Lea Henriksson and
Beatrix Niemeyer

 Routledge
Taylor & Francis Group

LONDON AND NEW YORK

This edition first published 2010
by Routledge
2 Park Square, Milton Park, Abingdon, Oxon OX14 4RN

Simultaneously published in the USA and Canada
by Routledge
270 Madison Avenue, New York, NY 10016

Routledge is an imprint of the Taylor & Francis Group, an informa business

Typeset in Galliard by
GreenGate Publishing Services, Tonbridge, Kent.
Printed and bound in Great Britain by
TJ International Ltd, Padstow, Cornwall.

British Library Cataloguing in Publication Data
A catalogue record for this book is available from the British Library

Library of Congress Cataloging-in-Publication Data
Seddon, Terri.
Learning and work and the politics of working life: global transformations and
collective identities in teaching, nursing and social work / Terri Seddon, Lea
Henriksson, and Beatrix Niemeyer.
p. cm.
1. Adult education—Cross-cultural studies. 2. Career education—Cross-cultural
studies. I. Henriksson, Lea. II. Niemeyer, Beatrix. III. Title.
LC5215.S46 2010
331.25'9—dc22
2009024908

ISBN10: 0-415-55752-6 (hbk)
ISBN10: 0-415-55753-4 (pbk)
ISBN10: 0-203-86312-7 (ebk)

ISBN13: 978-0-415-55752-8 (hbk)
ISBN13: 978-0-415-55753-5 (pbk)
ISBN13: 978-0-203-86312-1 (ebk)

# Contents

# Contributors

**Antje Barabasch** is Assistant Professor at the University of Magdeburg, Germany. She earned an MA in Vocational Education and Training/Adult Education from the University of Erfurt, Germany, and a PhD in Educational Policy Studies/ Social Foundations from Georgia State University, Atlanta, USA. Since 2007 she has been a visiting assistant professor at Ohio State University, Columbus, USA, the University of British Columbia, Vancouver, Canada, and Stanford University, Palo Alto, USA. Her dissertation focused on the school-to-work transition in Eastern Germany and the United States with an emphasis on risk perception regarding future opportunities in the labour market. In her comparative studies she focuses on governance structures in various VET systems, issues in career education in the United States, teachers' perception of education in Eastern Germany, policy transfer and academic cultures.

**Anita Devos** teaches in the areas of workplace learning, mentoring and coaching and research units in the Faculty of Education, Monash University, Australia, where she is also Director of Research Degrees. She has published in these areas, and in community and trade union education and higher education and research development. She brings a feminist analysis and an interest in gender to her work in each of these contexts. Some of her current projects address the experiences of women working and learning in regional Australia; workplace educators and occupational identities; and how students from diverse backgrounds succeed in higher education. Prior to starting work as an academic, she worked for trade unions as a researcher and advocate, in equal employment opportunity, and as a workplace educator.

**Lesley Farrell** is Associate Dean of Research and Development in the Faculty of Arts and Social Sciences, University of Technology, Sydney. Her research is in language and social change in globalising workplaces. Current projects focus on the impacts of globalisation on local workforces and work practices and on knowledge mobilisation across spatial and temporal domains. Her most recent books include *Making Knowledge Common* (Peter Lang 2006), *Educating the Global Workforce* (co-editor Tara Fenwick, Routledge 2007) and *English*

*Education in South Asia* (co-editors Udaya Narayana Singh and Ram Ashish Giri, Cambridge University Press, in press).

**Karin Filander** has been working as an Assistant Professor at the University of Kuopio, Finland. She has completed her PhD in adult education and she is a docent in adult education and work studies at the University of Tampere, where she will return to work in the Department of Education in autumn 2009. She has participated in the launching of a new academic discipline called social pedagogy in Finland. Her main interest has been to develop critical analysis on the traditions of adult education, which has become a kind of mainstream narrative of economical development. Her focus of research is on counter-discourses that move from the dominant cultural scripts and 'grand narratives' of lifelong learning.

**Frigga Haug** is Professor Emerita in Sociology and Social Psychology, University for Economics and Politics, Hamburg. She was a visiting scholar in Denmark, Austria, Canada and the USA. A founder of memory-work research, her early leadership in the field is reflected in the groundbreaking *Female Sexualisation: A Collective Work of Memory*. She is a member of numerous editorial boards including a series on Feminist Crime and Fiction, *Das Argument*, a journal of social theory, and the *Critical Dictionary on Marxism*, both of which she is currently co-editor. Her research has ranged from automation and work culture to social science methodology and learning to other areas of women's studies. Her most recent books deal with *Rosa Luxemburg's Art of Politics* (2007) and *The Four-in-One Perspective: Politics of Women for a New Left* (2008).

**Lea Henriksson** is a Docent in Social Policy and Academy of Finland Research Fellow. Her research contribution is related to welfare state change and the gendered politics of care work. In her research, policy trends are viewed as arenas of occupational and unionist struggles. Her work is cross-sectional in orientation, looking beyond the implications of retrenchment to welfare services, professional agency, cultures and identities. She examines the politics of occupations through the interlinkage of macro, meso and micro levels while adopting a history-, gender- and context-sensitive analysis. Reflections on her career as a teacher-researcher in the academic orders of social science and health research underline the importance of interdisciplinary and crosscultural inquiry and research partnership. Because of her double degree in social and health sciences, her research contributes to social policy, the sociology of work and occupations, the sociology of education, the sociology of health and illness and women's studies.

**Rudolf Husemann** is Professor for Further and Adult Education at the University of Erfurt, Germany, a position he has held at the Faculty of Education since 1998. In 1980 he gained his diploma in Sociology at the University of Bielefeld, Germany. He holds a PhD from the Technical University of Berlin gained in 1987, and completed his habilitation in 1997 at the University of

Duisburg, Germany. Since 1995 he has been an active member of the EUROVET Research Network, where his special focus of research is on governance and marketisation in vocational and adult education. Recent research projects include international comparison of adult and further education, regional development, ageing and qualification, employment and demographical change.

**Susan Kater** is the Director of Institutional Planning & Research at GateWay Community College, one of the Maricopa Community Colleges in Phoenix, Arizona. She has been both an adjunct faculty member and an administrator for 20 years within the Maricopa system. Her research interests and publications include issues related to faculty governance, student persistence and assessment. She has a PhD in Higher Education from the University of Arizona.

**Chris Kubiak** is an Open University Lecturer in Health and Social Care. He has a particular interest in practice and practice-based learning in health and social care, particularly in relation to care workers and assistants. Past involvements include research into brokerage in learning communities and networks. He originally trained in community psychology in New Zealand and has been involved in services for people with learning disabilities and mental health problems, volunteer-run telephone counselling, advice, education and advocacy services.

**John S. Levin** is the Bank of America Professor of Education Leadership and the Director and Principal Investigator of the California Community College Collaborative at the University of California, Riverside. His research addresses higher education in both the United States and Canada. His books during this decade – *Globalizing the Community College* (Palgrave 2001), *Community College Faculty: At Work in the New Economy* (Palgrave Macmillan 2006) and *Non-Traditional Students and Community Colleges: The Conflict of Justice and Neo-Liberalism* (Palgrave Macmillan 2007) – are empirically based examinations of community colleges. His latest book, with Virginia Montero Hernandez, is *Community Colleges and Their Students: Co-Construction and Institutional Identity* (Palgrave Macmillan 2009). His current projects include examination of university faculty professional identity, institutional practices at community colleges that contribute to equitable outcomes for student populations and graduate student career aspirations.

**Beatrix Niemeyer** completed her habilitation in Educational Science. She has studied Social Work, Educational Sciences and Sociology. As a senior researcher at the Institute of Technical Vocational Education at the University of Flensburg, Germany, she has coordinated a series of EU and regional projects, researching the educational space between general school and employment for social inclusive potentials. The books she has edited – *Reconnection – Countering Social Exclusion Through Situated Learning* (together with Karen

Evans, Kluwer 2004) and *New Learning Cultures in Europe* (Neue Lernkulturen in Europa, VS 2005) open a cultural-sensitive European perspective on differing transition regimes in Europe. In *Supporting Collaboration – Solving Dilemmas of Professional Education of Disadvantaged Young Persons* (Das Miteinander Fördern – Lösungsansätze für das Professionalisierungsdilemma in der Benachteiligtenförderung, Bielefeld 2008) she examines institutional boundaries and argues in favour of transprofessional networks, which place learning in a context that enables young learners to actively engage in the shaping of their life-course transitions.

**Päivi Niiranen-Linkama** has worked as a principal lecturer in Social Work Education at the Mikkeli University of Applied Sciences, Mikkeli, Finland, since 1999. She studied Education at the University of Turku, where she completed her Master's degree in 1988. This was followed until 1991 by a Teacher's Pedagogical Studies course at the Jyväskylä University of Applied Sciences. In 2005 she completed her PhD in Adult Education at the University of Jyväskylä. Her previous professional appointments were in Social Services and since 1991 in Social Work Education at the Institutes of Social Work in Seinäjoki and Otava, Finland.

**John Pardy** is a doctoral student at Monash University, whose research interests include vocational and technical education, the sociology of education, and knowledge and curriculum studies. John has worked for the past two decades as an educator in vocational and higher education, as a policy and project officer with state and national education departments and as a researcher. His PhD research is focused on examining knowledge and the curriculum in Australian working-class schooling.

**Terri Seddon** is a professor in the Faculty of Education at Monash University, Melbourne, Australia. She has built a research programme in the field of education (lifelong learning) and work with a special focus on policies and politics of teachers' work. Her work is cross-sectoral in orientation, looking at schools, vocational and higher education, and workplace and community learning spaces. She has built links with European research partners and is actively engaged in local and transnational partnership work. She co-edits the *Routledge World Yearbook of Education* with Professor Jenny Ozga (Edinburgh), Professor Agnés van Zanten (CNRS, Paris) and Professor Gita Steiner-Khamsi (Teacher's College Columbia). She has been a research assessor for the European Commission Framework programme and for the Australian Research Council.

**Sue Shore** is a senior lecturer at the University of South Australia and has been involved in Australian vocational and community education for three decades, first as a community educator and later as a university academic and researcher. Her research interests address racialised experiences of learning with particular reference to critical analyses of whiteness. She is well known for her work as a past director of the Adult Literacy and Numeracy Australian Research Consortium (ALNARC) and has been invited by the Australian Bureau of Statistics to advise on Australia's participation in the next international adult literacy survey – the Survey of Adult Competencies (SAC) – due to be conducted in 2011. Her understanding of vocational education has been enriched by conversations and projects with generous colleagues around the globe (see for example http://www.unisa.edu.au/hawkeinstitute/cslplc/research/Projects.asp).

**Richard L. Wagoner** is an assistant professor in the Higher Education and Organisational Change Division of the Graduate School of Education and Information Studies at the University of California, Los Angeles (UCLA). His research is concerned with how and to what extent globalisation and neoliberalism affect higher education institutions and their practices, particularly how the work faculties at all levels perform. His book *Community College Faculty: At Work in the New Economy,* co-authored with John Levin and Sue Kater, conceptualises community college faculties as New Economy workers particularly in terms of their use of technology, the increasing reliance on part-time contingent faculty, and the continual negotiation between academic and economic values which undergirds their work.

# Preface

This book has developed through a network of researchers distributed around the globe. It started as a loose invitation to people associated with the VET and Culture network, who worked in education, health, social work and youth work to come together to talk about and interrogate working life in human service work. Following some broad discussion of themes at the Joensuu workshop in Finland, participants went away to draft chapters, which were discussed a year later at the Gilleleje VET and Culture conference in Denmark. There was further discussion of chapters at the network's conference in Konstanz, Germany, a year later.

The initial impetus for this book project came through a VET and Culture curriculum development project funded by the EU. This project, CROSSLIFE, was focused on cross-cultural collaboration in lifelong learning and work. It aimed to develop an innovative global approach to academic apprenticeship for professionals and researchers working in the field of lifelong learning and work. This network activity brought participants from the University of Tampere, Finland, the Institute of Education, London, the University of Malta, the University of Zurich, Switzerland, the Danish Pedagogical University, Denmark, and Monash University, Australia, together in a formalised six-country partnership.

Preparing books was a way of making our research available to students and tutors involved in the teaching process in this CROSSLIFE partnership. Drawing chapter authors together from around the world to write about changes in learning and work and the politics of working life created a global space for dialogue and theorising. Thinking about learning, work and politics from within this global space opened up many issues and dilemmas that were not evident from locations anchored in any one country, institution or discipline. These spatial frames made us confront where we came from and who we were when we entered the global space of the book project, and the CROSSLIFE project. It was disturbing work but it opened up many new questions and conversations about experiences, which felt the same, but which were described and understood differently in different places.

Three titles were prepared in response to the CROSSLIFE project. Two are being published by Peter Lang: *Reworking Vocational Education: Policies,*

*Practice and Concepts* (Heikkinen and Kraus, forthcoming); and *Knowing Work: The Social Relations of Working and Knowing* (Weil, Koski and Mjelde, forthcoming). This suite of texts, developed separately by different editorial groups, offers a range of concepts and perspectives that reveal important insights into the changing patterns of local–global lifelong learning and work in national contexts.

Our process of working and learning together showed that doing academic work is tough today because it involves working at an unfamiliar globally networked scale. It means that individual academics, tutors and students must learn how to operate in a global space, how to listen and work across boundaries and how to engage in decision-making in uncertain and sometimes slippery contexts. There is a need for continuous problem solving, new strategies and people – working to make, build and sustain relationships. Yet resources for such work, with its high interpersonal and personal demands, are not readily available, either through funding sources or institutions.

This book opens a window on these disturbances in work and learning that accompany globalisation of working life. It provides resources that recognise the impact of innovation demanded of workers in global spaces and the challenges in forming spaces for reflexive learning and working that can bring fragmented working lives together in collective agency. *Learning and Work and the Politics of Working Life* is a contribution to practical politics that seeks more sustainable working lives.

*Terri Seddon, Lea Henriksson*
*and Beatrix Niemeyer*

# Acknowledgements

Discussions in a range of projects and places have informed our work in preparing *Learning and Work and the Politics of Working Life*. We thank those colleagues who wrote chapters for this book and showed great patience as it slowly moved towards completion. We also thank the members of the CROSSLIFE planning group: Professors Anja Heikkinen, Ronald Sultana, Lorna Unwin and Philip Gonon; and Drs Markus Weil, Katrin Kraus, Norman Lucas, Vibe Aakrog, Søren Ehlers, Philip Bonano and Vesa Korhonen. Special thanks are due to the CROSSLIFE project planner, Virve Kallioniemi-Chambers, and all the students from so many countries who attended the CROSSLIFE project workshops in London, Tampere and Malta. Dr Beverley Axford provided advice and editorial assistance in the preparation of this book.

We also acknowledge the support of the Academy of Finland (project numbers 207402 and 214430), the Jenny and Antti Wihuri Foundation, the University of Tampere, the University of Flensburg and Monash University in this project.

Chapter 13 includes two pages from Haug, Frigga (2009) 'The Four-in-One Perspective: A manifesto for a more just life', *Socialism and Democracy*, vol. 23, no. 1, Routledge, Taylor & Francis Ltd, http://www.informaworld.com, reprinted with permission of the publisher.

# Introduction – disturbing work and transforming politics

*Terri Seddon, Lea Henriksson and Beatrix Niemeyer*

This book is about politics and working life in a globalised world. It examines the way human service work – teaching, nursing and social work – is being disturbed today and how these disturbances both constrain and enable people's agency in everyday practical politics. Large-scale changes in work and education are key features of contemporary global transformations. They are also key features of the local lived experience of these changes in particular places – workplaces that are also learning places. It is our contention that these local places are sites where a significant politics of work are playing out.

We approach this agenda through detailed empirical research in human service work in Europe, Australia and the US and self-reflective theorising about doing academic work, cross-nationally, using a distinctive global research methodology. The book is structured by three main themes: disturbed work, disturbing work and transforming politics. We come to the view that this transforming politics is, at heart, a 'politics of we'.

## Disturbed work

Work and learning is being disturbed as a result of large-scale economic, political and social changes. These changes drive towards the development of competitive knowledge-based economies. Their impact re-shapes the way work has been traditionally patterned – through, for example, the organisation of skill, the categorisation and orchestration of work practices and the development of people's capacity to labour.

These disturbances in the older patterns of work have also played out in education and training for two reasons. First, schools, vocational colleges, universities and other learning spaces are also workplaces where employees live out their working lives within organised work practices and relationships. Second, knowledge-economy policy agendas have been used by national governments to reshape education and training policies and practices around ideas about 'lifelong learning'. This justificatory rhetoric presents 'learning' as a foundational competence required by citizens, communities and societies in globally competitive, knowledge-based economies. This competence is seen to be necessary for work and also for enabling individuals to negotiate rapid economic and social change. It has prompted an emphasis on work-related and applied learning for all learners, not just in formal institutions but also in workplaces and community settings. In this way, the metaphor of a knowledge economy, supported by lifelong learning policies and practices, is transforming established occupational and educational orders and the landscape within which employees traditionally navigate their lives.

## Disturbing work

The effects of these disturbances in work and learning are registered partly in the organisation of work, in workplace categories and hierarchies and in work practices. Sennett argues that these changes constitute an 'illegible regime of power'. This phrase acknowledges that changes accompanying flexible capitalism create new relations and practices of power, which are unfamiliar. For instance, the growth of the global economy has in some respects disturbed the policy-making processes of national governments. They must consider transnational factors, like the investment decisions of multinational companies, how to ensure labour supply when labour mobility is increasing and how to manage the movement of people and ideas across national boundaries.

They are also evident in the lived experiences of workers. Individuals confront changes in classifications and job roles and shifts in work expectations and relationships. These experiences have practical effects in the way people see themselves and on the ethical understandings of good practice that underpin their occupational identities. When work and learning is made-over in the rush to become 'knowledge-based economies' and 'lifelong learning societies', occupational landmarks are disrupted in ways that disturb the identities, practices and cultures. These disturbances play out in ways that destabilise occupations, their collective organisations and activities and the individuals that make up established occupational groups. As Sennett (1998: 10) argues: 'Flexible capitalism disturbs us because it corrodes character, our ethical sense of ourselves, and the personal traits we value in ourselves and seek to have valued by others.'

## Transforming politics through the 'politics of we'

A new kind of practical politics accompanies disturbed and disturbing work and learning. This politics embraces the everyday practical activities through which people confront different practices, cultures and identities, and negotiate relations of power and ways of using power responsibly. Drawing on Sennett's work, we have called this the 'politics of we'.

Sennett (1998) notes that 'we' is a 'dangerous pronoun' because it refers to forms of association that permit collective questioning of the status quo. It creates affiliations and belonging alongside inclusion and exclusion. It fuels mobilisations but with no guarantees about their social and cultural effects. One man's democratisation agenda is another woman's structural violence. Heavy-handed managerial prerogative may prompt individualisation and alienation in one place, conflict in another and, in others again, forms of collaborative engagement and dialogue.

This pronoun 'we' is a key theme in the book. It is not used in a rhetorical way, suggesting some abstract shared interest between authors and readers. Rather, 'we' captures issues about belonging and longing to belong. It draws attention to the way boundaries are negotiated and affirmed and the kinds of cultural anchor-points that individuals use to build relationships and narratives of affinity. The chapters document the conditions and locations that enable and disable the development and work of collectives across many different work and learning places. Thinking about our own research practices within global transformations also forced us to confront these processes in our own working lives.

In unpacking this 'politics of we' the authors and editors have actively used their location as a means for research. In writing this book we have drawn on knowledge traditions, occupational orientations, national identifications and social positioning as academics to create an interdisciplinary and cross-national dialogue. This dialogue has provided critical understandings of disturbing work and transforming politics.

This approach has also allowed an interrogation of the tension between, on the one hand, fragmentation and individual isolation and, on the other, new forms of collective agency. Sennett's work demonstrates the way global transformations constitute a new flexible capitalism that fragments work and working lives, and undercuts people's subjective sense of self. The implication is that these discursive practices play out as social practices. They construct relationships, identities and cultures, and also subordinate and govern subjects through dividing practices and classifications that encourage individualisation and self-management. Sennett describes these social and symbolic effects of the new capitalism as an 'illegible regime of power' (Sennett 1998).

Despite these powerful discourse effects, our work together has shown that policy steering and the imperatives of flexible capitalism are always incomplete. As Sennett suggests, despite the illegible regime of power, people find ways of 'speaking out of inner need' and coalescing in groups and networks that can use the term 'we'. So, along with fragmentation there is coalescing, which creates capacities for collective agency, at least for a period of time.

Interrogating this 'politics of we' is a primary objective in this book. The editors and authors have approached this work from a particular vantage point – as researchers and professional educators in human service occupations. Our disciplinary orientations, rooted in the sociology of work and occupations, the sociology of education and lifelong learning research, offer particular ways of understanding this collective identity formation and agency. Our working lives as educators mean that we see, first hand, the impact of re-ordering occupations and occupational learning on those who learn and those who teach. As human service professionals, we believe human service work can make a contribution to ameliorating the effects of global transformations. But in order for this to happen, those who work in these domains need to have more effective tools for reflecting on the nature of the work they do and the nature of the personal and professional identities this work helps construct.

## Interdisciplinary dialogue

The rationale for this work is, ultimately, about building a better world. This commitment recognises that; first, transforming politics is an everyday practice of power. Social conflicts and tensions are non-negotiable features of everyday life. They do not go away but require efforts at every scale to negotiate ways of living together that minimise insecurity, injustice and unhappiness. Yet, today, social inequality, cultural disregard and civil conflict are on the rise, alongside growing challenges of social and ecological sustainability. Moreover, governments around the world are radically overhauling traditional instruments, like work organisation and education, which have been used historically to govern populations and social division. In this context, we believe it is timely to consider how changes in work and learning are playing out in human service work.

## Research traditions

The sociology of work and occupations, and the sociology of education, share a discursive frame but offer different perspectives on transformative politics. The study of work foregrounds the idea of collectivity, whereas in education this achievement is more often seen as realised through particular processes of managing individuals (through, for example, the work of a teacher or academic). When these two perspectives are brought together in active dialogue they prompt questions about the nature of professional agency and how it anchors a politics based in collective action.

Classical and feminist research in the sociology of work and occupations emphasises the collective organisation of work through the division of labour. This orientation draws attention to social stratification, the way gender relations cut across work and working lives and the implications of these social processes for industrial and civil politics. The idea that work organises groups highlights principles of differentiation and the ways these are organised and coordinated to achieve particular economic and social outcomes, including sustainability and security. The concept of 'occupation', for instance, draws attention to the collective character of groups that are organised and coordinated through particular kinds of jobs. Each occupation is differentiated by expertise and develops particular moral and ethical understandings of their practices as a group. These occupational groupings interface with one another, negotiate and dispute boundaries and, through these processes of inter- and intra-occupational dialogue, create occupational orders and collective capacities for action.

Collectivity and collective occupational identity are almost premises in this research tradition. They exist and are anchored within a division of labour that is demarcated socially and culturally through classifications of work (e.g.

productive–reproductive, mental–manual) and of skill (e.g. unskilled, semi-skilled, skilled). The kind of work done and the scope for judgement is another differentiating principle. At one end of this classification is routine non-manual work (e.g. clerical) and at the other end of the scale is professional work in which effectiveness in the job depends upon complex judgements. These occupational divisions mean that the 'politics of we' are persistent features of the social land-scape and can never be taken for granted. To say 'we' is an expression of a collective identity, a feature of everyday life that is more or less consolidated in particular contexts, and a critical precondition for collective capacities for action.

The sociology of education approaches the idea of collectivity mostly as an outcome of educational processes. It is most obvious in the context of nation building, where education has been the instrument used by governments to develop identities and identifications as citizens and subjects. This emphasis on managing populations means that education is a critical institution in supporting people's development as workers and citizens, and in ameliorating civil conflict. Yet in education, research has tended to downplay politics and collective action. The focus is primarily on educational processes within schooling rather than on the institutional framing of education and its negotiation through practical politics. The result is more concern with individuals than groups, focusing partic-ularly on effective strategies that enable individual learning and development. This individualistic focus persists even in the sub-field of education and work. Research on education and work is mostly concerned with young people and their transition from school to work. The focus is on individuals and their learn-ing careers and the way these individuals are patterned by relations of gender, class, ethnicity and other social divisions. The institutional architecture of formal education and training is considered in relation to learner mobility, achievements and the regulatory reforms that may enhance performance. There is less atten-tion to the practical politics through which collective identities make and remake institutional arrangements and selective principles that sift and sort learners towards different social and economic outcomes.

A focus on groups emerges primarily through the documentation of individual achievements. This means that groups tend to be seen as collections of individuals rather than collectives with a collective identity. It also encourages research that is oriented towards making things better through ameliorative practices rather than understanding collective identities and capacities for action that make learning and development a governmental domain. These features of education research mean that talking about 'we' as a collective identity is relatively uncommon and a source of some ambivalence. The 'politics of we' cuts across the grain of 'governmentali-ty' that has been institutionalised through individualistic and ameliorative discourse. It is addressed in fields like institutional sociology of education, the study of teachers, industrial politics and social movements that mobilise schooling for social ends, and in notions of active citizenship. Yet these knowledge traditions often exist as counter-currents to dominant education discourses about individual development and learning for work.

Combining these insights from education and work research reveals the 'politics of we' in every work-learning place. The occupational frame shows the way global transformations are disturbing prior occupational identifications and dispersing established occupational identities and collectives. The educational frame shows the way dispersed individuals are prompted to learn and build relationships despite weak collective identities and capacities. These conceptual dialogues capture what is often rendered invisible and individualised by global reforms. They also draw attention to the way identities, acting alone as well as together, engage in practical politics outside the traditional practices of industrial politics, enabling self and others to achieve sustainable working lives and happiness.

This interdisciplinary dialogue reminds us that power and politics are always present in every work-learning place. Forgetting politics and political quiescence is a response to global transformations. It is, itself, a kind of politics – an induced amnesia that turns a blind-eye to the reordering of work and learning places, and the patterns of inclusion–exclusion, inequality and injustice that they sustain. The dialogue also prompts questions about ways of governing work and learning and the outcomes that are realised. It reminds us that the regulation of work and the mobilisation of learning can be turned towards building capacities for collective action. Through the book we suggest that remembering politics is neither just about head-to-head conflict nor its avoidance. Rather, it is about understanding and using practices of power throughout everyday life and developing collective capacities that use power responsibly through legitimate decision-making to build better societies.

## Global perspectives and the 'politics of we'

Understanding the 'politics of we' within global transformations creates further problems for education and work research. This becomes obvious in an edited collection that represents cases of disturbing work and transforming politics from around the world. Different chapters, prepared by authors in different parts of the world, not only describe different social worlds but also construct cultural representations that are framed in different ways. A global analysis of the 'politics of we' in human service work must acknowledge the way everyday life is spatially organised. Different practices in different places, and patterns of uneven development, are not natural features but outcomes of social and political practices in particular times and places.

The national framing of the chapters in this book is a consequence of the way human service work has emerged historically alongside the developing welfare state. Occupations like teaching and nursing support and collectivise prior dispersed reproductive and care work practices that were dispersed across families and communities. This work was, and remains, highly feminised and involves substantial levels of emotional labour and caring work essential for social continuity and security. This work is therefore significant because of its critical contribution to reproducing societies. Yet the social and cultural practices of human service work are now subject to welfare state restructuring which is a key feature of contemporary global transformations. Knowledge economy and lifelong learning reforms reorder collectivised human service work through market coordination, commodification and competitive relations. This privatisation reframes human service work. Its occupational practices, emotional labour and care work are subordinated to economic imperatives that maximise returns on investments in 'human services'.

These practical developments and national framings of human service work are both illustrated and interrogated in this book. Each chapter draws on a substantial body of empirical research to document disturbed and disturbing human service work and what this reveals about transforming politics. Yet each chapter is also a representation crafted by a researcher working in a particular location. They write from a specific place defined by its geography and history, anchored through their personal biography, in specific knowledge traditions and occupational cultures.

The process of interrogating the chapters as particular located representations provided a window on the 'politics of we'. As editors we used the chapter drafts as resources for two further levels of analysis. The first step involved digging into each chapter to identify unacknowledged spatial and historical assumptions and other gaps and silences in the chapter analysis. This strategy revealed things that had been rendered invisible in the account. For instance, representations commonly described workers or individuals abstractly without recognising the way these humans were gendered and classed. Similarly, authors identified their chapters with national contexts but without always explaining the particular location of the case in a specific city or region with a distinctive history and culture. The second step in this analysis involved reading across the chapters as representations to identify transversal themes. It is these themes that inform our conceptualisation of transforming politics as a 'politics of we'.

This process of writing, critique and analysis makes a distinctive contribution to the field of lifelong learning and work research. We build on cross-national and comparative research that documents national systems and cultures of work and learning (e.g. Heikkinen 1996; Green 1997) and on more grounded studies of policy reforms, professional projects and agency (Henriksson et al. 2006). We also draw on the methodological strategies of poststructural researchers who address the way language is implicated in social change and the discursive practices that constitute everyday life and its representation through research (e.g. Usher and Edwards 1994, 2007). In these ways we weave the nationally grounded chapters into a contribution that speaks specifically to the politics of lifelong learning and work within global transformations (Hughes et al. 2007; Jarvis 2008) and the wider field of global sociology (e.g. Edwards and Usher 2000; Farrell and Fenwick 2007; Epstein et al. 2008). These interfacing research traditions highlight the importance of seeing sociology as also a sociology of knowledge and approaching social action as an outcome of interactive effects at many scales (Burawoy 2000;

Massey 2005). This 'global' analytical frame recognises the way social practices of research, embedded in interfacing multi-scalar relations, contribute to politics within socially organised space and time. These representations based on research and evidence shape the way public knowledge is informed. Those at the margins of knowledge building are not heard like those occupying centres, creating knowledge practices that are ordered and differentiated across global North and South, mainstream and margins, cosmopolitan or indigenous, profit or care work. As Connell (2007: ix) notes, research representations exist and contribute to practices of knowing that are framed by relations of 'authority, exclusion and inclusion, hegemony, partnership, sponsorship, appropriation'. They shape, differentiate and order intellectuals and institutions in the metropole and those in the world's peripheries.

Our methodology implicates us – as authors and editors of this book – in the practical politics of work and learning. Using what we have called the 'politics of we' as a critical lens, we rediscover ourselves as collective actors by working together. 'We' are a global network of researcher-professionals working in the field of human service work and in research. 'We' prompted the idea for this book and wrote chapters. As editors we steered chapter writing to draw out what doing politics means today. This everyday work required us to commit to this project, to work together, to think about a better future by remembering the past and by realising our own institutional amnesia. Through our work together, we recognise that we are doing politics and actively intervening to inform and shape global transformations and their local effects in human service work. We are also intervening through our work as researchers, contributing to our knowledge traditions and also to public knowledge that can be taken up in everyday life. Recognising our own agency in a 'politics of we' is a powerful process. It reveals key features of contemporary work and learning and challenges constraints anchored in established mindsets. It also creates conditions for transgressing established frameworks that constitute everyday life and endorsing such transgressions in others.

## Transforming politics in human service work

Our global research methodology has opened up transforming politics in lifelong learning and work in globally connected times. This collective work has generated concepts for understanding the 'politics of we' in new ways. These concepts have grown out of the preparation and discussion of chapters and this is mirrored in the way the chapters are sequenced in this book. This introduction and Chapter 1 provide an overview of this book project and its contribution to the practical politics of work and learning. The remaining chapters are then grouped into four parts. Part I introduces key concepts, 'occupation', 'education'. It analyses their effects by examining the reconfiguration of occupational orders and the changing regulation of working lives. Part II includes five chapters that offer different windows on the politics of expertise. These cases, drawn from different parts of the world, and occupational and educational settings, reveal the ways occupational knowledge is being renegotiated in the context of flexible capitalism. Part III documents mobility stories. These chapters show the way individuals create careers as they navigate through transitions in learning and working life. Finally, we invited Frigga Haug to write the Coda, in recognition of her contribution to a feminist politics of work that has influenced our work as editors. This short chapter reflects on the collection and suggests a frame for practical politics in our global space-time.

Our global approach is also mirrored in the character of the chapters. Language is a complicated issue in a collection written by authors working in different disciplines and professional contexts from around the world. While English is our global language, there are many varieties of English and creating 'consistency' is always a difficult practical politics. The process of editing chapters was tensioned between respect for each author's national and disciplinary writing practices and the requirements of an English-language publication. In making the collection, we have accepted that a global book project has a 'multi-voice' global sound, which is anchored in different 'Englishes' and in different concepts and vocabularies. We have therefore tried to create commonalities across the chapters but not standardise them. Each chapter reflects the context and linguistic norms out of which it was written but is consistent within its own cultural frames.

The themes of fragmentation and agency that underpin the 'politics of we' are elaborated in Chapter 1. In order to better understand this contemporary dialectic, Seddon, Henriksson and Niemeyer draw on conceptual resources beyond Sennett to reflect critically on research, on the other chapters in the collection and on the experiences of working on this particular book project. Literatures from critical, feminist and cultural sociology provide ways of understanding this process of 'speaking from inner need' and its mobilising effects in terms of social action. Such dissonance or contradiction prompts action, ranging from retreat and alienation, passivity and conformity, through to active engagement and contestation. Reflecting on the chapters in this volume brought home the importance of who was being talked about and where they were located. This cross-national analytical work led us to question Sennett's 'Corrosion of Character'. We argue that it emphasises fragmentation at the expense of grounded examination of agency. By contrast, the chapters in this collection show that disturbing work also prompts questions and practical activities that contest social and symbolic practices within occupational and educational orders. Sennett's bleak analysis of flexible capitalism in terms of 'fragmentation' neglects the way reflexive engagement in working life provides ways of moving towards a transforming politics.

In Part I, this analytical groundwork is elaborated by focusing on specific concepts and the way they are problematised by disturbing work. Lea Henriksson uses the concepts of occupation and occupational order, developed within a sociology of occupations. This chapter shows how, with changes in the Finnish welfare state, the old occupational order and its collective agency is disintegrating. The impact of New Public Management in Finnish nursing and, in particular, the creation of new categories of ancillary nurses is examined. These 'practical nurses' do care work but fall below regular nurses in terms of skills, pay and conditions. Using the concepts of occupation and occupational order, Henriksson documents the way these developments disturb professional identities, the division of labour, skill profiles, salary levels and demographics. They also disturb traditional union politics, which are discomforted by these 'practical nurses' because they challenge conventional ways of thinking about occupational coverage and industrial strategies.

The next chapter by Karin Filander also documents Finnish experience but in education where welfare state reforms have affirmed new vocationalism. This chapter shows how the work ethics and occupational pride of vocational teachers are challenged by the rhetoric of lifelong learning. The detailed analysis shows how the work of Finnish teachers is disturbed by the introduction of polytechnics as a new institutional level in the ordering of education. Focusing on the analysis of discourse, the chapter shows how teachers have been redefined as salespersons, co-ordinators and managers of change. In this new educational order the students are defined as self-directed learners who 'self-service' their own learning choices and individual study plans. Teachers are positioned as subjects within neoliberal discourses but also act politically by using irony to re-anchor themselves in dissolving work organisation. Irony is a liberating strategy and counter-narrative in disturbing times.

It is not immediately obvious that these two chapters are both informed by and written into the practices and experience of work and education in Finland. The analyses focus on developments that are also occurring in other parts of the world. Yet there are traces of the practical context, a particular national space-time, within these texts. Finnish cultural traditions and national history are embedded in Henriksson's and Filander's normative assumptions that sit behind the words, for example in a particular view of the welfare state, its role and the way welfare and education are anchored in very practical understandings of citizenship. The next chapter is written from Australia. This Anglo-country has different welfare state traditions to Finland. It is a nation that has been subject to economic policy framing for a long time and where, we sense, these economic agendas find fertile ground in which to grow and take root. This cultural fertility is anchored in a particular history, as a (relatively) young white settler society. Here settlement meant carving out a place to live out of a hostile environment, in opposition to existing indigenous populations and where practices informed by established European traditions did not always work. While not explicit, there are differences in the words and descriptions which differ from the prior Finnish chapters. These cultural echoes are particularly evident in descriptions of the state and public culture. We note this interplay of texts and sub-texts because our global research methodology requires sharp sensitivity to the underlying themes and framing of texts as a prompt for interrogating taken-for-granted assumptions and analytical gaps and silences. This sensitivity is also needed with the other chapters in this collection, deriving as they do from other time-spaces.

The above-mentioned chapter is from Victoria in South East Australia. Anita Devos, Lesley Farrell and Terri Seddon focus on the multi-scalar regulation of work and the construction of spatialised narratives and worker identities within globally interconnected capitalism. The case analysis shows the pattern of national, transnational and individual regulatory frameworks and their contradictory effects in shaping narratives and practices of work and identity. The analysis shows the way employees sit at the nexus between the local workplace, with its person-to-person relationships and national industrial frameworks, and the globally networked workspace that operates largely through textual and technologically mediated practices and relationships. This nexus is illustrated by examining women's academic lives in university workplaces. These women employees negotiate contradictory discourses by 'shape-shifting' in terms of individual identity and also by identifying non-negotiable aspects of their everyday working lives that can serve as an anchor point for their 'flexibilised selves'.

The five chapters in Part II zoom in on specific work contexts and patterns of change. Written by authors from the US, Germany, England, Finland and Australia, these chapters draw attention to the global character of contemporary occupational and educational reconfigurations. The chapters document local effects of globalised flexible capitalism and its policy trajectories. They show differences between contexts of work and learning and also more consistent cross-cutting patterns of change. The chapters also vary in the way these changes are represented through processes of research and writing that are framed by different national, disciplinary and occupational traditions, which are evident as different linguistic practices within each text.

The first chapter in Part II is by Rick Wagoner, John Levin and Susan Kater who are located in California, another white settler society. It considers the disturbances in US community colleges, sometimes referred to as the 'democracy colleges' because of their role as a pathway to higher education and skilled employment for disadvantaged and second-chance learners. This chapter re-reads data from a large national study of changes experienced by staff (i.e. faculty) working in US community colleges. It shows the way work is disturbed by increased part-time employment, travel between worksites, increased managerial expectations and roles, and market-driven institutional hierarchies. Drawing on Sennett's (2006) work on culture, the chapter identifies 'narrative', 'usefulness' and 'craftsmanship' as ways of anchoring transforming politics in processes of building a preferred space for professional work.

Beatrix Niemeyer writes from Germany with its well-institutionalised dual sector vocational education and training system. She examines transformations in the work of education professionals working in the field of school-to-work transition. The chapter draws on two cases that show how the work of teachers working with so-called disadvantaged young people is being reconfigured by the introduction of 'regional centres of education'. In these centres vocational trainers, social and youth workers and other education professionals are required to work together. This means that teachers are forced to engage in inter-professional problem solving and coping strategies as they negotiate lifelong learning politics, employability and new qualification schemes for skilled workers. These changes challenge the strong anchoring of the German vocational education and training system and normative ideas about 'good' professional practice.

Chris Kubiak examines paraprofessionals in UK social and health care from a location in England. Through the Thatcher years, Britain was a pioneer in the kinds of market reform that drove flexible capitalism. British policies have reframed paraprofessional support workers, who help people with learning disabilities and mental problems in daily life, as 'professionals'. Yet these workers exist in marginal positions and are made invisible in work settings and research. The data from two case studies show how these support staff actively blur the boundaries between professionals and non-professionals. They actively engage with work practices and create learning practices and frontline authority through their hands-on work to make places where they can belong.

Päivi Niiranen-Linkama writes about patterns of change in the institutional and occupational ordering of social work in Finland. The chapter documents the disturbances created when polytechnics were constituted as places to learn and teach learners about social work. Using the concept of identity at a meso-level, the chapter shows how established norms and understandings of the 'social' were disrupted by neo-liberal welfare state reforms. The prior hegemonic discourse is challenged by the introduction of new learning practices and by pedagogic frameworks that privilege key competences. The chapter documents the implications of this shifting framework for professional identity and the kinds of learning involved in acting professionally.

Sue Shore considers the way Australian teachers of adult literacy negotiate a new policy-driven culture of competency-based workplace training. This shifting discourse of adult education is documented in the chapter through a self-reflexive analysis of processes that helped to define the occupation, adult literacy work and the knowledge base associated with that work. The chapter draws attention to the way policies, funding arrangements and the agency of adult literacy workers contributes the reordering of adult literacy teaching as a service within vocational education and training. It shows how policy texts are used as sites for occupational politics and how adult literacy teachers struggle to hold open a space for adult literacy occupational knowledge.

Part III includes three chapters, one from Australia and two from Germany. They offer different insights and ways of understanding disturbing work and its effects in terms of mobility. The first chapter by John Pardy tells the story of Frank, a Maltese-Australian, who started out in a fitting and turning apprenticeship and ended up completing a degree in Arts. Frank's narrative provides a window on large-scale changes in Australian manufacturing, shifting education and training policies and the way one individual has crafted a life from the resources at hand. The analysis focuses on the micro-practices through which Frank negotiates hurdles, constraints, desires and a sense of self-value to find a way of being in the world. While the analytical emphasis is on the individual, this individuality is anchored in I–we relationships and a valuing of self. In this work of crafting a life and a self, education and training offer important identity resources.

Rudolf Husemann highlights the way disturbances arising from social, economic and political changes impact on an ageing workforce. It documents the demographic challenges that are re-shaping German labour market policies and the implications they have in ordering working life in small and medium enterprises in the eastern part of Germany. The chapter focuses on new regional employment and personnel strategies that are developing under the combined influence of demographic changes and lifelong learning agendas. These disturbances mean uncertainty and insecurity for employees, which translate into experiences of ambivalence: should they stay in employment that they no longer recognise as their own? Should they go? How do they find out about their eligibility for a pension scheme?

Antje Barabasch focuses on structural disturbances and uncertainties in career prospects of young adults in Eastern Germany and the United States. The chapter documents and contrasts 'risk perceptions' in the two cultures by contrasting experiences of the global de-anchoring of work. When the 'rigid' East German norms and structures of vocational education and employment safety collapsed due to the reunification, the career orientations of the young adults in the two countries started to converge. The resulting insecurities related to the school-to-work transition mean that individuals in both countries are increasingly expected to act as choosers who direct their own lives in response to structural changes in the economy and society.

The final chapter in the collection, by Frigga Haug, reflects on the globalisation of work and its implications for the 'art of politics'. She draws attention to the fact that the preparation of this book has created its own global workplace. This workplace globalises and challenges participants' practices of academic work and also creates contexts where they can reflexively analyse and research the processes of 'speaking out of inner need' and moving towards transforming politics. Drawing attention to the parallel processes of change, and the way they are negotiated in everyday ways in the different chapters, and in a women's project in Germany, Haug highlights the critical question of how to create a 'space of orientation' within which all these fragmented struggles within everyday life can be recontextualised and brought into conversation with one another. Acknowledging the historic work of the women's and workers' movements, and political movements affirming individual development and the responsible use of power through democratic decision-making, she argues for a four-in-one politics of time. This politics of time is a call for equal recognition of different time demands, in employment, social continuity and care, our own development and democratic decision-making, and the need to align the sum of these times to the human constraints of a workable life.

Together, these chapters open up disturbing work and transforming politics today. They confirm Sennett's point that 'we' is a 'dangerous pronoun' but also raise questions about the conditions and capacities entailed in the 'politics of we' in global times. While 'we' can be dangerous, it is critical to fabricating collective identities and capacities for action in the world. As in the past, these capacities for collective agency develop in particular places; they exist in specific spaces and endure over finite times. Their agency may or may not last for long; they may be actively disrupted. But for a particular time and place, 'we' emerges within multiscalar relations to give effect to some kind of collective project.

The contemporary 'politics of we' embraces both the formation of collective identities and capacities to act and also their erosion in fragmented individualism. Neither option provides guarantees for the future. However, recognising the everyday nature of politics does open up questions. The challenges of our times are not simply technical problems that can be solved by good management. Rather, the challenge is to understand how we are seduced and implicated in flexible capitalism and change how we are positioned within these power relations. Remembering politics means using power and our capacity to act collectively in responsible ways. It is the first step towards building a better world where social and environmental sustainability and collective happiness are thinkable possibilities.

## References

Burawoy, M. (2000) *Global Ethnography: Forces, Connections, and Imaginations in a Postmodern World*, Berkeley: University of California Press.

Connell, R. (2007) *Southern Theory: The Global Dynamics of Knowledge in Social Science*, Sydney: Allen and Unwin.

Edwards, R. and Usher, R. (2000) *Globalisation and Pedagogy: Space, Place and Identity*, London: Routledge.

Epstein, D., Boden, R., Deem, R., Rizvi, F. and Wright, S. (2008) *Geographies of Knowledge, Geometries of Power: World Yearbook of Education 2008*, London: Routledge.

Farrell, L. and Fenwick, T. (eds) (2007) *Educating the Global Workforce*, London: Routledge.

Green, A. (1997) *Education, Globalization, and the Nation State*, New York: Palgrave St Martins.

Heikkinen, A. (1996) *Gendered History of (Vocational) Education*, Hämeenlinna: University of Tampere Press.

Henriksson, L., Wrede, S. and Burau, V. (2006) 'Understanding professional projects in welfare service work: Revival of old professionalism?', *Gender, Work and Organization*, 13(2): 174–192.

Hughes, J., Jewson, N. and Unwin, L. (2007) *Communities of Practice: Critical Perspectives*, London: Routledge.

Jarvis, P. (2008) *Democracy, Lifelong Learning and the Learning Society: Active Citizenship in a Late Modern Age*, London: Routledge.

Massey, D. (2005) *For Space*, London: Sage.

Sennett, R. (1998) *The Corrosion of Character: The Personal Consequences of Work in the New Capitalism*, New York: Norton.

Sennett, R. (2006) *The Culture of the New Capitalism*, New Haven: Yale University Press.

Usher, R. and Edwards, R. (1994) *Postmodernism and Education*, London: Routledge.

Usher, R. and Edwards, R. (2007) *Lifelong learning: Signs, Discourses, Practices*, Dordrecht: Springer.

Chapter 1

# Disturbing academic work
## Theorising a global book project

*Terri Seddon, Lea Henriksson and*
*Beatrix Niemeyer*

This chapter considers the way work is disturbed in global times by examining the process of preparing this book. We – the editorial group – reflect on our cross-national collaboration with the chapter authors to document the way work has been disturbed, and has been experienced as disturbing, as a consequence of what Sennett (1998) calls 'flexible capitalism'. Reflecting on this case has allowed us to investigate the way these disturbances in the way work is organised also prompts people to work together in transforming politics. The chapter also serves as background to the other chapters in the collection, which provide further cases of disturbing work and evidence of transforming politics in working lives.

## Building a platform for inquiry

We began work on this book at a Vocational Education and Training (VET) and Culture workshop by a lake in Finland. A group of eight researchers coalesced, talking about changes in the way work and education were organised. Two days in a workshop with intense discussions left us enthusiastic about doing cross-national collaborative research. The group made commitments – to prepare accounts of disturbing work in flexible capitalism from different occupational fields, educational settings and national jurisdictions and bring them into conversation with one another. Three of us agreed to take on the editorial role.

Yet once we got home, the impetus faltered. Six weeks on, with little to show, a tentative email conversation began amongst the editors. 'How do you feel about this book project?' we queried. 'Ambivalent,' we agreed. It all seemed so hard. There was so much else to do. This project came on top of other responsibilities – to work, families and other academic priorities. 'A transnational, even transcontinental, book project is a very ambitious aim,' said Beatrix. Lea responded, valuing the 'opportunity to reflect on why I have been so silent on this book project'. Yet, she said, 'I am also very eager to know how this book processing could be possible.'

We confronted a dilemma. On the one hand, we each faced our own university's institutional duties and performance demands. On the other, we glimpsed the tantalising possibility of an academic adventure that would engage us intellectually in new conversations, ideas and knowledge building. It was these activities that we each understood to lie at the heart of an academic's work. Yet it was these activities that were proving too hard to do in the face of workplace demands.

There were also practical challenges in actually doing this academic work across continents. It required us to find new ways of working across space, time and our separate academic cultures. Beatrix captured this. She noted that the book project had grown out of the general VET and Culture network rather than our common research experience. 'We have had no chance so far to experience ourselves as a "community of practice".' She was also unsure that just working via virtual communication would sustain our commitment. So:

> We should be aware that we need time and space to transform this general network 'spirit' into a working atmosphere of our editorial community. The practical question resulting from this: when and where will we meet again? How can we organise space and time for common reflecting? Will the network-meeting next year [at the VET and Culture conference] in Konstanz be early enough? I would be very happy if we could allow ourselves this time!

As this conversation progressed we became aware of interconnections. There were similarities between our own personal experiences in workplaces, occupations that were being re-ordered, and our research and writing. We agreed to read Sennett as a shared text, which provided a way of reflecting on our own working lives in academic terms. We recognised ourselves in his description of flexible capitalism:

> [The] emphasis on flexibility is changing the very meaning of work, and so the words we use for it. 'Career', for instance, in its English origins meant a road for carriages, and as eventually applied to labor meant a lifelong channel for one's economic pursuits. Flexible capitalism has blocked the straight roadway of career, diverting employees suddenly from one kind of work into another. The word 'job' in English of the fourteenth century meant a lump or piece of something which could be carted around. Flexibility today brings back this arcane sense of the job, as people do lumps of labor, pieces of work, over the course of a lifetime.
>
> (Sennett 1998: 9)

Working together across continents, we came to see the way contemporary changes in work and education have created a new global political regime that endorses flexibility and learning, albeit with national and local variations. Moreover, as researchers, educators and citizens, we have become as much subject to this regime as those that we talk about in the empirical studies that make up the later part of the book.

Yet it was Sennett's (1998: 148) concluding comment that resonated with our sense of frustration arising from the difficulties of doing our academic work. It focused our discussions and energies and gave this book its core agenda.

> If change occurs it happens on the ground, between persons speaking out of inner need, rather than through mass uprisings. What political programs follow from those inner needs, I simply don't know. But I do know a regime which provides human beings no deep reasons to care about one another cannot long preserve its legitimacy.

As a result of these discussions and our practical experiments in doing academic work by email, our work developed along three separate lines of inquiry:

- We dipped into various literatures in order to develop a lexicon to talk about our experiences of disturbing work, and to anchor and authorise our understandings and interpretations, in line with conventional research practice.
- We engaged with the various empirical studies that make up the body of this anthology – written from particular places across Europe, the US, UK and Australia and from across a range of human service occupations – from nursing, social work and education.
- And we talked together, mainly by email, sharing stories of our personal working lives and comparing our different experiences of flexible capitalism as it infected our academic workplaces and our country contexts.

We each saw the way different authors who wrote the empirical studies for this book sometimes took contexts for granted when interrogating their data, reworked concepts handed down from the past to fit new times and reproduced old silences by using old but authorised frameworks. Talking cross-nationally about these things made us aware of dissonance – in experience, histories and cultures and ways of understanding. These dissonances highlighted contradictions, jogged memories and pushed us back to ways of understanding that we felt we could trust outside the 'weasel words' of neoliberalism and managerialism.

Strikingly, we recognised that we, editors as well as chapter authors, were competent describing and analysing disturbing work, but much less able to see and discuss transforming politics. We began to see the way our work together, anchored in occupational fields, national contexts and disciplinary traditions, was constrained by place, time and culture, but also how that anchoring provided resources for understanding transforming politics, particularly when we worked with those resources across boundaries. Slowly, we realised that through our book project we were building important relationships, creating a space for transgressing familiar norms, and engaging in a 'politics of we'. In what follows, we review the literature we found most useful and then describe how we came to reposition ourselves as editors and to see our own professional locations and experiences as a valuable resource for analysing our own project.

## Dipping into literatures

Sennett's idea that people come together in troubling times to 'speak out of inner need' provided a provocative starting point for our reflections on the heavy literatures that the social sciences has handed down to us from the past. This phrase captured something about being caught in dilemmas, having 'no place to go', struggling to negotiate somewhere to stand and to act. It suggested the idea of 'contradiction'.

Points of contradiction when people experience disjuncture and speak out of inner need have long been recognised as a locus for collective coalescing and mobilisation. Marx (1845/1976: 619), for instance, talks of the 'inner strife and intrinsic contradictoriness' within social life that revolutionises practice. Giddens (1984: 165–166) gives voice to this theme, saying:

> We have to grasp how history is made through the active involvements and struggles of human beings, and yet at the same time both forms those human beings and produces outcomes which they neither intend nor foresee.

C. W. Mills (1971) describes the articulation of inner need as a process of moving from personal troubles to public issues. Troubles afflict individuals, in their sense of self, their immediate relationships and in those environments in which they are directly involved and aware. They give rise to the individual's sense of being caught in a trap, locked in by larger-scale processes over which they have little control. In this respect troubles are private matters, an individual's recognition that cherished values are threatened. Issues transcend these local personal environments and are instead evident in broader aspects of social life, in organisations and institutional arrangements, and in the way these coalesce to form larger social structures and histories. Issues are evident in the public domain, as publics become aware that their values are threatened. Initially this awareness may be diffuse and almost unarticulated, a pervasive 'structure of feeling' (Williams 1977) that is ephemeral and hard to pin down.

Yet as threats to values becomes more evident, this diffuse unease crystallises, sometimes in withdrawal and passivity and sometimes in talk and action. This awakening marks the recognition that each of us stands at the intersection of biography, history and social structure and that a self-consciousness of ourselves in history and society gives us more embracing ways of understanding the world and sharper insights into sensible courses of action. Mills describes this awakening:

> [People] whose mentalities have swept only a series of limited orbits often come to feel as if suddenly awakened in a house with which they had only supposed themselves to be familiar. Correctly or incorrectly, they come to feel that they can now provide themselves with adequate summations, cohesive assessments, comprehensive orientations. Older decisions that once appeared sound, now seem to them products of a mind unaccountably

dense. Their capacity for astonishment is made lively again. They acquire a
new way of thinking, they experience a transvaluation of values.

(Mills 1971: 14)

Haug and her colleagues (1987) argue that these processes through which people awake from their personal troubles to see public issues can become a
transforming politics. Yet whether and how this happens depends upon the way
subjects actively write themselves into social relations of domination and subordination, and the practical work of turning heteronomy, 'a state of social
relations that marks out barriers to women's [and men's] strivings for autonomy
and liberation' (Carter 1987: 18) into autonomy or self-determination. They
argue that we are not victims in these processes, as subjects subordinated to social
structures. Rather, we are active makers of our subjectification as a consequence
of the process through which we 'perceive any given situation, approve or vali-
date it, assess its goals as proper or worthy, repugnant or reprehensible . . .
[which sets up] a field of conflict between dominant cultural values and opposi-
tional attempts to wrest cultural meaning and pleasure from life' (Haug et al.
1987: 41).

This tension between living dominant cultural norms compliantly or in conflict with them creates contradictions in experience which are felt in embodied
ways as well as being evident in language and action. The challenge, Haug
argues, is not to harmonise these contradictions, finding ways of living that erase
their disturbing impact, creating numbness and amnesia and confirming our sub-
jection within relations of power. Instead, the task is to 'live historically', refusing
'to accept ourselves as "pieces of nature", given and unquestioned', and 'to see
ourselves as subjects who have become what they are and who are therefore subject to change' (Haug et al. 1987: 51). This process of living historically means
becoming aware of the way changes in work and life are formed historically, con-
textualised and experienced across social divisions. This awareness forms a basis
for an everyday practical politics of working life – what might once have been
called a 'politics of liberation' that contests social relations of domination and
subordination as an everyday pursuit of social justice and collective happiness.

Yet as Haug (1984) argues, living contradictions through practical politics
rather than accepting subjectification is not easy, especially given the slipperiness
of norms within flexible capitalism. Dominant cultural norms are embedded in
language that is mediated through texts and text-based systems of communication. 'Information, knowledge, reasoning, decision-making, "culture", scientific
theorising, and the like become properties of organization' and coordinate and
regulate activity across local sites (Smith 1999: 79). These 'textual practices of
power' create the familiar world of talk and tradition, becoming part of everyday
life and lived in ways that are taken for granted, unless we are prompted to
actively consider and question them. Even then, the experience of dissonance
may not be enough to prompt us to live contradictions historically by asserting
our own meanings and pleasures from living. As Haug (1984: 79) says, while

changes in work and life may rupture established forms of living, this does not necessarily lead to change:

> Whether people grasp the changing conditions and construct new forms [depends upon] practical politics. The forms of the old society are obstacles and, at the same time, shelters for the individual . . . It is this entanglement, the protecting character of the fetters and the fettering character of the protections which can make liberation a catastrophe. The shattering of the old forms . . . engenders tasks of reorganisation, it creates conditions which must be seized. But it does not produce liberation itself.

## Cross-cultural readings

Our book project was conceived as an interrogation of transformations in lifelong learning and work. Yet our cross-national comparative conversations opened up our shared experience of global policy discourses. We recognised that the change in terminology, from education and work to lifelong learning and employment, is itself a significant feature of the (not so) illegible regime of flexible capitalism. We reflected on the way lifelong learning positioned us all as learners in a learning process. We were expected to learn all the time, about everything, exhaustively and exhaustingly, throughout our lives. Yet in becoming learners, we never became learned. We were not expected to arrive at a state of knowledge, which would give us a place to stand as 'knower', with authority to speak and a basis for respect (Sennett 2003). Instead, the treadmill defined by neoliberal lifelong learning positions us as always with things to learn, as not able, as a beginner to others' authority.

We read Sennett's *Corrosion of Character* as a starting point for our work together because it provided an *entrée* to the way work was being disturbed. But Sennett was writing about the US, while we were reading from Finland, Germany and Australia, countries that have different, more and less convergent, relationships with Anglo-American capitalism. Sennett was also writing about particular kinds of workers, largely in manufacturing, who were already organised and working in flexible networks and in which disturbances arose from technological progress and dislocation of knowledge. His examples were taken from specific sections of the working world/labour society and they present a male perspective. Although Sennett occasionally adds female examples, he does not reflect the gendering effects of neoliberal reforms, nor the gender structures in the dominant organisation of work/labour, nor does he reflect the possible gendering or de-gendering outcomes of reconfigurations of work. This is because – surprise – he does not see the established gendered societal labour division.

Sennett's analysis of work also does not consider established education and other kinds of human service work. Instead, he focuses on the relationship between work and learning along just one dimension, which is related to learning to work by acting as a flexible self-entrepreneur. This leaves out the fact that modern societies have institutionalised education systems so that education itself plays a crucial role in the continuity of societies, reforming and renewing knowledge skills and dispositions over time within publicly endorsed frameworks. It means that Sennett does not pay all that much attention to the reproductive role that education plays in society and working life. Yet this educational work contributes to the configuration of occupational orders through vocational and professional education, and is critical in developing the skills necessary to coordinate staffing. It also contributes to social renewal and security across generations.

This institutionalisation of educational work has become an occupation/profession itself with a distinct occupational order. Education, particularly education for work through apprenticeships and technical training, has always had a particular division of labour. In the 'society of orders' men and women both had an acknowledged place in the mainly home-based economy. The master and his wife both were responsible for maintaining the common business, although with an established labour division between them. With industrialisation and the development of administrative bureaucracies the division of workplaces for men and women was further delineated. Now men left their home to work in offices or factories and earned the family's living, while women did the home and family work without pay. In Germany, but also elsewhere, this was a crucial process in the eighteenth century, when the sustaining model of the bourgeois family developed into a normative orientation. The bourgeois ideal of the role of woman shaped the form of the 'breadwinner state' and the German idea of education and the educational system. The 'ideal occupation of a woman as a mother and housewife' is still shining through institutional arrangements, for example school hours ending at 1 p.m. and kindergartens open only for children over the age of three, patterns that only recently started to change.

This division between breadwinning productive work outside of the home and unpaid reproductive work – one visible, the other invisible, one serving as a defining frame and blueprint for education and training, the other to be developed 'by nature' – persists. It persists not just in practice but in the framing of Sennett's account of flexible capitalism and its effects. His account is a textual practice of power which sees some things and also has blind spots. This means that it is important to re-write education and care work back in to public understandings of flexible capitalism, along with the necessary contribution that schools, teachers and other forms of reproductive human service work make to the renewal of society across generations. For without this work, how can societies perpetuate themselves over time? Teachers' work is disturbed if education is transformed into self-responsible life-wide learning, but with what other effects? Will the learners of tomorrow's flexible, entrepreneurial, 'self-service' world need teachers at all? What will be lost or gained by this transformation? Who will benefit? And how are other forms of emotional labour and caring work, which contribute to social continuity and security, disturbed and reconfigured alongside these reorganisations of educational work?

Reading Sennett from places other than the US confronted our place-based experiences. These dissonances pressed us to reflect on our own taken-for-granted assumptions about the world and the way we generalised them across space, time and experience. Similar things happened when we read contributors' early chapter drafts, sharpening our sensitivity to the way we had each come to know disturbing work and why we seemed blind to transforming politics.

Chapters from Germany told stories about disturbing work but without considering the implications of the geographic division into East and West and the subsequent effects of reintegration. Yet, at that time, people from the East who could be mobile moved to the West. It meant that disturbing work in Germany was tied up with mobility and the kind of bodies that could move. The movers were young and the professionals, leaving older, less mobile workers in the old East Germany. Understanding disturbing work, and the kinds of transforming politics that could be sustained there, depended upon understanding these movements and bodies and the power relations that orchestrated them.

Chapters from Anglo-countries highlighted the effects of unbounded entrepreneurialism and individualistic responses but also the way people were supported through particular kinds of social mobility opportunities organised through education. The significance of fees in regulating access to these pathways distinguished these Anglo-practices from established European education, even though fees for learning are being endorsed in European neoliberalism. It suggested a greater accommodation to markets and the commodification of education in the Anglo-world compared to continental Europe. The representation of democracy was contentious, too. Some chapters echoed neoliberal attitudes to states and the idea of democracy being anchored in individual citizen participatory action, which confronted European notions that saw a central state, nation and civic life as critical features of living together.

These processes of reading cross-culturally as we worked together created dissonances, sometimes through recognition of similarity and sometimes difference. Yet through these cross-national processes of working and learning together we began to see how disturbing work framed and constrained transforming politics. We recalled the way people's eyes glazed over when someone talked about educational practices and principles in their own countries – as if there were no continuities or interesting discontinuities between places and practices. It helped us to recognise the everydayness of living contradictions and acknowledge that by working together we had grasped something important about how to listen, how to feel, and how then to interrogate, rather than harmonise, contradiction.

This revealed another feature of the increasingly legible regime of power within flexible capitalism – that when time is squeezed through work intensification, funding cuts and the erosion of people's commitment to work, acknowledging contradictions adds to workload. Harmonising contradictions, smoothing things out, through pragmatic problem solving with minimal effort seems much more attractive than the struggle to work with contradictions. We recognised that dealing with dissonance required us to 'take time' – a stance which immediately set us at odds with the intensified imperatives within our neoliberal workplaces and which we found deliciously enjoyable and energising.

Our process of working together had taken the hard road of engaging actively with dissonance but it enabled us to see the tension between 'doing it right' and 'just doing it'. It became obvious that these different styles of work were two ends of a spectrum and we had to decide, consciously, on a task-by-task basis how to frame our effort and define boundaries in relation to our work. Through these processes of working, reflecting and learning together we began to tease out a methodology for disrupting the enchantment induced by neoliberal flexible capitalism and awakening ourselves to ways of seeing transforming politics in working life.

## Living contradictions historically

The texts from the past, and our engagement with the empirical studies from our contributors, offered certain ways of thinking in relation to our work as editors in this book project. Yet it was our practical conversations which prompted our 'awakening' and reflections on how we were 'living contradictions historically'. Each of us, located in Finland, Germany and Australia, spoke from our own places, our different cultures and traditions, and through this process we became sharply aware of the textual practices of power and how we were enmeshed in them. As Sennett says, place is geography, which becomes a location for politics when the inhabitants experience contradiction and begin to talk together. 'A place becomes a community when people use the word "we"' (Sennett 1998: 137).

These conversations began as we struggled to take up this book project alongside our everyday working lives. Through emails we compared experiences of our working lives in academic workplaces and our frustrations at work. While this talk offered some relief, it also fuelled our growing awareness of a shared experience of work intensification and of us running out of control.

Terri's situation was as a tenured professor in a small faculty (about 100 education academics). She reflected:

> I had been Associate Dean of Research (theoretically 50 per cent of my workload) plus teaching and research projects but the workload got out of control. When this 50 per cent formal teaching and administrative workload (but not research) reached 197 per cent, with no evidence that the institution would act to ameliorate the pressure, I almost unconsciously drew a 'line in the sand'. Resigning from the administrative position was met with disbelief from colleagues and had costs – my access to information stopped, my connections with university-level networks fell away. The experience felt like a kind of exile but institutional marginality provided the opportunity to rebuild a working life on my terms. It broke the spell of managerialism that drives people to inhuman levels of self-exploitation under the guise of being responsible, making things happen, supporting colleagues and ensuring institutional survival.

This personal experience of working life gone mad was paralleled for Lea and Beatrix. We agreed to extend our email correspondence to write short narratives about our working lives. The themes of work intensification, pressure to get funding and to do projects were common across our experience but the women in the European Research Area – Lea and Beatrix – were in long-term contract employment, caught in the cracks between god-professors and their acolytes and handmaidens. As Beatrix noted, these features of academic work were not just personal troubles, they were

> an effect of general academic working conditions. You need to be a lonesome fighter and most of the time you are alone with your reports and chapters to be written, with your students, with your field research, when presenting in a conference. In addition, when placed in the middle field of the academic hierarchy, i.e. as a senior researcher but not as a professor, part of what I do is counting as reward for the professor, not as my own achievement. And there is no real culture of valuing, e.g. quality in teaching. So, what disturbs me most is: 1. not having a permanent contract and therefore I am repeatedly forced to rethink my perspective; 2. the lack of a supportive network at my workplace; 3. the lack of affirmation; and 4. the fragmentation of work and, as a result, the lack of time for intense reflection.

Lea, in her short-hand way, captured these contradictory themes:

- shortage of academic positions and greater dependence on outside funding
- double standard: flexible practices and orthodox faith in science and discipline
- what is loyalty? To whom to be loyal? The ethic of university employer? Network ethics?
- science fractions/subcultures follow the rules of patriarchal family order.

As she said:

> Goodbye to the democratic university and peer practices originating from the women's studies pioneers in the late 80s and early 90s! When the supervisor of my PhD, the female professor, retired I was thrown out as an old-timer as well. New Public Management – local managerialism – step in!

What emerged from these narratives was a sense of the similarities of our experience, despite our global spread. We each experienced our own workplaces as onerous and damaging. We deployed all kinds of strategies to protect those practices of work and learning that we valued, as we protected ourselves from the destructive effects of this 'flexibilised' regime of power. We began to recognise that, despite Sennett's claims, this regime of power was not so 'illegible' after all. It hinged in familiar ways on exploitation anchored in social divisions, particularly gender divisions of labour. Living these relations and textual practices of power on a day-to-day basis had rendered us incapable of seeing our way through this subordination in our everyday lives.

While our email correspondence and self-writing provided a sideline link to sanity, our attention turned more and more to chapter drafts and the textual practices used to represent lifelong learning and work. As we talked and reviewed drafts of this introduction and contributors' chapters, we again confronted dissonance as a result of the place from which we wrote, read and spoke.

## Toward a transforming politics

Reading, talking and emailing together enabled us to clarify the purposes of our book project. The formal aims were to:

- clarify the conditions and contradictions of work, education and the way we live it all today within an increasingly global, illegible regime of power;
- identify the places and conceptual platforms from which we might be able to take tentative steps towards a transforming politics of education and work – what in flexible capitalism is characterised as lifelong learning and employment; and
- document examples of the transforming politics within lifelong learning and employment.

Yet what motivated us was the struggle to find ways of understanding contemporary changes in work and education as we articulated private troubles as public issues in ways that let us see transforming politics. Through this work we began to crystallise a methodology and conceptualisation of transforming politics in globalised flexible capitalism.

The process of working together energised us and reconfirmed the social significance of academic research. First, it alerted us to dissonances: in our experience and in the interface between experience and textual practices. That we each came from different countries accentuated the surprise of similarities as well as differences. It was exciting work, which turned our conversations into a kind of adventure where we discovered new things about our own and each other's worlds. Talking about these dissonances with this spirit of curiosity and adventure meant that we engaged with them actively rather than glossing them over. So we did not routinely harmonise these contradictions but, instead, problematised our taken-for-granted ways of understanding as we spoke and heard from different places. Active listening opened up ways of recognising these framings and how they shaped our ways of living, in conformity with the embrace of neoliberal flexible capitalism. Finally, this process of talking and hearing our differences affirmed us as knowers in relation to our places. We could speak as knowers in relation to our occupations, countries and disciplinary traditions, and also the extra-local practices of coordination and regulation that shaped our working lives – the global discourses of lifelong learning, quality, the governing by numbers, and the ways we lived inside these text-based systems of knowledge. Through listening and talking we authorised each other to speak, hear and critique as knowers within our own working lives and our work with others.

What emerged was a much clearer sense of transforming politics and a sharp awareness that we need to find ways of seeing and doing the 'politics of we' in our everyday life situations, rather than endlessly reiterating the story of disturbed work, troubled experience, and individualised subordination within relations of power. Instead, what is required is an active grasping of agency; a choice to be agentic in our everyday lives and to assert ourselves as knowers in practice and our capacity to know and be expert in relation to others. This practice of knowing acknowledges dependencies but also engages with (walking a tightrope between) respect and disrespect. It permits a sceptical and critical collaborative dialogue with those who came before us as well as those with whom we live and work.

We can see that globalised neoliberalism is disturbing work in different occupations and countries, creating micro-level disturbances in individual experience and meso-level disturbances in organisational settings and practices. The disruption of these individual and occupational identities and the entities through which they are embodied means that the old 'we' of collective action and industrial-occupational politics is no longer available as a collectivity for politics to the extent it was in the past.

Yet alongside these processes of fragmentation and new inclusions and exclusions, there is plenty of evidence of new clusters of people coming together to create 'wes' that are more fluid, light, networked and mobile than in the past. Some of the chapters talk about these new 'wes' in terms of teachers in casual employment who drive from place to place to teach, or who come together for temporary periods to work on projects. Others talk about the way 'wes' are formed by stratification processes that operate through definitions of skill, knowledge, ethnicity, age and seniority.

The process of fragmentation is disturbing but so is the absence of a familiar old-styled 'we' that we can recognise. This absence is confirmed because we do not always see the new fluid coalescing clusters, occupants of job categories and transient project groups as 'wes', and they (we) do not always recognise themselves as 'wes'. Because we cannot recognise these emergent 'wes', we do not know or acknowledge them as collective actors, and so we do not endorse and authorise their agency within transforming politics. This means that we do not support them as actors in everyday practical politics, find ways of linking them into established traditions and decision-making structures and build on them in further political agency through those dimensions of our everyday work and lives which reproduce social continuity and security.

Yet, our bottom-up reading of the draft chapters and discussions about these emerging light and fluid 'wes' suggest that they do open up some kind of counter-politics within flexible capitalism. Some of the patterns that indicate these contradictory fragmenting and coalescing 'wes' are:

- fragmentation of old occupational orders and de-centring of social spaces;
- hollowing out of occupational identities and diversification of occupational entities;

- struggles over boundaries and contents, boundary definition and belonging, and the authority to define boundaries;
- inequalities, patterns of inclusion/exclusion in occupations, divisions of labour and working life;
- emerging groupings, clusters, project groups, job category sub-groups, and networks;
- shifting conditions which bring identities (individuals, occupations, organisations) together even though they may not recognise themselves as a collectivity;
- individual choice and the sense that this is a non-choice (for example taking part-time employment which may have been a choice but also is taken because there are no other options);
- privatisation of living, depression, but also health and well-being, lifestyle management, spirituality, personalisation of the workplace/space;
- fears and fantasies about the centre when there is no centre, and about being in- or out-side when there are multiple spaces and boundaries;
- pressures around positioning and priorities – what you should have, where you should be, how you should manage your effort, and how you can focus;
- ethical dilemmas in work and work ethos because established values and what is valued are challenged and problematised;
- changes in work practices, work organisation, hierarchies, with new challenges
- patterns of networking based on task and function, but also on affiliation, external collegialities, access to and use of social spaces;
- strategies that create fragmentation-fabrication and how they are used, by whom, with what effects; and
- resources (economic, cultural, knowledge, social, political) which are used in these strategies for and against fragmentation-fabrication.

These emerging themes highlight the importance of an active 'politics of fabrication' to counter the effects and preoccupations with fragmentation. This fabrication of 'wes' involves processes of cultural and organisational construction and of building collective capacity – even if only transiently. It suggests a politics of sociality: that affirms mutuality and collective happiness in place of neoliberal betterment through individual achievement, laughter to counter depression, remembering rather than forgetting and belonging rather than individualised alienation.

The cultural and organisational work of fabrication focuses attention on the importance of education, which engages critically with dominant cultural norms and textual practices and the identities they form. The process of crafting social spaces which induct people into ways of living actively and critically in relation to the extra-local coordination and regulation of everyday living and sustainable societies is fundamental to a politics of education. It might be called an education for civil, civic and sustainable living.

What is at stake in this politics is the deployment of learning as an organised strategy in all contexts to form and endorse knowers, with public recognition and authority to act within the social processes that make up and shape working lives. It is not about producing learners as individualised identities who always learn but never know, who remain beginners but not authorised and agentic players in their space-time collectivities. And it is not about privileging schools, universities and other sites where knowers are formed and ordered as part of a national project and staffing strategy. Rather, becoming a knower is a process that is intrinsic to the formation of 'wes' in every place. It depends upon the way we recognise and respect, sceptically engage with and act within accepted social constructions and structures to endorse one another in our everyday interactions and living together.

This politics of education for social fabrication acknowledges, and is anchored in, the important work of social construction and of renewing social continuity and security over time. For it is only by passing on the wisdom of the past and subjecting it to the critiques of the present that collective capacity can move, in the future, beyond transience to sustainability. In this way, our work together presses us to recognise the historic structuring of society by gender and class, and to work against the death-wish discourses that operate as if work that privileges productivity and profitability can exist without reproductive and care work, the kinds of human service work that support life itself.

# References

Carter, E. (1987) 'Translator's foreword', in F. Haug et al. (eds) Female Sexualisation: A Collective Work of Memory, London: Verso, 11–19.

Haug, F. (1984) 'Marx and work: The immiseration discourse of the logic of ruptures and contradictions', in S. Hanninen and L. Paldán (eds) Rethinking Marx, Hamburg: Argument Verlag, 76–80.

Haug, F. et al. (1987) Female Sexualisation: A Collective Work of Memory, London: Verso.

Giddens, A. (1984) Constitution of Society: Outline of the Theory of Structuration, Berkeley: University of California Press.

Marx, K. (1845/1976) Theses on Feuerbach, Moscow: Progress Publishers.

Mills, C. W. (1971) The Sociological Imagination, London: Penguin.

Sennett, R. (1998) The Corrosion of Character: The Personal Consequences of Work in the New Capitalism, New York: W.W. Norton.

Sennett, R. (2003) Respect: The Formation of Character in a World of Inequality, London: Penguin.

Smith, D. E. (1999) Writing the Social: Critique, Theory and Investigation, Toronto: University of Toronto Press.

Williams, R. (1977) Marxism and Literature, Oxford: Oxford University Press.

# Part I

# Reconfiguring occupational orders

# Chapter 2

# Human service labour force in the making

## Spotlight on Finnish practical nurses

*Lea Henriksson*

The universal welfare state of the Nordic type and its comprehensive public services have played a central role in professionalising human service work and empowering its citizen-employees. Starting with short training courses, nursing and social work – like teaching – have gradually become integrated into national education systems. This development has resulted in increasing expectations about formal competence and ethical commitment.

Complexities and controversies around the neoliberal turn in Finland since the 1990s have, however, shaken the terms and conditions of work and learning in human services. The policy shift has questioned the institutional anchoring of public service provision, the gendered legacies of occupational and educational developments, and labour force protection related to comprehensive public employment for which the trade unions have traditionally fought.

Developments in Finland roughly match those of the other Nordic countries, although the intensity seems to be somewhat more thoroughgoing. Perspectives highlighting these transformations in occupational, educational and unionist orders underline the multi-layered nature, and the historical, cultural and gendered institutional embeddedness, of work and learning in human services.

The concept of human service work (Hughes 1958; Stacey 1981, 1984) is applied here as an inclusive frame to consider the making of a new labour force from two perspectives. First, the concept opens up a view of the career as an occupation, consisting of changes in its internal organisation and its place in the societal division of labour. Second, it captures the careers of individuals and professional groups within the organised systems of welfare provision; the social and cultural processes that are lived through everyday settings of work and learning. The intention is to present disturbances in the work and labour aspects of human services, linked to the policy interplay – or lack of coordination – among service policy, education policy and employment policy.

In welfare policy and research, lower-level professionals are often an invisible group of actors (Thornley 2003; see Kubiak, this volume). Yet these lower ranks also face immediate global transformations through the restructuring of services and the vulnerability of employment relations (Seccombe 1995; Walford 1995). Therefore it is important to take a closer look at what the contemporary policy incentives and management procedures imply for this labour force. The education reform of 'practical nurses for social and health care' (in Finnish '*lähihoitaja*' – the 'carer nearest to you') is introduced as an example of a neoliberal policy reform disturbing social orders, collective agency and professional identity in human service work. The reform is an illuminating example of fixing together economy, life-long learning and active unemployment policies in a societal context defined by welfare service restructuring.

## Changes to the Finnish welfare state

The development of the Finnish welfare state is tightly bound to nation building and citizenship. As a small, poor and agrarian country, Finland faced modernisation relatively late, but quickly. The building of a welfare state infrastructure since the Second World War was a piecemeal activity, characterised by conflicts and bargaining processes between various social interest groups, which led to corporatist negotiation structures. State-steered expansion of the public service system was blooming in the heyday of the welfare state in the 1970s and 1980s, helping the values of democracy, solidarity and mutual responsibility to filter into professional and unionist agency (Henriksson *et al.* 2006). It is important to recognise that education is a key strategy for regulating human service work and how the 'cultural projects of vocational education' (Heikkinen 1995) have evolved alongside the growth of the nation state.

A shift in emphasis from state-regulated and professionally driven public welfare service systems to managerially driven ones has occurred across large parts of Europe (Lewis and Surender 2004; van Oorschot *et al.* 2008). This development, here referred to as a neoliberal policy shift, has emphasised the reorganising of human services to increase cost-effectiveness through marketisation and outsourcing. In Finland this shift started in the early 1990s. Along with the regulation of the money market, a deep economic crisis and recession was associated with mass unemployment, helping the neoliberal ideology to gain hegemony (Patomäki 2007). Despite positive trends, unemployment has remained high (at 16.6 per cent in 1994 and 7.0 per cent in January 2009; Statistics Finland 2009). Although in macroeconomic terms post-recession Finland continues to follow the European and Nordic developments (Heikkilä and Kautto 2006), far-reaching institutional changes caused by welfare cuts and pruning occurred.

Global pressures have pushed national policy measures to rearrange the responsibilities among the state, municipalities, employers and the citizens. As elsewhere in Europe (Finlayson *et al.* 2002; Bleich *et al.* 2003), the Finnish public sector employers, educational actors and stakeholders and trade unions are persuaded to act in a coordinated manner. The call for partnerships with strategic actors and a 'multi-layering' of political authority is especially justified by emphasising the need to safeguard the supply of labour for the future labour force. The policy rhetoric reflects these developments surrounding what is currently recognised as a crisis of recruitment – labour mismatches in EU terms – in human service work and is creating special types of appeals about work and learning. The shift from a welfare state to a 'competition state' (Kettunen 2006) is documented and arguments about the welfare state crisis are introduced. But contrary to what the theories about the legitimacy of the welfare state had predicted, there continues to be a widespread support for the welfare state all over Europe, including Finland.

## The case of practical nurses:
## a three-scene approach

The occupation titled a 'practical nurse for social and health care' provides a case example of the interfacing social, economic and cultural transformations related to the disturbances in work and learning in human service work. The national landscape highlights the importance of policy-induced change in the terms and conditions of collective agency, professional identity and value commitments in human service work. The case comprises three elements. First, the education reform is introduced as a contested policy instrument that created both amalgamation and fragmentation of a professional group. The unionist policy inventory, in the second scene, mirrors the way education reform disturbs craft unionism and the lived experiences of employees at the organisational and workplace level. This inquiry is restricted to the unionist 'politics of we', tailored by the leadership to union members. In the third scene, the focus is on the interplay between policy changes and professional projects as collective mobility projects. Conclusions about social polarisation sum up the complex and contested nature of the making of a new labour force in human service work. The purpose of the three-scene approach is to use different analytical lenses that highlight what kind of social group or collective force practical nurses form. Who constitutes the 'we' that makes up practical nurses and what is this 'we' like in terms of social status, professional agency and identity?

The making of a new labour force is portrayed through policy documents and a trade union journal. The documents, revealing the governmental split in terms of sectoral and institutional trajectories, are concerned with welfare services and education strategies, which are linked to scenarios of national service policy and employment concerns (Ministry of Labour (ML) 2003; Committee for the Future of the Finnish Parliament 2004). In the health sector (Ministry of Social Affairs and Health (MSAH) 2001, 2002, 2007a), the focus is on the upper levels of the professional hierarchy; the licensed health care professionals who have longer traditions and are usually more educated and regulated than the social care professionals. In the social sector (The Finnish National Board of Education (FNBE) 1995, 2001; MSAH 2003, 2007b; Ministry of Education (ME) 2006), documents address the three grades of social care professionals whose eligibility is less regulated compared with the health professionals and is therefore demonstrated by qualifications.

The trade union journal for practical nurses, titled *Super* (volumes 2000–2006, 11 numbers per year), is a former journal of the craft union. The union was exclusive to one occupation, the primary nurses (1985–1995) and their forerunners, the auxiliary nurses (1946–1985). Both of these occupations function primarily in health care, occupying the roles of nurses' aides. Editorials are explicit about health care and craft union trajectories, although the journal as a whole gives a more inclusive picture of the occupational field for union members. In 2009, the union has about 70,000 members who are predominantly women (96 per cent) working in primary care health centres and elderly care (73 per cent) and hospitals (14 per cent). They are mainly (78 per cent) employed by the municipalities (Super 2009). 'Super' is one of the five trade unions practical nurses could join.

## Who are the practical nurses?

Throughout the 1990s and early 2000s unemployment, the threatening labour shortage and declining attraction of human service occupations have increased policy interest in tightening the linkages between educational restructuring, employment incentives and public service provision (MSAH 2001, 2003). In order to dismantle rigid professional hierarchies and sector boundaries, the practical nurse occupation was designed to be a 'new-born educational field of social and health care' (MSAH 2001: 42). In the name of relevance to working life (FNBE 1995), social inclusion and skill upgrading (MSAH 2003, 2007b), a variety of education pathways at the upper secondary school level, adult education and vocational training were tied together in the career of an occupation following the command of employability.

As part of this streamlining of welfare service provision, the upper secondary vocational curriculum for practical nurses was established in 1995. It combined three social care (homemaker, day care worker, carer for the disabled) and seven health care occupations (primary nurse, paediatric nurse assistant, psychiatric nurse assistant, dental assistant, first aid care worker, rehabilitation nurse assistant and podiatrist) under one umbrella title (FNBE 2001). The reform lengthened the training and stretched the occupational spectrum, which currently includes nine sub-fields: care for the disabled, care for the elderly, children's and youth care, customer service, emergency care, mental health and social work with intoxicant abusers, nursing and care, oral and dental care and rehabilitation (HESOTE 2009). Practical nurses were to work in the declining primary care and hospital settings and the growing community care settings following the restructuring of human services. In the context of service pruning, these new professionals were also expected to become entrepreneurs, to create their own occupational careers, employ themselves and bear the risks of service provision, in the growing private sector labour market, which is developing slowly in Finland. In spite of the aims of the reform, to produce cross-sector, generalist professionals, it is noticeable that national policy-making and local administration structures are slowly discarding the sectoral split and practices, although the preference of health care over social care continues (Henriksson 2008).

Occupational protection and regulation of health care professionals in Finland include different categories of professional practice rights reflecting professional hierarchies. Following the reform of practical nurse training, this regulatory frame extended to practical nurses and thus to social care. Licensed professionals (17 titles in total), such as physicians (university degree) and nurses (polytechnic/higher-education degree), receive the right to practise a profession by virtue of law (Act 559/1994, Decree 564/1994). This right has to be applied for and is granted by the National Supervisory Authority for Welfare and Health (Valvira 2009). According to the rules, the practical nurses are professionals with a protected occupational title (13 titles in total). Although the regulation encompasses practical nurses, their employment security is rather different from other regulated professionals. Other persons with required training, experience and skills and knowledge can enter this occupation but are not entitled to use the protected occupational title. Within the terms of the cut-back economy and crisis of recruitment, the employers benefit by continuing to use old job titles, such as home helper or primary nurse, because it permits the hiring of less-educated and less-expensive workers instead of qualified practical nurses.

The policy aim of preventing social marginalisation is strongly embedded in the reform of practical nurse training. Broad recruitment through diverse curricula and education tracks has created different occupational careers and status. The social mixture of the recruits opened a variety of occupational opportunities up to youngsters and adults through schools-based learning or apprenticeship and competence tests. For the 'elite' of the recruits who entered a three-year curriculum (120 credits), the qualification fulfilled the ideal of a gradual step-by-step education. This included, for instance, an option for the qualified practical nurses to further educate themselves by entering higher education and graduate from polytechnics, for instance, as registered nurses or social work professionals (see Niiranen-Linkama, this volume). Nevertheless the education policy target, which seems to have been realised, was for about one-third of the recruits to continue their vocational education upwards (MSAH 2001; ME 2006). Due to this multi-channel recruitment, the employment patterns of practical nurses vary enormously. For a few, the qualification made permanent employment possible. For some, especially for the youngsters, the qualification led to low-paid, unattractive temporary jobs. Too many became unemployed (about 16 per cent in 2003) – a rate that is significantly higher than at any other educational level (ML 2003: 57).

Reducing unemployment in accordance with the European Union policy incentives, by emphasising active employment measures, was strongly encouraged in the education reform. Special funding arrangements, such as national unemployment and rehabilitation schemes and the European Social Fund, were used for this purpose. A partial training of 40 credits, one-third of the total qualification, was used as a policy instrument to promote social inclusion and prevent or reduce unemployment (MSAH 2007a). These training courses were organised especially in elderly care, which was most affected by the labour shortage and its unattractiveness as an occupational choice. The partial qualification is, however, a contested policy instrument. Although the partial education was intended to break a period of unemployment or otherwise marginalised labour market participation (Pitkänen 2005), it created a para-professional category (see Kubiak, this volume) of 'would-be professionals' (Hughes 1958: 8) in a more general sense. These would-be professionals compete for the same jobs as the qualified ones but are less expensive and may be more agreeable to accept temporary work. The partial qualification may also contribute to the overall degradation and lack of appeal in this female-dominated occupation, while being hyped up as an instrument of active employment policy.

These developments show how the neoliberal policy shift annuls the legacies of the former practical nurses – those homemakers in social care and primary nurses in health care – whose occupational standing was strengthened with the rise of the Finnish welfare state (Wrede and Henriksson 2005; Henriksson and Wrede 2008). In a comparative Nordic perspective, however, this nationally contested development appears in a new scale. Practical nurses seem to have the longest education in Finland and the shortest in Sweden (Wrede *et al.* 2008). The education reform discussed here has complex national, sectoral and professional segmentation consequences. Yet at the Nordic and international scale this policy-induced change means that in Finland the lower-level human service professionals continue to be well qualified and regulated. As citizen-employees with comprehensive education rights and access to active unemployment measures, human service professionals hold on to institutional anchorage within the welfare state, which is even strengthened by new inclusion policies. But how does this picture show up in the unionist scene?

## The unionist 'politics of we'

The editorials in *Super*, the trade union journal for practical nurses, introduced here, are published under the name of the union leader, a woman (until number 6/2000) and then a man, himself a primary nurse. In these accounts the union leader articulates global, national and organisational transformations and reconstructs the 'politics of we' for the union members. Editorials as institutional texts highlight how a trade union leader can act as a kind of 'identity entrepreneur' (see Alasuutari 2004) by rearticulating the policy and identity challenges faced by the union members. In this position, the identity entrepreneurs have rhetorical power to convince the members by offering their brief policy inventory. Unionist texts not only provide arguments on policy-making but also serve as accounts of how to comprehend and legitimate the agency and commitment of the professional collective in question. The examination of the editorials is here compressed into two concerns. First, how is the union agenda articulating the changes in global and national policy-making? Second, how does the union leadership express the implications of these transformations for collective agency, for the terms and conditions of the labour market and for the lived experiences and identity of practical nurses in work organisations?

In the editorials, the dangers of global policy-making portrayed by the union leader emphasised that, although Finland was a small country, trans-national enterprises had some opportunities to cut down the prices and penetrate the health services market, since it is health, not social, care services that provide 'business opportunities' for trans-national enterprises. The leadership agenda thus advocated that service provision should be kept under national governance. This claim reflects the tones of a universal welfare state tradition: comprehensive public services and equal access for a wide array of citizens. Editorial accounts clearly stressed that everything should not be outsourced and marketised (6/2004). Instead, the union leadership demonstrated the negative outcomes of policy-induced change by pointing out how decentralisation and understaffing went hand-in-hand. State-centred steering should therefore be restored to safeguard a reasonable amount of educated personnel in workplaces. It was repeated that it was not the duty of the workers to raise national competitiveness. Workers did not have any obligation to devote themselves solely to the public good! Unquestionably, it was ethically improper to appeal to employee commitment and public responsibility (4/2006). The following argument crystallises the leadership stance on the policy shift: it is not the employees' duty to participate in national saving campaigns, particularly when employers' actions become heavy-handed and workers' needs have been ignored (6–7/2006).

Continuing to criticise decentralisation, the union leadership claimed that health care policy was far too focused on redesigning organisational models instead of attending to employment relations and salaries. The declining ethic of the municipalities as public sector employers was bitterly spotlighted. It was signposted that the problems the municipalities faced were implications of the downsizing of 'ear-marked' state subsidies, critically needed for public services (4/2006). At a time when public health care was being eroded, recommendations for good professional practices or bare minimum staffing levels were policy measures absolutely insufficient to defend public service provision. Stronger manoeuvres should therefore be taken up because the cutback economy was nibbling away employment safety. The union agenda, however, noted that there had already been some severe cases in elderly care where understaffing and the neglect of care provision had attracted negative attention in the media.

In general, the editorials argued that the policy shift was having a disturbing impact on employment relations in the public service labour market. Increasing competition was creating unemployment and unwanted temporary work contracts. The question was whether practical nurses would have to resort to force to keep their jobs (1/2001; 5/2001). There was also an impending labour shortage but the competence of practical nurses was underused and undervalued. The union leader asked (1/2001: 15; 5/2001: 33): 'Why are practical nurses not good enough but the untrained workers are?' The scale of low-wage untrained service workers – the would-be professionals, the trainees, apprentices, partly qualified – showed how the leadership was bargaining for full-time, permanent jobs for the qualified professionals at a time when 46 per cent of practical nurses working in the municipalities had temporary employment contracts (5/2003). The outcry from the leadership indicated how the practical nurse occupation was becoming disregarded; the occupation was unknown and also carried a 'bad reputation' due to its broad recruitment basis and its hallmark as a cross-sector occupation in sector-divided working life settings.

The reasons for this breaking down of the potential of collective agency were attributed to national recruitment policy. 'Why are there short courses with narrow competence for the unemployed at the same time when the qualified ones have big difficulties in finding employment?' the leader asked (9/2004: 5). 'How can one attend to the recruitment of young people in this situation and how will those already working in this field keep their skills and competence updated for future work?' But it was not only the untrained workers and trainees who endangered the labour market eligibility of practical nurses. The integrity and legitimating of the occupation was also to be protected against more educated nurses (2/2000). One editorial crystallised these inter-professional tensions as follows:

> Practical nurses complain of being treated unfairly in most hospitals. Their first line managers [nurses/LH] do not act rightfully and fail to give any support. Not to mention any concern for them. The work of practical nurses is not appreciated. Work tasks are taken from their hands. Practical nurses are forced to work on the level of minimal competence.
>
> (2/2002: 7)

Employment competition seems to have created unionist anger against the nursing hierarchy; rank-and-file nurses, nurse-managers and nursing science were promoted and upgraded in hospitals while the practical nurses were excluded, according to the leadership. In the editorials the union leader pointed out the necessity of practical nurses having opportunities to use their education, skills and competence to the fullest extent (1/2002; 2/2002). It was also in the interest of the union leadership to repeat the claims about the declining status of practical nurses in hospitals. Although it was argued that the social and health sectors should be integrated organisationally to enable the skills and competence of practical nurses to be used fully (3/2004), the main campaign for the licence and mandate of the professionals was focused on hospital work. Unlike their forerunners in health care – the auxiliary nurses and primary nurses – cross-sector practical nurses had difficulties in keeping their former health care roles and job vacancies. These were abolished or taken over by nurses, the union agenda underlined.

While the corporate negotiation structures were being eroded in Finland, the union leadership adopted new modes of policy-making and lobbying practices. Appeals were made to governmental agencies, policy stakeholders and partners representing work organisations, employers and managers to get publicity and support for the idea of an umbrella occupation. However, as late as 2006 one editorial mentioned for the first time that there are three rudiments that constitute the broad competence of practical nurses: nursing (health care), caring (social care) and interaction (pedagogical aspects) (9/2006). Instead, what the union agenda emphasised was the perception that decades of secure public sector employment – in place since the 1970s – were over in Finland. The changes due to marketisation had created risks for the very foundations of the labour force protection and collective agency. In this new situation 'a healthy place of work' was marked up as an important 'trump card' in this new culture of competition (6/2006).

Studying the editorials highlights the way practical nurses were positioned within the global transformations and the restructuring of human service work in Finland. It was clearly claimed that the new qualification fulfilled the unionist goal of skill upgrading by offering new employment options and more demanding but highly contested work tasks. Collectively, practical nurses shared increasing employment competition and insecurity, but also faced the loss of job opportunities, especially in health care. The burden of being an unknown newcomer in institutional settings with a rigid sector-bound social order created disturbances in employment relations and status as public service employees. Especially in elderly care, the qualified practical nurses, and even the partially trained ones, augmented their usefulness as a flexible labour force that was able, in some situations, to replace the nurses (see Suominen and Henriksson 2008). Contrary to the policy documents on social care that advocated the need to 'clarify the profile of social care' (MSAH 2003: 33), this concern was not raised in the editorials.

What is notable here is that the education reform that created an umbrella occupation did not attract much attention in the leadership agenda established on the footholds of craft unionism. The contested development constructed by the union leadership, however, dispersed the agency of practical nurses as a new type of collective. In the editorials, the core members of the union, who were employed by the health sector – and carried the legacy of the union predecessors – were presented extravagantly as 'the' collective losing professional legitimation and mandate. The others, having worked and being forced to transfer to work within ambulatory settings and the social sector, were kept invisible as non-existent union members not being worthy of a special interest. In that sense a somewhat modest basis for collective agency and identity anchorage was created by the leadership in the struggle over the renegotiation of contested boundaries between social and health care. The agenda reinforced past craft unionist tradition rather than openly designing a new type of multi-rooted, cross-sector unionism. Some of this craft-unionist order may be due to the background of the union leader himself as a former primary nurse working in a hospital, and partly due to the complex set of demands the education reform created for the legacy of craft unionism based on one occupation.

## The rise and fragmentation of professional projects

Sociological literature provides evidence of how the Nordic welfare states and professions have evolved in a particularly close relationship. It has been argued that the welfare states were arenas of gendered relations and practices that constructed the societal division of labour but also made room for women's political and professional interests. It is recognised internationally that the Nordic developments made way for women's collective agency, conceptualised as professional projects (see Larson 1977) in human service work, for instance in nursing, midwifery, public health nursing and social care. It is also worth mentioning that in Finland these developments included the accomplishments of the short-trained professionals such as homemakers in social care and primary nurses in health care.

The last two decades have, however, witnessed disintegration and undermining of the former 'women-friendly' (Hernes 1984) and 'care-worker-friendly' (Henriksson and Wrede 2008) trajectories. Anglo-American literature argued that women's professional projects failed because of the way patriarchal relations are institutionalised in the state (Witz 1992). In Nordic theorising, it is argued that welfare states have sponsored and shaped the professional projects of women-dominated professional groups when these have been in line with welfare policy (Evertsson 2000; Henriksson *et al.* 2006; Wrede *et al.* 2008). This claim underlines that welfare policies structure service provision and that consequently they enable and shape the professional licence (permission to carry on certain activities) and mandate (the elbow room while doing the work; see Hughes 1958: 78–87) of human service professionals that might not otherwise even exist. It is therefore exciting to take a closer look at how the neoliberal policy shift changed the collective agency of practical nurses and challenged their professional status and identity.

Global trends and unstable national economy and employment, together with workplace vulnerability, generate gendered and generational consequences. The existence of occupational gender segregation – the tendency for men and women to work in different occupational fields and to have unequal pay and positions in the hierarchies of working life – has been strengthened in Finland by the neoliberal policy shift (Julkunen 2004). The inclusive aims of the education reform induced by the policies and media plainly documented the contradictory sets of messages and manoeuvres related to the crisis of recruitment. For instance, in the media there have been repeated calls for retrenched IT workers and unemployed paper mill workers to become recruited as practical nurses for elderly care. In this context, elderly care is downgraded as an occupational choice and regarded as a kind of national solution to prevent marginalisation caused by global business cycles. Degradation is witnessed by the kind of public 'sale' of these jobs. Ignoring the risks of 'forced education' pushed by the active employment policy thus endangers the status and dignity of the professionals working in the field. Policy coordination incentives have led to a complex set of outcomes:

anyone in danger of being unemployed or marginalised – also in the name of gender equality – is urged to enter the education of practical nurses, or at least complete portions of it.

As Margaret Stacey (1981) pointed out, the service ethic is about recognising the ways in which 'work for' might routinely become 'work to' because of institutional transformations. This notion corresponds to the way in which the 'cult of efficiency' (Stein 2001) postulated by the neoliberal shift is impacting on value commitments in service provision where the questions 'efficient at what?' or 'for whom?' are not asked. Reflecting Nordic theorising, the case of practical nurses demonstrates how public service policy, restoring care to women's unpaid chores to be accomplished in their homes and private relationships, has facilitated transitions that also do not make adequate provision for those remaining in low-paid jobs (see Daly and Lewis 2000; Lewis 2002). As argued, marketised service production has a tendency to generate 'junk jobs', thereby contributing to social polarisation (see Crompton 2001, 2002; Theobald 2002). In the international and Nordic perspectives, the Finnish practical nurse reform showed the consolidating of traditions of fostering and upgrading of qualifications in human services. Nationally the development is more ambiguous. For groups of qualified practical nurses, a number of career opportunities were provided, thus leading to social mobility. One fraction became the flexible and easily movable core of front-line service workers and ended up in junk jobs. Some of the qualified and the partly trained would-be professionals became or stayed marginalised, possibly ending up at the less powerful borderlands of unemployment, rehabilitation or other social ills.

There is, however, evidence pointing to increasing gendered problems related to public sector employment: increasing requirements and workload, unemployment and lack of workforce safety (Lehto and Sutela 1998). Demographic challenges, the retirement of baby boomers and the exhaustion of the ageing workforce are contributing to labour shortages. New recruitment and employment patterns simultaneously challenge the way in which people can reconcile their occupational and personal lives (Kauhanen 2002). The ethos of work and the protection of public employment are vanishing as managerialism strengthens its hold. There are signals showing the decline of professional pride and the loss of trust in service quality. It is therefore important to consider what is happening to value commitments in an era when it seems to be a luxury to ask who has the right to professional pride and dignity in human service work. Under the circumstances it is appropriate to ask if there is any time, space and place for vocational development and collective accomplishment (Heikkinen *et al.* 2001).

On the macro level, the making of a new labour force in human services has concentrated on policy coordination and organisational modelling instead of investing in employment relations. On the organisational level, the transformations were aimed at dismantling old distinctions, demarcations, hierarchies and the 'house rules'. Flexibilisation and streamlining was followed with repeated calls for new ways of working (also Davies 2003). The evidence shows, however, that establishing new workforce designs builds on divisions among individual employees rather than their professional collectives. In ambulatory settings, new staff roles are put into practice without any rigorous consideration of their wider implications. For the practical nurses, new subtle workplace and situation-bound everyday practices are created, especially in elderly care (Suominen and Henriksson 2008). Organisational structures and cultures in hospitals are more fixed and slowly changing.

Although research has addressed various rudiments of welfare state development related to collective agency of female-dominated professional groups in Finland, it is important to emphasise that professional groups are not equally strong collectives of actors. Compared to more established, licensed professionals, such as physicians and nurses, the lower-level professionals seem to have their positions shaped by policy reforms and the professional strategies of the more powerful actors. The increasing pressures to deregulate the market may also contribute to the fact that individual professionals in a competitive labour market find it difficult to resist organisational demands and are therefore highly unlikely to develop collective strategies to improve their situation (Crompton 2002). As shown, the neoliberal policy shift curtailed the agency for middle-class white-collar work in human services, but this was especially true for the lower-level professionals. The stronger projects of nurses and nurse managers were becoming stronger (Wrede and Henriksson 2004; 2005), whereas more fragile professional projects were dissolving and fragmenting as the case of practical nurses indicates.

## Social polarisation and legitimacy gap

Even though the reforms implemented in Nordic and Finnish welfare policies are inspired by global trends and the same OECD and EU policies, the way these ideas have been put into practice may differ. The portrayal introduced here shows the complex ways in which policy-induced changes are filtered nationally and organisationally. Through this citizen-focused, three-scene approach I unpacked the Finnish neoliberal policy shift and argued that a significant restructuring of human service work occurred through active policy-making. However, this trajectory seemed to be in need of coordination, was sector-steered, focused on higher-level occupational groups and touched core value commitments. All the way through these changes, there were a variety of implications for the future of an occupation and the careers of the groups of professionals. These changes also matter for the client-citizens and citizen-employees in human service work. There has been an erosion of the public sector ethos which, to some extent, had been the glue binding public sector employees and service users and has protected certain value commitments: integrity, due process, fairness, probity, loyalty, care-friendliness. The blurring of policy demarcations, administrative sectors, educational grades and professional mandates opened up a legitimacy gap which was debated in policy and experienced in the disturbances of working life and education. Shifting terms and conditions of employment and differences in value commitments and morality between expectations of the citizens and managerialist organisations reshaped professional agency, identity and belongings.

Polarisation, in terms of inclusion and exclusion, offers useful lenses for understanding the complex nature of social change related to the making of a new labour force in human service work (Hobson 2000; Woodward and Kohli 2004). This dynamic extends to thinking towards the broader European and global landscapes that are challenging national policies and the agency of the citizen-employees. Inclusion–exclusion also extends into the growing fragmentation of professional collectives and increasing individualisation in work and learning. Nationally, education has been an important social means to decrease marginalisation and social exclusion. When building the welfare state, education policy was a core part of welfare policy. Education of the citizens was to remove poverty from the social agenda. There has been an enormous trust in education in Finland and this has been especially true for women. The 'occupation of one's own' (Henriksson 1998: 1) has been an important constituent of citizenship for better-off, better-educated urban women. But in Finland, it has also been an important avenue for lower-class, peasant-background women who only had access to shorter vocational training programmes.

The same neoliberal policy trend faced in Western European welfare states has increased the income gap and created cultural cleavages and social ills, such as job insecurity, unemployment and poverty (Charles and James 2003; Woodward and Kohli 2004). This development is also well documented in Finland: marginalisation has not been removed from the national agenda. During the 1970s and 1980s the significance of education was argued in terms of promoting enlightenment and economic growth especially in the name of equality (Heikkinen 1995). Since the 1990s, considerable credential inflation has taken place. While the education level of citizens was increasing, the borderline between a good labour market position and a poor one moved upwards (Rinne and Kivirauma 2003). As the case of practical nurses demonstrates, the labour market value that a shorter training previously guaranteed was curtailed and new social processes, making an educated service-class, were produced. It is therefore important to recognise how human service reforms promote comprehensive rights, for instance access to services and training, but simultaneously create processes that create inequalities between the citizen-employees.

The making of a new labour force implied the categorisation of 'insider and outsider labour market positions' (Esping-Andersen 1996: 82) and re-sorted citizen-employees into the ones eligible for employment and social mobility and the non-eligible ones. Among practical nurses, inter- and intra-professional polarisation occurred, with new options for moving upwards in educational hierarchies for some and marginal employment or unemployment, incapable of guaranteeing a decent living, for others. The diversity of recruitment routes and educational pathways enabled a mixture of labour market positions, increased status competition for some and impugned professional recognition for others. The cross-sector nature of the occupation also seemed to deepen polarisation by questioning the generalist profile of practical nurses, especially in health care settings.

Structural changes are, however, connected to the wider cultural change and the lived experiences of individuals. As Hughes (1958: 56) points out, 'no individual becomes a moral person until he has a sense of his own station and the ways proper to it'. Status assigns individuals and collectives to various accepted social categories. The case of practical nurses shows how neoliberal education reform shaped the lived disturbances of individuals and different segments and generations of professionals. Uncertainties of social anchorage, belonging and ethical commitment were related to the institutional restructuring and policy mismatch which augmented horizontal and vertical fragmentation of practical nurses. Despite the aims of upgrading education, the occupation's diverse social composition, together with the inflation of credentials, contributed to the decline of 'professional respectability' (Aldridge and Evetts 2003). Managing professionals in workplaces according to new criteria of formal competence, hardiness, proper commitment, grade and career histories – the well-known recruitment criteria in the legacy of female-dominated professional groups – has challenged professional identity and the ethical underpinnings of human service work. In the context of the policy shift and institutional restructuring, traditionally appealing human service work has faced a new type of employment competition and lack of attractiveness. Generational gaps have emerged between the pre-reform mono-occupational professionals and the post-reform cross-sector ones, which has profoundly challenged the patterning of collective agency interests and unionism.

Culturally, the making of a new labour force is also about 'othering' processes through managing of identities (Davies 2002a). New managing strategies are explicit in the national policy claims and practices of managerialist organisations, but they are also invented by the professional groups themselves. As the union inventory highlights, there was a 'devalued other', symbolically located outside the boundary of a specific identity but, in practice, helping to give meaning to it (Davies 2002b). The union leadership valued the legacy of one membership category – the two health care forerunners – and implicitly silenced the occupational legacies of other sub-groups integrated into the new-born hybrid occupation. In a situation in which a new occupational constellation was designed based on a variety of former occupations, the trade unions played a major role in terms of professional identity and belonging.

Nevertheless, policy has been contested in its aim of compiling a hybrid occupation within the lower levels of occupational rankings in institutional settings that embrace 'mono-professional' and hierarchic sector trajectories. The intricate nature of the reform shook occupational, educational and unionist orders, thereby fuelling debates on educational grades and competence constellations in human service work. But the hybrid nature of an occupation also teased out reflection on the changing nature of collective agency fixed in union trajectories. The history of the demise of the former auxiliary and primary nurses (who both worked in health care and in hospitals) suggests that craft unions will need to confront this issue of many silenced 'out-groups' working within different territories and sector cultures of health and social care. It is important to note that status is never peculiar to the individual but is historically anchored as the informal and unique become formal and collective. As Hughes (1958) points out, careers in society are thought about mainly in terms of jobs or a series of business and professional achievements, for these are the characteristics and crucial connections of the individual within institutional structures. The case of practical nurses shows that, in the course of one's educational, occupational and moral career, one's life touches the multi-layered social order, and other lines of social accomplishment – influence, responsibility and recognition. In this landscape the societal ethos of human service work is lived through individual experience and filtered into professional identity and belonging.

## References

Alasuutari, P. (2004) *Social Theory and Human Reality*, London: Sage.

Aldridge, M. and Evetts, J. (2003) 'Rethinking the concept of professionalism: The case of journalism', *British Journal of Sociology*, 54(4): 547–564.

Bleich, M., Hewlett, P., Santos, S., Rice, R., Cox, K. and Richmeier, S. (2003) 'Analysis of the nursing workforce crisis: A call to action', *American Journal of Nursing*, 103(4): 66–74.

Charles, N. and James, E. (2003) 'Gender and work orientations in conditions of job insecurity', *British Journal of Sociology*, 54(2): 239–257.

Committee for the Future of the Finnish Parliament (2004) *Suomen terveydenhuollon tulevaisuudet, Eduskunnan kanslian julkaisu 8*, Helsinki: Edita Priima.

Crompton, R. (2001) 'Gender restructuring, employment, and caring', *Social Politics*, 8(3): 265–291.

Crompton, R. (2002) 'Employment, flexible working and the family', *British Journal of Sociology*, 53(4): 537–558.

Daly, M. and Lewis, J. (2000) 'The concept of social care and the analysis of contemporary welfare states', *British Journal of Sociology*, 51(2): 281–298.

Davies, C. (2002a) 'Managing identities: Workers, professions and identity', *Nursing Management*, 9(5): 31–34.

Davies, C. (2002b) 'Continuing to manage professional identities', *Nursing Management*, 9(6): 31–34.

Davies, C. (ed.) (2003) *The Future Health Workforce*, London: Palgrave Macmillan.

Esping-Andersen, G. (ed.) (1996) *Welfare States in Transition: National Adaptations in Global Economies*, London: Sage.

Evertsson, L. (2000) 'The Swedish welfare state and the emergence of female welfare state occupations', *Gender, Work and Organization*, 7(4): 230–241.

Finlayson, B., Dixon, J., Meadows, S. and Blair, G. (2002) 'Mind the gap: The extent of the NHS nursing shortage', *British Medical Journal*, 325(7): 538–541.

FNBE, The Finnish National Board of Education (1995) *Työelämän edustajien näkemyksiä lähihoitajakoulutuksesta*, Moniste 41, Helsinki: Painatuskeskus.

FNBE, The Finnish National Board of Education (2001) *Sosiaali- ja terveysalan perustutkinto*, Opetushallituksen määräys 7/11/2001.

Heikkilä, M. and Kautto, M. (eds) (2006) *Welfare in Finland*, Helsinki: Stakes.

Heikkinen, A. (1995) *Lähtökohtia ammattikasvatuksen kulttuuriseen tarkasteluun* (1840–1940), Acta Universitatis Tamperensis ser A vol 442, Tampere: Tampereen yliopisto.

Heikkinen, A., Borgman, M., Henriksson, L., Korkiakangas, M., Kuusisto, L., Nuotio, P. and Tiilikkala, L. (eds) (2001) *Niin vähän on aikaa – ammatillisen kasvun katoava aika, paikka ja tila?*, Tampere: Ammattikasvatuksen tutkimus- ja koulutuskeskus.

Henriksson, L. (1998) *Naisten terveystyö ja ammatillistumisen politiikka*, Tutkimuksia 88, Helsinki: Stakes.

Henriksson, L. (2008) 'Reconfiguring Finnish welfare service workforce: Inequalities and identity', *Equal Opportunities International*, 27(1): 49–63.

Henriksson, L. and Wrede, S. (2008) 'Care work in the context of transforming welfare state', in S. Wrede, L. Henriksson, H. Høst, S. Johansson and B. Dybbroe (eds) *Care Work in Crisis*, Lund: Studentlitteratur, 121–152.

Henriksson, L., Wrede, S. and Burau, V. (2006) 'Understanding professional projects in welfare service work: Revival of old professionalism?', *Gender, Work and Organization*, 13(2): 174–192.

Hernes, H. (1984) 'Women and welfare state: The transition from private to public dependence', in H. Holter (ed.) *Patriarchy in a Welfare Society*, Oslo: Universitetsforlaget, 26–45.

HESOTE, Helsingin sosiaali- ja terveysalan oppilaitos (2009) Vocational qualifications. Available at: http://www.hel.fi/wps/portal/Koulut/Ammatilliset _oppilaitokset/Hesote/Artikkeli?WCM_GLOBAL_CONTEXT=/hesote/fi/ Hesote+In+English (retrieved 23 September 2009)

Hobson, B. (2000) 'Introduction. Special issue: Faces of inequality', *Social Politics*, 7(2): 125–126.

Hughes, E. C. (1958) *Men and their Work*, Glencoe, Illinois: The Free Press.

Julkunen, R. (2004) 'Hyvinvointipalvelujen uusi politiikka', in L. Henriksson and S. Wrede (eds) *Hyvinvointityön ammatit*, Helsinki: Gaudeamus, 168–209.

Kauhanen, M. (2002) *Määräaikaiset työsuhteet ja toimeentulon riskit*, Sosiaali- ja terveysturvan tutkimuksia 69, Helsinki: Kela.

Kettunen, P. (2006) 'The power of international comparison. A perspective on the making and challenging of the Nordic welfare state', in N. F. Christiansen, K. Petersen, N. Edling and P. Haave (eds) *The Nordic Model of Welfare: A Historical Reappraisal*, Copenhagen: Museum Tusculanum Press, 31–65.

Larson, M. (1977) *The Rise of Professionalism*, Berkeley: University of California Press.

Lehto, A.-M. and Sutela, H. (1998) *Tehokas, tehokkaampi, uupunut: työolotutkimusten tuloksia 1977–1997*, Työmarkkinat 12, Helsinki: Tilastokeskus.

Lewis, J. (2002) 'Gender and welfare state change', *European Societies*, 4(4): 331–357.

Lewis, J. and Surender, R. (2004) *Welfare State Change: Towards a Third Way?*, Oxford: Oxford University Press.

ME, Ministry of Education (2006) *Sosiaalialan osaajat 2015* SOTENNA: loppuraportti, Sosiaalityön julkaisusarja 4, Jyväskylä: Jyväskylän yliopisto.

ML, Ministry of Labour (2003) *Työpolitiikan strategia 2003–2007–2010*, Työministeriö Nro 334, Helsinki.

MSAH, Ministry of Social Affairs and Health (2001) *Sosiaali- ja terveydenhuollon työvoimatarpeen ennakointitoimikunnan mietintö. Komiteanmietintö 7*, Helsinki.

MSAH, Ministry of Social Affairs and Health (2002) *Kansallinen projekti terveydenhuollon tulevaisuuden turvaamiseksi. Työvoiman tarve ja keskinäinen työnjako. Työolosuhteiden kehittäminen ja täydennyskoulutuksen järjestäminen 15.1.2002*, STM:n julkaisuja 125, Helsinki.

MSAH, Ministry of Social Affairs and Health (2003) *Kansallinen sosiaalialan kehittämisprojekti*, STM:n työryhmämuistioita 11, Helsinki.

MSAH, Ministry of Social Affairs and Health (2007a) *Hyvinvointi 2015. Sosiaalialan pitkän aikavälin tavoitteita*, STM:n julkaisuja 3, Helsinki.

MSAH, Ministry of Social Affairs and Health (2007b) *Kansallisen terveydenhuollon hankkeen seurantaryhmän raportti*, STM:n selvityksiä 51, Helsinki.

Patomäki, H. (2007) *Uusliberalismi Suomessa*, Helsinki: WSOY.

Pitkänen, M. (2005) *Raskasta mutta antoisaa*. Sosiaalityön pro gradu, Tampere: Tampereen yliopisto.

Rinne, R. and Kivirauma, J. (eds) (2003) *Koulutuksellista alaluokkaa etsimässä*, Turku: Suomen Kasvatustieteellinen Seura.

Seccombe, I. (1995) 'Still a job for life?', *Nursing Standard*, 9(29): 21.

Stacey, M. (1981) 'The division of labour revisited or overcoming the two Adams', in P. Abrams, R. Beem, J. Finch and P. Roch (eds) *Practice and Progress: British Sociology 1950–1980*, London: Allen and Unwin, 172–190.

Stacey, M. (1984) 'Who are the health workers? Patients and other unpaid workers in health care', *Economic and Industrial Democracy*, 5(2): 157–184.

Statistics Finland (2009) *Labour Force Survey*. Available at: http://www.stat.fi/til/tyti/index_en.html (accessed 15 January 2009).

Stein, J. G. (2001) *The Cult of Efficiency*, Toronto: Anansi Press.

Suominen, T. and Henriksson, L. (2008) 'Työnjako vanhusten kotihoidossa', *Yhteiskuntapolitiikka*, 73(6): 625–639.

Super (2009) *Suomen lähi- ja perushoitajaliitto*. Available at: http://www.superliitto.fi/ (retrieved 23 September 2009).

Theobald, H. (2002) 'Care for the elderly: Welfare systems, professionalisation and the question of inequality', paper presented at the 5th conference of the ESA 'Visions and Divisions: Challenges to European Sociology', Helsinki, Aug. 28–Sept. 1.

Thornley, C. (2003) 'What future for health care assistants: High road or low road?', in C. Davies (ed.) *The Future Health Workforce*, London: Palgrave Macmillan, 143–160.

Valvira, National Supervisory Authority for Welfare and Health (2009) *Licence to Make a Difference*. Available at: http://www.valvira.fi/en (accessed 28 April 2009).

van Oorschot, W., Opielka, M. and Pfau-Effinger, B. (eds) (2008) *Culture and Welfare State: Values and Social Policy in Comparative Perspective*, Cheltenham: Edward Elgar.

Walford, J. (1995) 'Changes lead to fears on jobs and wages', *Nursing Standard*, 9(24): 16.

Witz, A. (1992) *Professions and Patriarchy*, London: Routledge.

Woodward, A. and Kohli, M. (eds) (2004) *Inclusions and Exclusions in European Societies*, London: Routledge.

Wrede, S. and Henriksson, L. (2004) 'Kahden kerroksen väkeä: kotihoidon ammatillinen uusjako', in L. Henriksson and S. Wrede (eds) *Hyvinvointityön ammatit*, Helsinki: Gaudeamus, 210–234.

Wrede, S. and Henriksson, L. (2005) 'Finnish home care in transition: The changing terms of welfare service work', in H.-M. Dahl and T. R. Eriksen (eds) *Dilemmas of Care in the Nordic Welfare State*, Aldershot: Ashgate, 62–79.

Wrede, S., Henriksson, L., Høst, H., Johansson, S. and Dybbroe, B. (eds) (2008) *Care Work in Crisis: Reclaiming the Nordic Ethos of Care*, Lund: Studentlitteratur.

# Chapter 3

# Disputing managerial architecture in educational work

## Irony as a liberating strategy for Finnish vocational teachers

*Karin Filander*

The changes that took place in Finland in the 1990s are consistent with occupational changes taking place elsewhere. According to Richard Sennett (1998: 70–72), the new practical realities of labour require acceptance that work identities are weaker and lighter than before and marked by indifference and improvised skills. Still, at the same time, this kind of more superficial work orientation requires the particular strength of character, confidence to dwell in disorder and to flourish in the midst of dislocation. This kind of 'expertise in uncertainty' (Filander 2003, 2005) requires acceptance of instability as a normal everyday practice in which every individual must be able to adapt, and even enjoy, in their everyday life (Bauman 1992). Bauman (1996: 18–24) argues that the post-modern 'problem of identity' is primarily that of how to avoid fixation and keep the options open. In the life-game of the post-modern consumers and entrepreneurs, one has to live one day at a time without long-term commitments and vocations. What are then important are continuous presence and the capacity to move swiftly where the action is and to be ready to take in experiences as they come. One has to discover, invent, construct, assemble and even buy an identity and, first of all, prevent it from sticking.

In the early 1990s when Finnish society was in the throes of the deepest economic recession in the Western world, the public sector experienced an intense managerial turn. This turn was part of broader European efforts to transform welfare services according to the new principles of New Public Management and emphasised individualistic entrepreneurship and market-oriented forms of action. The older Nordic welfare state model confronted the ideology of neoliberalism – an ideology that stressed the minimal role of the state, deregulation and the replacement of government regulation with market competition and the privatisation of the functions of the public sector (Naschold 1996; Clarke and Newman 1997; Filander 2003).

This chapter identifies counter-discursive resources of irony that challenge the dominant black-and-white rhetoric of the 'new managerialism' that accompanied the structural reforms within the Finnish vocational education sector during the 1990s. Ironic statements are one way to find alternative patterns and voices from the dominant discourses when it is introduced as the only way to frame future developments. The focus of my interest is in identifying the resources that enabled Finnish vocational teachers to develop counter-narratives for challenging the mainstream talk on occupational order and the future of occupations during a period when the 'new managerial' discourse was dominant.

## The new architecture of educational order

The managerial turn was evident particularly in the field of education, where several structural reforms were made at all levels of the education system. Among the most prominent was the reform in the non-university sector of higher education covering the upper secondary vocational education, called the polytechnics (Niiranen-Linkama, this volume). The aims of the education reforms were to decrease institutional school-based education and to increase both the individual responsibility of students and the co-operative undertakings with regional developments and industry. Individual students were regarded as lifelong learners capable of carrying on the main responsibility for their own learning as self-directed and active learners. They were also expected to have the ability to compete and be co-operative at the same time. Concepts that belonged to the older times of the centralised welfare state – such as school-based study plans, teacher-centred models of teaching and an emphasis on knowledge structures (on understanding why rather than just how) – became redundant. Individual students were now supposed to choose their own paths and their own individual study plans from several alternatives offered by the supermarket of educational institutions.

Education as lifelong learning became defined as a kind of salvation programme and a strategy for survival for the whole society (Rinne and Salmi 1998: 141; Edwards et al. 2001, 417–418). In the public rhetoric of decision makers of educational reforms, education and learning for their own sake, and on their own terms, no longer had any justification. The whole education system was increasingly understood as a basic instrument serving a competitive state and economic necessities. The new aim was to produce a flexible and entrepreneurial workforce and innovations for industry to improve possibilities for better competition on globalised markets. Employees were supposed to be adaptive and innovative at the same time. Personal qualities and qualifications were to be more on the agenda than the older, collectively defined, qualification requirements of occupational knowledge structures.

The education system of the Nordic welfare state tradition, developed earlier as a free and extensive system of equality, was to be abandoned. This earlier tradition, which held that education was a basic and universalistic right and duty of every citizen and as a cornerstone of decreasing inequality, faced strong pressures to adapt to the new labour market demands and the ethos of managerialism (Esping-Andersen 1990; Rinne and Salmi 1998: 38). The question of what education is and what it is for was redefined more narrowly according to the values of a market economy. The formal vocational education system now faced more direct work-related and instrumental demands set by the labour markets in new capitalism. This, in turn, led to the emergence of a 'new professionalism' of teachers. This meant a flexible acceptance of continuous change and a new kind of skill mix aimed at producing a multi-skilled workforce (Brooks and MacDonald 2000: 222, 227; Filander 2007). The multi-skilled orientation of the new workplace was an integral part of the flexible regime in which qualities of being a skilled worker seemed to be more difficult to define. In the flexible system of working life and vocational education, the traditional expectations of skilled work were gradually losing their social standing and social character.

In Finland, occupational knowledge structures and stable professional identity structures have increasingly become subject to this 'burden of flexibility' in which tolerance of change and uncertainty are offered as compensation for the more traditional values and basic assumptions of vocational autonomy, professional respect and honour. Self-evident trust in occupations is increasingly questioned. Occupations and professions are defined more or less as cultural and social structures and solidarities of the old industrial order. As Finnish writer Vehviläinen (2001: 81) points out, teachers have learned to serve two masters concurrently: they both educate and develop skilled practitioners for occupations in society and try to fulfil the direct needs set by both the economy and industry at the same time.

For vocational teachers, the new reforms forced a re-evaluation of their occupational know-how as well as their work as teachers of occupational skills and occupational identity. The black-and-white distance from the past to the idealised future was a typical rhetorical accompaniment to managerial change (Filander 2003, 2007). According to this neoliberal rhetoric, the traditional role of the teacher was compensated with new roles as tutors or advisers for individual students who were supposed to be able to develop their individual study paths and study plans. The New Public Management regimes offered vocational teachers subject positions as training managers who could sell their educational products in the markets of education under the pressure of 'healthy' market competition. The concept of learning organisations was part of the managerial framework that espoused a drive towards 'learning economies' and 'learning societies'.

## The methodological framework of irony

In what follows I draw on three sets of interviews to provide an analysis of the ironic discourses some participants brought to the changes they experienced. The interviews drawn on here were collected in a research project, financed by the European Social Fund (ESF) of the European Union, that aimed to develop networking between vocational institutions, enterprises and companies. During the project, vocational teachers organised and developed the system of work-based and practice-based learning for their students and for themselves (Filander and Jokinen 2004). A series of interviews conducted with 24 teachers between 2002 and 2004 are drawn on from our total interview data (N = 40). Other interviewees were students, headmasters and on-the-job instructors. From these 24 teacher interviews I have chosen three as 'cases' for studying the way teachers use irony as a counter-narrative. By selecting these key interviews with the teachers of different skilled occupations in the upper-secondary-level painting and surface treatment, health care and social services and economics and trade, some counter-narratives that contradict the dominant managerial rhetoric are explored through particularly selected key interviews that I call 'special' cases or 'deviant' cases (Billig 1987; Potter 1996). Dialectical irony can be an act of emancipation and counter-discourse on managerial change (see also Brown 1987: 172). In what follows, I wish to show how irony functions as a tool for redefinition of and negotiation for meanings in situations in which alternatives are difficult to find. Irony can work as an instrument of counter-narratives that help keep a distance from the dominant culture of managerialism and managerial governance. This meta-perspective of irony is needed in the processes of producing new possibilities for alternative understanding (Burke 1945; see Summa 1996: 55). Irony as a method creates some new gaps and ruptures in governing the meta-narratives that have previously been taken for granted.

Ironical analysis may be explored as a particular rhetorical-responsive version of social constructionism (Shotter 1993: 7). It refers to a methodology in which we craft our own unique selves in relation to one another in communication. Challenging communication enables us to see new connections between different kinds of frameworks and positions. It makes it possible to understand and justify one's own credibility as a rhetorical achievement. In the tradition of active interviewing, the interviewer is activating cultural scripts potentially available for the interviewee, however contradictory they may be (Holstein and Gubrium 1995: 3–4; 1997). Stimulated accounts are polyphonic discussions about things that, under the pressure of the hegemonic mode of talk, are easily reduced to the mechanical application of the prevailing discourse. The interviewer's role is to encourage the interviewees to shift their ground repeatedly during the interview so as to explore alternative perspectives and knowledge bases linked with their social and cultural setting (Holstein and Gubrium 1995: 37; see also Filander 2003). In this way, the interviewee is helped to identify and recognise different possibilities and potentials that give insight into alternative framing, which can also be seen as an emancipatory and therapeutic process (Silverman 1991: 32).

In the cases described below basic argumentation strategies include categorisation and, on the other hand, particularisation (Billig 1987: 6). Categories are used to generalise about the transitional period, to bring order into the transition process and to make it more manageable. Particularisation, by contrast, emphasises the unique features of a given issue or problem. In this context, the strategy of the special case is an approach founded on the methodological assumption that special cases make it possible to deconstruct shared stereotypical conceptualisations and generalisations (Billig 1987: 139–141).

Different argumentative positions of selected key interviews are a way of demonstrating the limitations of black-and-white generalisations of dominant managerial discourses. Such definitions are always formulated and argued in a rhetorical context of justification and criticism (Billig 1987: 94; see also Jokinen 1999: 46). In this case, the context, broadly taken, consists of the market-oriented turn occurring in vocational education and the transformation of occupational identities into the direction of corporate culture and flexible workforce. In this process, education and teaching are shown to be losing their respectability and legitimacy. Teachers are no longer rewarded for their dedication to their basic work as teachers but rather for their project activities and extra achievements that are part of the trendy development of vocational education (Filander and Jokinen 2004; see also Filander 2003).

## Case 1: Teachers in the field of painting and surface treatment

Manual skills and the practical know-how of work-related issues are highly valued in the field of painting and surface treatment. This was evident in the interviews with five teachers and a department head in this field. The teachers identified themselves as foremen or entrepreneurs who, after acquiring their basic vocational qualifications, had gained a long work experience in their own field as skilled workers or as entrepreneurs.

For different reasons they had found their way to teacher positions in their own occupational field. Despite this change, they still identified themselves as skilled and experienced workers more often than teachers. They had improved their basic hands-on knowledge by acquiring further vocational qualifications; they had qualified as vocational teachers through brief teacher training programmes, usually completed along with their basic work activities. These teachers identified themselves above all as skilled workers able to control and master their activities in their own occupational field. For example, according to the teachers, the basic skills required in painting and surface treatment have not changed at all in recent years (group interview 03: 5). In this craft, it is about the old kind of learning by 'starting from the basics ( . . . ) the old apprenticeship thing (---). This is the way it's been before forever and this is the way it'll continue' (group interview 03: 28).

In this male-dominated field, these vocational teachers, who had earlier worked as craftsmen, can be seen to be committed to an 'assorted circle of skilled workers' (group interview 03: 7). In the following extract, I describe an episode in which these vocational teachers react against the central idea of development work, according to which the pedagogical work of these vocational teachers will expand to include consultation in working life and online use of information and communication technologies in guiding and teaching their students:

*Extract 1*

Interviewer:    Is it so that in this (---) [learning-at-work] developmental project there has been a kind of idea that schools would go and consult workplaces [in issues of learning at work]?

Teacher A:   Sure, there is a little also . . .

Teacher B:   That in the air . . .

Teacher A:   . . . and they [the entrepreneurs and skilled workers in the field of painting and surface treatment] don't take anyone to consul[t] them . . . (laughing)

Teacher B:   What will we do when we consult a firm and it goes bankrupt – what then?

> And visions of students having a portable computer and going to those mucky construction sites to finger it and send messages from there about what he or she has done and us [at the institutes of vocational education] writing it down . . .
>
> . . . with no electricity through any extension cords . . .
>
> There are several small-scale entrepreneurs who have just recently acquired for themselves a computer with which they try to deal mainly with their bills and then do some invoicing for contracts.
>
> But it is out of the question that at the site they would have . . .
>
> The responsible manager of the construction site can have a computer in his site hut, but nobody else who works there.

(Group interview 02: 26–27)

In the interview situation, the teachers of painting and surface treatment produced a shared counter-talk to the dominant discourse on learning at work. They maintained that the reform of learning at work means mainly retrenchment that would reduce the possibilities of teachers visiting workplaces and supervising their students' learning-at-work periods. Traditionally, co-operation between schools and workplaces has been based on a useful division of labour for both parties and only those students who were already capable of using their basic occupational skills transferred to enterprises to work and improve their skills at work. According to the interviewed teachers, the recent reforms were destroying this fruitful co-operation between vocational schools and firms. Now schools needed to send to work also those students who, according to the teachers, were not yet ready to cope with the demands of the workplaces.

These teachers in the field of painting and surface treatment were constructing a collective male counter-talk based on occupational pride and honour. They use this as their resource when keeping themselves at arm's length from the dominant development talk. By contrasting new pedagogical ideas with the 'wretched realities' and hierarchical arrangements of their work in practice, it becomes ridiculous for them even to think about these new arrangements. The teachers considered it to be quite clear that students and teachers of vocational institutions were not in a position to consult experienced entrepreneurs or skilled workers about their own craft. The idea of such consultation is seen as amusing but also threatening because what is at stake is the honour of the entrepreneurs and skilled practitioners whose task is to control the limits and conditions of work in their own area. 'Fingering' the computers at the construction site is the responsibility of the managers and entrepreneurs alone, not of the secondary labour force from vocational schools.

In the interview situation, these teaichers of painting and surface treatment found for themselves resources to contradict the dominant talk that positioned them as managers of new training practices. They positioned themselves as a team that collectively guarded the traditional codes of honour and team spirit by constructing a counter-talk anchored in their masculine craft. Their world of hard business has no extra space, time or money to train students in basic occupational skills. The teachers were of the opinion that workplaces needed to have competent 'fellows' already from the beginning. Only those students can survive who have learned already – at school – the basic skills that are needed in this field. 'They do not have [at the workplaces] any extra trainers, they [the students] must be able to get along and (---) carry on as part of the whole system' (group of teachers 03: 15).

## Case 2: Teachers in the field of health care and social services

Vocational institutions of health care and social services are parts of colleges that, at the beginning of the 1990s, shared the Finnish structural reforms of the polytechnics. During this process, the work communities of the institutes were divided into higher- and lower-level colleges. The whole process was very difficult for the employees. According to the teachers who were interviewed for our study, a division like this was 'stupid, particularly in economic terms' in small institutions (Teacher B 02: 3). Teachers who had earlier worked in the same college-level training were now classified as either 'first-class' or 'second-class' teachers. The teachers of health care and social services did not agree with the absolute nature of this division. In interview, the teachers emphasised the fact that they would naturally still co-operate a lot. 'Teachers go and teach there and those of the polytechnics come here' (Teacher B 02: 3).

Before this structural division, the curricula reform had already taken place at the beginning of the 1990s. Many areas of more specialised care were collected together to produce broader, more general, and also more flexible, qualifications for practical nurses. These new kinds of occupations were the ones that vocational schools and teachers were now forced to 'introduce (---) to the practices of working life' (Teacher B 02: 2). The teachers of these basic-level care work students were quite highly qualified practitioners, and included nurses, social scientists and psychologists. Their task, as they saw it, was to train the students to become qualified practical nurses in the female-dominated field of care work.

According to the teachers, the work of practical nurses required, above all, hard work and the ability to cope in situations in which they had to face their customers and deal with highly intimate issues. In the field of health care and social services, the most important thing for these teachers was to teach the students how to grow into ethically highly developed personalities who could face customers with respect and treat them respectfully in all situations. The teachers thought that students who applied to study in these fields presented with a certain type of personality and with an ability to face the special demands of this field of practice.

The ethical nature of the work was a central theme during the interviews. Teachers emphasised the importance of co-operation – of 'pulling together' – and a need to quickly intervene in the possible problems of students in the work practices: 'Of course we train [students] together [with experienced practitioners of working life]. We cannot train [them] alone, we have always trained [them] together' (Teacher B 02: 6).

It was typical of these interviews in the field of health care and social services that interviewees identified and committed themselves to continuous development of their work. Even the question of possible resistance created some confusion. When I asked whether the teachers were always ready to involve themselves in development work projects, one teacher emphasised strongly that: 'At least our teachers are. As a matter of fact, I don't really know . . . this must be [maybe] a little bit weird when nobody here ever says no' (Teacher B 02: 26). 'We people in the field of health care and social services are . . . ; I believe that nobody works as dutifully as we do in our field' (Teacher B 02: 22).

The same ethical and dutiful attitude is present in the interview when the teacher comments on possible problems that students may face during their periods of learning at work:

> Somehow I do trust our . . . [experienced practitioners] (---) If some problems arise during those periods of learning at work, they will contact us *at once* and the teacher will go there *at once* and try to solve the problem.
> (Teacher B 02: 10)

It is possible to distinguish the special characteristics of this collective and ethical practice in a counter-narrative by one teacher (here identified as Maria) who defined her work attitude as being 'selfish'. The ironical nature of her statement becomes evident when Maria starts to describe more closely her period of learning at work when she, a teacher, joined a group of practical nurses to work with them. When Maria describes her position during the period of learning at work, she distances herself from the dominant ethos of absolute consent and commitment of the field of health care and social services. As a psychologist, Maria holds on to her autonomous right to define her own relationship to the development demands of her work. She reveals her desire to acquire for herself first-hand knowledge of the field in which she works as a teacher. Maria talks about her steps in care work when she 'risked herself and made herself vulnerable' by working in a very ordinary position of a practical nurse. This position required of her a special kind of boldness. According to her, it depended on whether the person had the guts to work in a situation like that without being protected by his or her position as a teacher. It depended on whether the person had the courage to throw herself into work as one of the 'workforce' and to 'offer those hands, eyes and arms' that are the most important qualities in a practical nurse's work (Teacher A 03: 7). Maria challenges the ethos of consent in health care and social services with the following counter-discourse:

*Extract 2*

But as I've already said in those [development project meetings], is it possible to learn anything in those things?. . . .

. . . so I do have a pretty selfish agenda of my own in the background . . .

. . . so it is for myself that I get up-to-date knowledge and wisdom of what the work's about . . .

. . . and maybe you also wanna understand and make sense . . . of those things.

(Teacher A 03: 3)

We are accustomed to think that the autonomy and responsibility to develop one's own work is a natural part of professional and occupational work. Professionals are able to acquire for themselves the wisdom and new knowledge that is needed in their work. Professionals are also supposed to have some autonomous space for counter-arguments that are independent and can differ from the shared visions of workplaces (Casey 2003: 622). Maria's counter-narratives concern her own responsibility for her developmental work orientation, which in the managerial order is defined as a 'selfish' activity.

When defining her professional needs to improve as selfish, Maria uses the developmental talk of managerialism. With this move she restores to herself the feeling of professional autonomy. She takes herself a permission to work as a selfish teacher who listens first of all to her personal needs to develop herself as a sensitive teacher. According to Casey (2003: 622–624), the managerial framework does not recognise organisations as a contested terrain where workers and practitioners can also have divergent and potentially counter-organisational rationalities of their own. Dominant strategic models of human resource management and organisational learning models have created an image of individual workers as human resources whose individual learning needs are legitimated solely when the learning is useful and contributes to organisational purposes.

Professionals like Maria are facing new narrow strategic imperatives. In other words, their individual needs to develop their work are interpreted inside the developmental talk of managerialism as selfish action. Maria is consciously developing for herself an ironical counter-narrative by using the very vocabulary and categories of dominant discourse ('being selfish') in order to restore the feeling of democratic citizenship as a central part of her professional identity. As a psychologist Maria is able to work as a subject-worker (Casey 2003: 629) with her own professional and personal values and needs to develop her work as a teacher. According to Casey (2003), the talk on learning organisations and developing human resources is destroying this kind of subjectivity and democratic citizenship as autonomic professional work. Managerial discourse is turning employees into human resources that are expected to commit themselves to the shared visions of the workplace. The personal development needs are legitimate only when they are significant to the whole organisation (Casey 2003: 620–234; see also Casey 1995, 2002).

## Case 3: Teachers in the field of economics and trade

During the 1990s the field of economics and trade training was also facing the massive structural reforms that took place at polytechnics. College-level institutions were divided into two parts: the higher education system and the secondary-level vocational education system. Teachers in these institutes, who mainly had academic Master's degrees, were also classified as 'first-class' and 'second-class' teachers. Some teachers were appointed to the posts of higher-level vocational education and some stayed on the lower level of secondary vocational education. Higher-level 'first-class' schools had better buildings, more resources, more valued positions and better students. If the teachers stayed in secondary-level vocational education, they did not need to apply for their old posts again.

In the general rhetoric, secondary-level teachers did not admit that their vocation as a teacher decisively changed. As far as co-operation with firms and enterprises was concerned:

> I think that the firms have not really noticed that [the education system] has changed. They have not realised that it is different from the old [degree]. They feel that they search for a graduate for the task, and a person with this title applies for the job, and they want to give him or her that job. [The new degree titles provided by polytechnics] as such are considered to be incoherent, I don't know anything about them.
>
> (Teacher C 02: 9)

Markus belongs to the ones who remained as 'second-class' teachers in lower-level vocational education. He was one of those academically educated teachers who, after the changes, was teaching students with very low grades and low motivation. Markus, who had worked as a teacher of economics and trade for 20 years, denied that he was now training students just to become only shop assistants, although many students seems to '[work] in these [tasks]' (Teacher D 03: 8). Still, Markus admitted that 'my student material is now totally different, as is the nature of my work. Our work changed totally' (Teacher D 03: 10).

After the structural division of vocational institutions, many teachers felt that they had been cheated. They had been working extra hours to develop new study plans for the new polytechnics and still many of them had been left outside. In addition, many had been forced to move out of their dignified college buildings to totally new and more modest places. They had lost the contexts that earlier created the pride and honour of their work. They had lost the old images and traditions that had prevailed in commercial colleges. For example, in unofficial conversations with a group of teachers from the commercial college, I was told a very memorable story about a group of secondary-level teachers who had together decided that they would not leave their old and dignified college building with bare hands. In the early morning hours one of these teachers went into their old building and collected the portraits of the earlier headmasters from the walls, put them into plastic bags and brought them to the new secondary-level building of their vocational education institute. Nobody asked for the portraits and the teachers were able to secure for themselves, and for their institution, the symbolic legitimation of their institution as the natural successor of the old commercial college and its traditions.

In Markus's case, he interpreted the situation of this educational reform differently. He said that he was not eager to become a teacher on the polytechnic level, because 'I prefer to stay in a sinking ship in order to learn to swim' (Teacher D 03: 10). He admits, nevertheless, that:

> . . . for years I regretted and thought that I made a stupid choice and thought that I should have applied for a post there. In the polytechnics I would have had a chance to develop my professional knowledge.
>
> (Teacher D 03: 29)

Later he realised: 'Actually, I stayed on the lower level intentionally and did not apply vigorously for teachers' posts in the polytechnics' (Teacher D 03: 29). According to Markus, this was because of his ethos and his need to help the weaker students.

In his counter-talk, Markus created a very colourful picture of the situation in a secondary-level vocational institution in which the leaders of the institute and the ordinary teachers were living in 'totally different spheres' that did not communicate with each other. Ordinary teachers, with whom Markus identifies, 'teach students of different nationalities with grade point averages of 6' (low in the scale of 4–10) who should be able to make for themselves personal study plans and choose courses from the online study programmes of the institutions. The teachers had to teach according to five different timetables in the modules with 150 students at the same time. Markus compares his teaching job to working 'in an assembly line':

> [You] jump from the bus stop, then you continue for a while, then you jump away and then you take another line. [When the] teacher starts to know them [his students] a bit and [he realises] which strings to pull [what to do next], [the group of the students in the module changes again and] you start from the beginning again. You start to learn the names [again].
>
> (Teacher D 03: 11)

At the same time, the leaders of the institute were moving 'into a totally different sphere in which they are trying to create a kind of small . . . higher institution for these small, small ones' (Teacher D 03: 11).

According to Markus, it was no longer possible to hear the real voice of the teacher in the classroom, where the students were asked to collect new information only from the Internet. According to Markus, books were gone: 'Nobody reads books any more. (---) The only thing that is important is the Internet and internationality' (Teacher D 03: 17–18).

Markus justified his criticism by using repeatedly the phrase 'I am exaggerating now again' (Teacher D 03: 11; 03: 12; 03: 28). He said that he was in a way consciously giving a worse impression of their situation in his workplace than the other teachers would do (Teacher D 03: 28). According to Markus, they would describe the situation quite differently and give a more positive perspective. With these excuses of exaggeration he created for himself a free space that legitimised alternative criticism and irony that were targeted at the inspirational rhetoric of the general developmental work of the management.

In his counter-narrative Markus keeps a multi-level distance from his own biography and life choices. He had been a teacher for about 20 years, although he had 'never intended to become a teacher' (Teacher D 03: 5). He felt different from the rest of his organisation and he defined himself as 'a kind of individual freethinker' who has always been different from others (Teacher D 03: 18). Markus taught entrepreneurship and this is one of the central themes from which he distances himself. He says that, as a child of a working-class family, he felt that 'I was like a student of divinity without faith in God' (Teacher D 03: 5) when he studied economics at the university. He defined himself as a person who had difficulty connecting to the world of marketing and enterprises.

On the other hand, he defined himself 'as a preacher' (Teacher D 03: 5). He knew that he was super-good in selling, especially 'spiritual selling' (03: 6). He felt like a person who took everything emotionally (03: 5). He had committed himself to the ethos of 'humble serving' that he had learned from his mother and father (03: 6). He was also applying the idea of humble serving in his teaching; he was teaching his students to be ready to serve their clients as well as possible. Although he had never intended to become a teacher of economics, he considered himself to be a quite good educator. He really wanted to touch the souls of young people and make his mark on their young minds. He said that the headmaster of his institution once said to him: 'Markus, you are the kind of teacher who makes his mark on the pupil' (03: 20). Markus commented on these words of his headmaster with acceptance. He defined himself first of all 'as an educator' and it was clear that for Markus this was almost as central a position as 'being a father', which was the most important identity for him (03: 19). Educating was the most valuable and important task of his work. 'I increasingly think that [a teacher's work] is above all an educational task' (03: 19).

According to Markus, schools had 'lost the idea of parenthood' and peer support in upper-level comprehensive schools (seventh to ninth grade). Pupils were left alone in a situation in which they needed stable relationships with adults and teachers. This had led to a situation in which pupils had to rely on themselves more than before. According to Markus, the change from the tradition of students having a permanent learning environment where they worked together with the same classmates to one characterised by short modules and continuous admission may be good for the financial situation of the institute but was not good for the students. Individually selected modules and courses did not offer a safe and permanent learning environment, especially for the young boys who most needed it (03: 11).

In the following extract, Markus constructs his ironical counter-narrative by using metaphors. Markus compared the effectiveness of the existing vocational education system 'to a Soviet kind of "efficiency"' (Teacher D 03: 12). This brisk comparison was a result of this small story that is, in Markus's words, also part of his exaggeration and a story that was not really meant to be told in public:

*Extract 3*

Interviewer:   What do you think about the situation about which another teacher I interviewed told me, a situation in which she had a class of 18 students and that only eight or nine of them were able to complete their degrees? Half of the students could not manage to complete their studies in time.

Markus:   So?

Interviewer:   Is this kind of situation possible at your educational institute?

Markus:   Yes, of course . . . but now different kinds of means to prevent this have been developed. Nowadays, I mean, well . . . this story is not meant to be told publicly . . . but . . . the situation is that those study advisers work with us in a very efficient way. . . . in fact, the degrees are today churned out. In other words, when they miss courses in spring time . . . they can be third-year or even fourth-year students. . . . but when they come, they go first to the study adviser and then they go from one teacher to another and . . . they apply for compensation for their uncompleted courses accordingly, the demand level has been lowered briskly, and so, these degrees, according to my interpretation, are being churned out. In this way, the number of accepted degrees can be raised. . . .

so this is one of the reasons . . . I sometimes wonder . . . when there are only 40 per cent of the whole class present . . . sometimes over half of the class is missing . . . and still the percentage of degrees is high. So, I think that this is in fact like, so I exaggerate again on purpose, but anyway I am able to say that I think that these kinds of activities are somewhat similar to the Soviet 'efficiency'.

(03: 11–12)

Markus heavily mocks the new teaching system of his institution and the new direction of change. He invents apt comparisons that are very impressive and convincing rhetorical achievements. He creates a kind of counter-picture to the trends of development work and change that he confronts. He opens up new ruptures to the prevailing pretty story of self-directed learning (Filander 2003) and the sympathetic talk on tutoring and guidance systems. According to the counter-picture created by Markus, the Finnish vocational education system was in the middle of developmental trends of global competition, stronger management and leadership with continuous evaluation and strategies of quality, top expertise and benchmarking. Teachers were increasingly positioned in the institutional settings of vocational education as persons not able to work as educators any more. For Markus, the rhetoric of lifelong learning positions students to be self-directed learners who are themselves responsible for their success and failure. However, according to the counter-picture given by Markus, the students in secondary-level vocational education are not necessarily able to carry the main responsibility for their own learning and continuous renewal through into the different phases of their studies.

## Irony as an emancipatory discourse

In this chapter irony is understood as an emancipatory discourse that has become a necessary dimension of the new politics (Marcuse 1969; see Brown 1987: 172). From this perspective, when such self-evident 'truths' as those of the Finnish 'New Public Management' movement of the 1990s was presented as a one-dimensional and orthodox mode of thought, there is a need for alternative talk and for the creation of spaces for envisioning an alternative future. Irony is considered as a liberating metanarrative that makes it possible to question the basic and self-evident assumptions of unchallenged governing narratives of individualistic vocabularies of learning on managerial governance. This metaperspective is needed in the processes of producing new possibilities for alternative understandings (Burke 1945; see Summa 1996: 55). Irony works here as a method to create some new gaps and ruptures in governing metanarratives that have previously been taken for granted.

This way of thinking about the role of irony stands in contrast to Rorty's (1989) idea of irony as a state of mind of flexible order is which people are never quite able to take themselves seriously (quoted in Sennett 1998: 116). From this perspective, ironic persons are always aware of the contingency and fragility of their final vocabularies and thus also of themselves. Sennett argues that irony understood like this does not stimulate people to challenge power; they challenge themselves instead (Sennett 1998: 116).

In the case studies, the emancipatory elements of an ironic stance are clear. With their individual counter-narratives, the trade teachers Maria and Markus make it possible to see the connections and contradictions inside the dominant cultural manuscript of managerial development work of vocational education. Irony helps them to create an alternative space and gives them permission to justify their agency through voices that have to be listened to in their own right (see Shotter 1993: 10).

In the first case, the work orientation in painting and surface treatment can be defined as a traditional craft with hands-on knowledge and skilled know-how combined with the idea of constant evolution of skills (see Sennett 1998: 34–35). The teachers' task is to produce skilled workers able to gradually master their own craft and find for themselves the skills needed by repetition and practice. The study demonstrated the collective and shared masculine distress the teachers shared and that they tried to control with the help of their collective ironical counter-narratives. They used a very simple turn of narrative to show how impossible and ridiculous the whole idea of online use of information and communication technologies in teaching and learning is in painting and surface treatment. They use a shared strategy of counter-narratives that aims to keep the division of labour between the schools and workplaces unchanged with the help of traditional collective strategies of occupational order.

In the second case, Maria, coming from the field of care and social services, constructs a highly individual counter-narrative. Compared to the traditional collective craft of painting and surface treatment Maria provides a highly individualistic advocacy of her professional and individual rights but her ironical statements raise questions about the changed meaning of professional autonomy and democratic citizenship. What has actually happened if a teacher has to define herself as selfish when she is determined to understand better the field in which she teaches? In such circumstances, subject-workers (Casey 2003: 629) who commit themselves as professionals to develop their personal work and competences are forced to defend their autonomous space with the reverse discourses in which they use managerial vocabularies in an ironic manner.

Markus, coming from the field of economics and trade, distances himself from the dominant individualistic hype-talk on development work that forgets the moral and essential ethos of the educator. Markus uses the vocabulary of education and parenthood that positions both teachers and vocational schools as responsible actors for those students who are not able to cope as individual and self-directed learners at schools and workplaces.

Casey (2003: 621) argues that the discourse of human resource management is an important factor in producing a new symbolic order that requires more intensive integration into, and commitment to, the corporate culture. Irony works here as a creative repositioning of the dominant managerial narratives and makes it possible to frame managerial imperative in a new light. According to Andrews (2004: 1–2), people often construct personal stories that go against the social grain with a consciousness of being a member of an outside group. When they position themselves as being in the margin or part of the significant other, they bring with them alternative resources that they use when challenging the dominant cultural narratives. In my own data, Markus perhaps best represents this kind of counter-narrative. Markus's whole life story seems to be an exception and a special case in relation to the dominant discourses and master narratives of his field in economics and trade. His experience of difference is based on the feeling of divergence and uniqueness that prevented him from identifying the dominant narratives of managerial talk on learning. The narrative resources of an educator and a father provide Markus with resources that help him to reframe the phrases of dominant development work as a regression, preventing the institutes of vocational education from concentrating on their most important work: teaching the students to become good practitioners and citizens.

We live in a situation in which it is difficult to define the ethical dimension of our work and to maintain personal integration and a feeling of occupational identity. According to Sennett, the fragmentation of occupational identity, self and experience is threatening the ability of people to form their characters into sustained narratives. People have to improvise their life in order to survive (Sennett 1998: 31). They have to learn to use new vocabularies, when the meaning of the responsibility and collective identity in which they have earlier positioned themselves is changing into something profoundly different. According to Hall (1996), identities are now more about questions of using the resources of history, language and culture in the process of becoming rather than being. It is more important to ask what we might become, or how we might represent ourselves, than 'who we are' or 'where we came from' (Hall 1996: 4).

Narrating professional and occupational ownership in specific historical and institutional sites has become a continuous and rather individual process with no clear collective points of identification. In this process, irony can teach us that nothing is known absolutely and that everything is reversed when overextended (Brown 1987: 192). Irony can work as a strategy for critical analysis that can raise new questions concerning the choices we make. In vocational education, it can help to understand the possible consequences of agreeing with mainstream ideas of flexible managerialism, a new culture of neoliberal vocational education and a post-modern multi-skilled process-worker orientation. All three counter-narratives examined here challenge the constraints of the dominant narratives of development work. These collective and individual counter-narratives of defence and resistance mirror and challenge the dominant cultural script of developmental narratives by questioning the value of occupational belongings, teacher work, democratic citizenship and occupational autonomy. In this way, these counter-narratives can also expand the boundaries of the dominant talk and challenge the mainstream understanding of the future of occupations and of vocational education.

## References

Andrews, M. (2004) 'Opening to the original contributions: Counter-narratives and the power to oppose', in M. Bamberg and M. Andrews (eds) *Considering Counter-Narratives: Narrating, Resisting, Making Sense*, Amsterdam/ Philadelphia: John Benjamins Publishing Company, 1–6.

Bauman, Z. (1992) *Intimations of Postmodernity*, London: Routledge.

Bauman, Z. (1996) 'From pilgrim to tourist – or a short history of identity', in S. Hall and P. du Gay (1996) *Questions of Cultural Identity*, London: Sage, 18–36.

Billig, M. (1987) *Arguing and Thinking: A Rhetorical Approach to Social Psychology*, Cambridge: Cambridge University Press.

Brooks, I. and MacDonald, S. (2000) 'Doing life': Gender relations in a night nursing sub-culture', *Gender, Work and Organizations*, 7(4): 221–229.

Brown, R. H. (1987) *Society as Text: Essays on Rhetoric, Reason, and Reality*, Chicago: University of Chicago Press.

Burke, K. (1945) *A Grammar of Motives*, New York: Prentice Hall.

Casey, C. (1995) *Work, Self and Society: After Industrialism*, London: Routledge.

Casey C. (2002) *Critical Analysis of Organizations: Theory, Practice, Revitalization*, London: Sage.

Casey, C. (2003) 'The learning worker, organizations and democracy', *International Journal of Lifelong Education*, 22(6): 620–634.

Clarke, J. and Newman, J. (1997) *The Managerial State: Power, Politics and Ideology in the Remaking of Social Welfare*, London: Sage.

Edwards, R., Armstrong, P. and Miller, N. (2001) 'Include me out: Critical readings of social exclusion, social inclusion and lifelong learning', *International Journal of Lifelong Education*, 20(5): 417–428.

Esping-Andersen, G. (1990) *The Three Worlds of Welfare Capitalism*, Princeton: Princeton University Press.

Filander, K. (2003) *Vocabularies of Change – Analysing Talk on Change and Agency in Developmental Work*, Roskilde: Roskilde University Press.

Filander, K. (2005) 'Experts in uncertainty: Making cultural analysis of identities in adult education', in A. Bron, E. Kurantowicz, H. Olesen and L. West (eds) *'Old' and 'New' Worlds of Adult Learning*. Wroclaw, Poland: Wydawnictwo Naukowe, 56–69.

Filander, K. (2007) 'Deconstructing dominant discourses on vocational education', in R. Rinne, A. Heikkinen and P. Salo (eds) *Adult Education – Liberty, Fraternity, Equality? Nordic Views on Lifelong Learning*, Turku: Finnish Educational Research Association, 261–274.

Filander, K. and Jokinen, E. (2004) *Tekemällä oppimisen kokeita – Ammattiopettajat työssäoppimisen kentillä*. Toimintatutkimus Opekon kehittämishankkeista, Loppuraportti. Työraportteja/Working Papers 99/2004. Tampere: Tampereen yliopisto, Yhteiskuntatieteiden tutkimuslaitos. Työelämän tutkimuskeskus.

Hall, S. (1996) 'Introduction: Who needs "identity"?', in S. Hall and P. du Gay (eds) *Questions of Cultural Identity*, London: Sage, 1–17.

Holstein, J. A. and Gubrium, J. F. (1995) *The Active Interview*, Qualitative Research Methods, vol. 37, London: Sage.

Holstein, J. A. and Gubrium, J. F. (1997) 'Active interviewing', in D. Silverman (ed.) *Qualitative Research: Theory, Method and Practice*, London: Sage, 113–129.

Jokinen, A. (1999) 'Vakuuttelevan ja suostuttelevan retoriikan analysoiminen', in A. Jokinen, K. Juhila and E. Suoninen (eds) *Diskurssianalyysi liikkeessä*, Tampere: Vastapaino, 126–159.

Marcuse, H. (1969) *An Essay on Liberation*, Boston: Beacon.

Naschold, F. (1996) *New Frontiers in Public Sector Management: Trends and Issues in State and Local Government in Europe*, New York: Walter de Gruyter.

Potter, J. (1996) 'Discourse analysis and constructionist approaches: Theoretical background', in J. T. E. Richardson (ed.) *Handbook of Qualitative Research Methods for Psychology and the Social Sciences*, Leicester: BPS Books, 129–140.

Rinne, R. and Salmi, E. (1998) *Oppimisen uusi järjestys: Uhkien ja verkostojen maailma koulun ja elämänmittaisen opiskelun haasteena*, Tampere: Vastapaino.

Rorty, R. (1989) *Contingency, Irony and Solidarity*, Cambridge, UK: Cambridge University Press.

Sennett, R. (1998) *The Corrosion of Character: The Personal Consequences of Work in the New Capitalism*, London: W.W. Norton and Company.

Shotter, J. (1993) 'Becoming someone: Identity and belonging', in N. Coupland and J. F. Nussbaum (eds) *Discourse and Lifespan Identity: Language and Language Behaviors*, Newbury Park, London and New Delhi: Sage Publications, 5–27.

Silverman, D. (1991) 'Sociology and the community: A dialogue of the deaf?', in H. Forsberg, A. Jokinen, K. Juhila, H. Järviluoma, M. Kuronen, T. Pösö, A. Ritala-Koskinen, I. Roivainen, I. Rostila, D. Silverman and R. Suoninen (eds) *Sosiaalisia käytäntöjä tutkimassa*. Katkelmia empiirisen tutkimuksenteon vaiheista. Tutkimuksia Sarja A, Nro 1, Tampere: Tampereen yliopiston sosiaalipolitiikan laitos, 11–34.

Summa, H. (1996) 'Kolme näkökulmaa uuteen retoriikkaan: Burke, Perelman, Toulmin ja retoriikan kunnianpalautus', in K. Palonen and H. Summa (eds) *Pelkkää retoriikkaa: Tutkimuksen ja politiikan retoriikat*, Tampere: Vastapaino, 51–83.

Vehviläinen, J. (2001) *Innolla ammattiin? Ammatillisten oppilaitosten innovatiiviset työpajat- ESR-projekti*. Opetushallitus, Moniste 21/2001, Helsinki: Edita.

# Chapter 4

# Disturbing work, workspaces and working lives

## Three Australian case studies

*Anita Devos, Lesley Farrell and Terri Seddon*

The focus of this chapter is the forms and politics of regulation of work in contemporary Australia. We explore the ways that new regimes of regulation affect work and learning through three distinct case studies from very different regulatory levels. The first case examines National Government 'Work Choices' legislation introduced in 2006. The second takes a very different approach to the issue of workplace regulation by examining what happened when a new 'virtual' regulatory regime was introduced into the car industry. Looking at the issue through a completely different lens, our third example draws on a study of mentoring programmes for academic women to focus even more specifically on the issue of what Foucault (1988) calls 'technologies of the self'.

Taken together, these three very different examples of new regulatory regimes help us identify new pressures in work and new contexts for learning at every level, from the nation state, the global corporation, the local worksite and the individual work group. The changes are neither straightforward nor consistent. Neither are they uniformly, nor even usually passively, accepted, but are frequently contested, both collectively and by individuals. These changes, and, more specifically, the ways in which education and work-related learning is implicated in them and shaped and constrained by them, need exploration and analysis. In that sense, work is disturbing but also needs to be disturbed. The three cases we have used to explore the politics of work and learning reflect our current research agendas. Reflecting on these varied research projects has helped us to identify some of the paths that analysis might take.

In this chapter, we are not arguing that the explicit economic agenda driving workplace change or education and training means that its goals or effects are pre-determined and not subject to renegotiation or change. Much evidence suggests that workers actively manage their own learning in ways that will be most productive for them in spite of, or in addition to, the priorities identified by the organisations in which they work and learn. Rather, we are arguing that it is important to understand the complex interrelationships between regulatory regimes, workers and work practice if we are to understand learning at work.

## Case 1: Work choices and the national regulation of work

In 2006, the Commonwealth Government in Australia passed new 'Work Choices' legislation. Its broad thrust was to increase the flexibility of the Australian labour market by increasing the use of individual employment contracts – Australian Workplace Agreements (AWAs) – rather than industrial awards based on collective bargaining. Among other measures, the new rules reduced the number of established work conditions from 20 to five.

Despite government claims that this legislation would benefit Australia, early evidence suggested that individual Australians were losing out from these changes. At least one protected award condition had been negotiated out of each of the first 250 contracts signed off and all award conditions had been removed in 16 per cent of AWAs, leaving only five minimum conditions (Australian Council of Trade Unions 2006). The press carried stories of disadvantage. For example, Spotlight, a fabric retailer, offered new employees contracts that reduced prevailing work conditions in return for an extra two cents an hour. Another woman, returning from unpaid leave, was offered an AWA that meant she would lose $90 per week in penalty rates (*The Age*, 14 June 2006).

These legislative changes in industrial relations disturbed work and were disturbing, particularly for the individuals directly affected by AWAs. Yet these disturbances were felt well beyond those individuals and the parties directly involved in industrial relations. This was in part because, as Mills (1971) points out, there are connections between 'personal troubles', like losing a job or having pay reduced, and 'public issues'. Personal troubles are often private matters in which deeply held values and commitments are challenged or thrown into crisis. Public issues relate to institutional arrangements that organise societies. Understanding disturbance means locating individual experience in contested processes of institutionalisation that regulate social practices.

Connections between individuals and their contexts have been understood since the nineteenth century, as constituted by the interactive effects of social structures, history and biography (Mills 1971). Yet these are not simple 'things' that are static and known before analysis. Rather, they are processes that change across time and space and appear as trajectories of things and narratives of meaning (Seddon 1993). So we see categories (such as 'society', 'individual' or 'institution') relationally, as social time-spaces that are always in open-ended processes of formation. These time-spaces are constituted by social relations, which shape social and symbolic practices, and sediment as particular places, distinguished by their culture, relations and practices. These social relations of place are manifested at different scales (the body, local, national, global) and through many voices. Massey (2005: 10) captures this relational understanding by emphasising the way 'identities-entities, the relations "between" them, and the spatiality that is part of them, are all co-constitutive'.

Drawing these ideas together suggests that 'Work Choices' legislation was disturbing because it destabilised the co-constitutive effects of social relations relayed through trajectories of things and narratives in ways that affected not only individuals' lives but also institutions and their regulatory effects. We can track these disturbances into three contested formations: the national regulatory state, the national imaginary and education.

'Work Choices' was one element in successive industrial relations reforms in Australia that, since the mid-1980s, and under various governments, have driven flexibilisation and deregulation of the labour market to open up the Australian economy to global competition. These changes have unpicked the distinctive Australian industrial relations system originally established after the 1890s strikes and laid down in the constitution that formed Australia as a Commonwealth of six states with a distinct federal-state division of powers. That system of industrial relations assumed conflict between capital and labour. It sought to manage this relationality by extending the common law basis of employment, embodied in the individual employment contract, through judge-made law that recognised and drew out the rights and duties of the industrial parties. The aim was to redress the bias inherent in individual employment contracts that tended to benefit employers (Plowman 1992).

This twentieth-century industrial relations system produced high levels of unionisation and complementary employer organisation, compulsory adjudication of industrial disputes that were binding on each party, comparative wage justice and wage indexation. It also engendered a strong sense of duty toward the public interest and equitable distribution of productivity. This was confirmed by the broader orchestration of economic, work and welfare policy. The outcome was a distinctive kind of 'wage-earners' welfare state (Castles 1988) that anchored social protection to the breadwinner and basic wage, and provided residualised welfare support for dependants (mostly women and children) and for those who fell beyond the world of work. This public policy framework, anchored in State and Commonwealth jurisdictions and division of labour, underpinned social and symbolic practices at the national scale, establishing national practices of social protection and giving a sense of nation – an 'Australian Way' in government, markets and civil society (Smyth and Cass 1998).

'Work Choices' overturned those established industrial rules of the game by asserting efficiency over equality and privileging individual employment contracts, irrespective of employer–employee power relations. It went hand in hand with a re-formed regulatory state that had opened up the Australian economy to international competition by removing tariffs, endorsing free trade, driving a particular kind of industry restructuring and up-skilling the workforce. It was accompanied by wide-ranging welfare reforms that redefined universal entitlements available to categories of disadvantaged in terms of mutual obligations, and learning and earning.

These disturbances in social and economic arrangements also disturbed normative and cultural expectations. National myths about Australia's system of social protection shifted over time. Sometimes described as mean and divisive, it is now being affirmed and defended in the face of privatisation, individualisation and growing inequality (Roe 1998). The old logics of a job for life, universalistic schooling for the young and a pension in old age were never the only narratives about the Australian Way (Pixley 1993). This history disregarded 'her-stories': the experiences of women and indigenous Australians who were never well served by the 'breadwinner' state. The limitations of these monocultural claims failed to acknowledge that universalistic services like schooling systematically disadvantaged those who fell outside the preferred norms defined by Anglo-Celtic, classed, gendered, able bodies. Yet both national myths and counter-narratives were being compromised by shifts in the rationalities of government. The ideology of globalisation contested the Australian Way and its gendered stories of 'mateship' and a 'fair go'. Trans-national economic changes and cultural flows re-scaled lived horizons, while governments remained locked within historic, national jurisdictions and national geographic boundaries.

People's identities were formed through and against these social and symbolic practices that accompanied patterns of institutionalisation and regulation. The changed rules of the game were lived in disturbing ways, mediated by the discursive rules and historical narratives that had come to represent institutional arrangements that helped frame ways of understanding work, life and citizenship.

New economic and social policies had already co-opted education as an instrument of economic reform before the advent of 'Work Choices'. These education reforms were initially aimed at up-skilling the workforce to enhance Australia's international competitiveness. They later shifted discursively to create a competitive knowledge economy that was to be more innovative and individualistic. Policy acknowledged the collapse of the full-time youth labour market (Freeland 1986). Institutional experimentation complemented these trends (Axford and Seddon 2006). Early efforts focused on reconfiguring the senior secondary curriculum to accommodate the increasingly diverse young people who were staying on beyond the compulsory years of schooling. Decentralisation, programme budgeting and school choice followed, pressing schools to be responsive to local communities, newly endorsed as choosers and consumers.

Continuing evidence that young people were falling between the cracks of education, training and the labour market helped to ratchet up the case for diversification and deinstitutionalisation of learning (Dussledorp Skills Forum 1998, 1999). There was growing endorsement of work-related learning. Participation in work-related training increased, despite employer contributions to training as a percentage of pay-roll remaining static at 1.3 per cent, although government subsidies increased. The vocational education and training (VET) sector grew with public and private training providers treated as equivalent Registered Training Organisations (RTOs). VET in school enrolments grew, with students moving between schools and local RTOs. Opportunities for young people to continue their education outside school grew with support for community-based programmes and formalised recognition of this learning credentialed through

VET qualifications and new school-based credentials in applied learning. Higher education enrolments grew rapidly and substantially, particularly in vocational fields. And private education enrolments also grew as middle Australia sought to shore up educational opportunities for its own children (Watson *et al.* 2003).

Education as a social institution was decentred and its normative capacity turned away from traditional national concerns: universalistic public ethics, equality of opportunity and the formation of knowledgeable national citizens (Ferguson and Seddon 2006). New institutional arrangements endorsed the formation of particularistic knowing and self-regulating identities who worked across patch-worked learning spaces. Yet decentring did not diminish the normative power of education. While globalisation diffracted educational provision to accommodate internationalisation, and employers could now receive subsidies to support work-based learning, education remained underpinned by the resources and rule-making powers consolidated in national state formations. What changed was not the power of the national state to assert and drive learning as normative identity formation but its orientation. This shifted in line with other forms of 'graduated or variegated sovereignty' to provide differentiated 'sites of entitlement' differently invested with economic and political resources (Ong 2006).

'Work Choices' was just one element in the reconstruction of national regulation. The process remains uneven and contested. Industrial, economic, social and education reforms, effected through the nation-state, disrupted the slow cadence of everyday practices and engagements that constitute institutional and identity time-spaces. They also disorganised the allegro play of practical politics. But a deep structure of feeling remained ambiguously anchored in the older national regulation that continued to underwrite a sense of public duty to others, a fair go and what it means to be Australian. These variable rhythms of change created dissonances in experience. They disturbed because they were lived as moral dilemmas with contradictory political effects. Yet these changes in a national regulatory regime are not the full story. The contradictory effects that disturbed work and working life were compounded by global flows that further disrupted the familiar frames of reference.

We turn now to consider some of the ways in which these contradictory effects were manifested in one particular contemporary globally distributed, technologically enabled, workspace.

## Case 2: The regulation of a globally distributed workspace

One of the most fundamental challenges to national regulatory regimes of work has been the development of the technologically enabled, globally distributed workspace that sits alongside and augments the more familiar idea of the workplace:

> . . . work*places* [form] local nodes of a complex network of people, technologies and practices that constitute a potentially globally distributed

> work*space*. . . . workspaces [can be understood as] dynamic, fluid, often transient, working units defined and bounded by regular routine information communication technology routes (telephone, E-mail, hardcopy print materials, palmtop computers, pagers etc), not bounded by geography and not even by commercial organization, no matter how extensive and complicated the corporate legal ties might be.
>
> (Farrell 2006: 17)

Work and technology have had an uneasy relationship since at least the industrial revolution. The whole question of the body, embodied knowledge and the relationship between the labouring body and the machine has been debated and worried over for 200 years (Zuboff 1988). The machine has been seen as both potentially oppressive (in that it controls the exertion of the body) and potentially liberating (in that it replaces injurious or dangerous work).

Communications technologies reproduce some of these debates and generate new ones. One persistent debate (familiar since the industrial revolution) focuses on the disembodiment and technologisation of working knowledge and the implications for what counts as knowledge, who owns it, and what it means for the power and autonomy of individual workers in physical, historically located workspaces. Sewing machines, mechanical harvesters, production lines and industrial robots (to name a very few examples to technologisation) have each had a profound impact on what counts as valuable knowledge at work, on how work is done and how the power relationships in working life (and outside it) are calibrated. Communications technologies generate different debates because they have the potential to dislodge working knowledge (or at least some of it) from its physical context as well as the individual, 'the knower', in whom it may be embodied. This technology has the added dimension that it can reconstitute this working knowledge in words, numbers and symbols that can be transmitted and reformulated moment by moment as it shifts around the communications network (and the world). This has impacted on what it is to know, what it takes to use knowledge and how anyone gets to be acknowledged as 'someone who knows'.

Workplaces are one of the oldest learning spaces we have, and work-related learning, of both the formally accredited and the on-the-job, 'sitting next to Nellie' kinds, has been a powerful means of regulating the way work is done, relationships between people and between how people and institutions are managed, and working identities are developed and produced. Place still matters (and national regulatory regimes are critically important) but place matters differently. The incorporation of the virtual into existing physical workspaces fundamentally changes the way work is done, the relationships that are possible and necessary, and the kinds (and varieties) of identities that need to be produced and managed by ordinary workers in ordinary workplaces. However, while these changes may be fundamental, they change things in ways that are by no means obvious or consistent across sites or cultures (e.g. Arunachalam 1999; Sholtz and Prinsloo 2001; Farrell and Holkner 2004).

The ideas of the learning organisation and of knowledge-based economies have foregrounded the workplace as a site of learning and knowledge production and they have led to the promotion of certain forms of learning – such as innovation and problem-solving – as key productive behaviours (Brown and Duguid 2002). This approach to learning (which has as its hallmark the capacity of a learner to produce new knowledge and use established knowledge collaboratively 'just in time') has been explicitly recruited to the project of creating and maintaining globally distributed workspaces.

A key feature of the contemporary physical workplace is the extent to which it is integrated into a global, technologically enabled environment. In contemporary workplaces it is usually the case that the physical and the virtual are mutually constitutive around a project or a practice and this seems more or less taken for granted, unlike school education where virtual environments are often treated as exotic. If a distinction is made it is generally a dangerous one: that the virtual workspace is unproblematically neutral, that it is an exclusively technological phenomenon in which the social, political or cultural meanings of the physical world can be erased. The development of the 'Virtual Workspace Project' described below questions these assumptions and problematises the role of the work-related education that prepares people to operate in technologically enabled working environments (for a much more comprehensive account of this project see Farrell 2006).

The 'Virtual Workspace Project' is a suite of applications (including a 'problem solver', a 'collaboration manager' and a 'quote manager') developed for the automotive industry by a company specialising in e-commerce. (It is called a B2B or business to business exchange and they exist in most industries that operate in globally distributed environments.) Because car companies outsource almost all their operations, including the design and development of components and materials, and because they are designing and developing at the same time as they are manufacturing, they need a virtual environment where the changes to the design can be monitored and modelled and relevant adjustments tried out. The moulded components manufacturer in Melbourne and the hydraulic system manufacturer in Johannesburg and all the people in between need to be able to log on and 'walk through' the car to see what has changed and how their proposed changes might work.

The aim of the 'Virtual Workspace Project' is to streamline the production of the global car in a network of production that extends throughout the even moderately industrialised world. It is partly about creating a collaborative interface and partly about trying to get people to 'buy in' to a particular way of interacting with each other, collaborating in design and solving problems. It is usually presented as a technical problem (dealing with time and space) with a technical solution.

The 'Virtual Workspace Project' was a huge co-operative undertaking developed by Ford, General Motors Holden and Daimler-Chrysler. The online industry press (which appears to operate under ambiguous libel laws) described their relationship as 'bitter enmity'. They took three months to agree on what to call the project and much longer to decide whose software system would be used. This was exacerbated because the chairmen of two of the software companies were described as 'dire enemies'. When the technicians came to design the software they were already constrained by negotiations, compromises and decisions that were political and historical (and related to specific physical environments) rather than purely technical in nature.

By the time negotiations were completed the cost had blown out so much that the 'Virtual Workspace Project' had to be presented as an absolutely comprehensive problem-solving environment even though the software designers had not been able to ask the suppliers what kinds of problems they thought might need to be solved.

So, to participate in the virtual workspace, a worker needs to enter the virtual environment with a problem that has occurred at their physical workplace, reconfigure it in terms that can be understood in the virtual workspace and go through the mandated problem-solving processes. They then need to translate the solution back to the physical workspace, making the minor or major adjustments that take account of local manufacturing conditions without reference to the virtual workspace, although they might telephone or email colleagues in Johannesburg or Melbourne to sort out the details.

The globally distributed workspace regulates people's work practice and working identities. It also regulates the learning people can do 'on the job' and the learning they need to do to operate within the virtual space. This does not mean that industry and national regulatory regimes are rendered neutral. Each regulatory regime is in many ways constitutive of the other, and each worker is shaped by, and shapes, all of them. The histories and politics of the global automotive industry could not be erased from the 'Virtual Workspace', as they were embedded in its whole orientation from the design of the software to the assumptions that were made about work practices and physical (and social and political) working conditions.

The problem was not that it was not a neutral environment – since it could never have been one. The problem was that the history and politics of the many specific, physical locations in which various versions of virtual workspaces were taken up was neither erased nor acknowledged. The histories and politics of global cities were unknowingly taken up by people operating in physical workspaces like Melbourne, Johannesburg, Mumbai and Malaysia, places that had their own histories and politics to contend with. The explicit national regulatory regimes under which they operated mattered too. The regulatory regimes that operated in each of these spatial scales were in complex interaction in global workspaces, disturbing established work practices, processes and regulatory regimes and the working identities that went with them.

What the case of the 'Virtual Workspace' programme shows is that virtual workspaces are, as they are intended to be, sites of learning in which particular subject positions are made available and others are actively discouraged by making them technologically impossible, or very difficult, to produce. In this way, global corporations attempt to regulate work practice and working identity at a distance, over-riding prevailing local practices where they can. Workplace education is often implicated in this process (Jackson 2004; Farrell 2006; Scheeres and Solomon 2006). This raises important questions for workplace educators and for workplace education more generally. Specifically, what role does workplace education have in regulating workers operating in global webs of production, and what role do workplace educators play in constraining or expanding working identities and working relationships?

The globally distributed workspace is a politically complex and contradictory phenomenon. As the foregoing suggests, it is significantly less monolithic and comprehensive than it appears to be. In the light of these contradictions, local work practices have proven to be surprisingly resilient in the face of co-ordinated efforts to impose standardised global systems. A potentially productive approach to work-related education could be for work-related educators to exploit the contradictions inherent in attempts to standardise working knowledge, supporting workers in exercising some autonomy over their working lives, at least at the local level. So how do these inter-spatial regulatory regimes and their contradictory effects play out for individuals? We now explore these questions through one prominent and powerful form of work-related learning – the pedagogy of workplace mentoring.

## Case 3: Regulation of the self at work

Mentoring has become a very widely practised form of workplace education, across a range of industries, occupations and nations. The model of mentoring used varies from site to site but usually involves a process where a more experienced person is paired with a less experienced worker for a defined period of time to transfer and build knowledge and support career development. In mentoring, the role of 'workplace educator' is dispersed, enacted in the role of mentor by any number of people in the organisation who may, or may not, fill a formal workplace education role. Many people learn at work through mentoring. But what exactly do they learn? This section draws on data from a qualitative study of women, mentoring and the construction of academic identities, to respond to this question.

Clearly there may be skills and knowledge that are learnt or produced through mentoring that are specific to the profession or the workspace or place. However, the study discussed here argues that mentoring also generates new knowledge of the self or identities for the workers involved and that these identities are related to the specific time and the place. In mentoring, possible working identities may be modelled, or they may be confronted. In either case, these identities are framed by the political and institutional contexts in which they are produced, and so mentoring is always implicated in a wider political agenda. It never occupies a neutral or value-free zone. This is the case, whether mentoring has as its aim the development of new leaders in a global corporation, the induction of new schoolteachers, or – as in the study reported here – a feminist goal of supporting women's career progression in academia.

Recent years have seen the development of a body of research that looks at the ways in which work and workers have been reshaped during the last half of the twentieth century. A number of writers have noted how new forms of workplace governance and regulation and new work demands create new forms of subjectivities (Rose 1989, 2nd edn 1999; du Gay 1996). In this research literature the management of the ways in which workers understand and construct their identities is acknowledged as a central task of contemporary organisations, the goal being to create apparent congruence between workers' own goals and those of the organisation. The active subjects produced in this way will, it is argued, be more productive (Usher and Solomon 1999).

The goals of educational institutions have been reshaped in line with economic goals, leading to a situation in universities (as in the public sector more broadly) where efficiency is the new bottom line (Blackmore and Sachs 2001: 45). Workplace education has assumed a critical role in driving and supporting agendas of contemporary universities, as institutions hunt for ways to increase productivity through closer monitoring and measurement of worker performance directed towards specific institutional goals. Importantly, human resources technologies are used as a means to not only manage workers, but to encourage them to manage themselves. The focus has shifted in many industries from regulation via external means, such as time clocks, to self-regulation.

For these technologies to work, workers must believe their own needs and desires are the same as those of their institution and actively take on a project of self-improvement in line with institutional imperatives. In some respects this is not an entirely new development. Any workplace education invariably involves an element of self-formation and change, containing 'implicit theorisations concerning the nature of the self, its development or capacity for change and the way the self relates to others or to society more generally' (Chappell *et al.* 2003: 9).

Foucault (1988) called these devices we use to act upon ourselves 'technologies of the self', which he described as those technologies

> which permit individuals to effect by their own means or with the help of others a certain number of operations on their own bodies and souls, thought, conduct and way of being, so as to transform themselves in order to attain a certain state of happiness, purity, wisdom, perfection, or immortality.
>
> (Foucault 1988: 18)

When we work on ourselves in these ways, we situate and define ourselves by becoming tied to a particular identity (Foucault 1983). New work contexts do, however, promote new working identities that reflect dominant values. Rose (1989, 2nd edn 1999) argues that the new forms of subjectivities that characterise contemporary workplaces have developed alongside a culture of liberal freedom that celebrates values of autonomy and self-realisation. Within this culture humans are 'obliged' to pursue their autonomy and self-actualisation, to make their life meaningful, 'as if it were the outcome of individual choices made in furtherance of a biographical project of self-realisation' (p. ix).

In workplaces, technologies such as performance appraisal systems and training programmes provide the means for workers to come to 'understand' and act upon themselves within the discourses of their workplaces, creating order and knowledge, and ultimately to produce power (Townley 1994). Self-regulation is central to this task.

In his study of a knowledge-intensive unit undergoing change in a large corporation, Deetz (1998) suggests knowledge-intensive organisations are characterised by high levels of autonomy and self-management, rely primarily on individual and collective forms of intellectual capital, and rely more heavily on normative forms of control, exercised more through self-surveillance and self-control than by the exercise of sovereign or external power by management. The products of most work processes in such organisations are hard to measure. They are not tangible either, leading him to suggest: 'The often hidden and mysterious work, plus the absence of a clear physical product with measurable characteristics, leaves identity to be acquired from the projection of the subject rather than drawn from the product or work activity' (Deetz 1998: 157).

This 'work on ourselves' was well illustrated in a study that looked at how a number of women academics in Australian universities had taken up the task of self-improvement through self-regulation in mentoring relationships. Seventeen women from a number of universities across Australia were interviewed about their experiences of mentoring. They were responding to an invitation to participate in the study, circulated via the National Tertiary Education Union (NTEU) and the Higher Education Research and Development Society of Australasia (HERDSA). A few had been mentored as a result of relationships that developed naturally within their universities, for example where a more senior person offered to provide advice and guidance in regard to their work. Most of the women in the study were mentored in the context of formal programmes established with the explicit goal of supporting career development in the context of the continuing low representation of women in senior positions.

The study demonstrated the ways women may take action in and through their mentoring relationships to produce behaviours and outcomes they and others desire. The study findings also point to the iterative and ongoing process of shaping and reshaping the self to produce desired identities. These identities may include more productive researchers, better-evaluated teachers and better time managers to name a few. These identities are projected on to the mentoring relationship and sometimes the mentor too. In the research discussed, desired identities are also characterised by particular forms of being or conduct at work. A number of the women interviewed used words such as 'calm', 'serene' and 'not manic' to describe the forms of conduct they admire, especially in other women, and in the face of numerous conflicting priorities and expectations.

In their engagement with the discourses of academic careers and mentoring, the interview data pointed to the ways women moved back and forth between two subject positions. This was demonstrated by the women taking up the position of the active subject, trying to manage themselves better through mentoring as a productive academic worker of the times. The second position many women spoke about in the interviews was of one who is 'taken on board' in a mentoring relationship. These two positions are not contradictory but work together to produce the active academic worker. Further, these elements are necessarily present in mentoring, in that mentoring requires an active subject whilst also embodying a desire to be acted on by another (Devos 2004). The self is produced through social relations, in this case in relation with another in mentoring.

A key finding of the study is that the self produced in mentoring is not a unitary conception but is fluid, shifting and many faceted, framed through the discourses of the women's workplaces, and in terms of what it means to be a woman (and sometimes a migrant or lesbian) in those workplaces. This means the project is ongoing as the demands of work, and the regimes of truth which go hand in hand with those demands, change over time. In mentoring the production of the self becomes the curriculum or material with which mentor and mentored work to produce desired identities. This process is not even or uncontested as women confront the possible meanings of work and of themselves made available to them in discourse. Some participants in this study upset expectations of desired identities and behaviours promoted through mentoring, and set out to disturb normative gendered and racialised forms of conduct at work. In doing this they assumed power, both individually and sometimes collectively with other women, by 'outing' discourses and practices which undermine their integrity as working women, feminists, lesbians, and so on. The practical forms such politics take vary, as women – again sometimes individually and sometimes collectively with others – look to secure a future for themselves as academic workers in ways that reflect their desire for integrity in working life.

The study showed that this work of self-improvement may be 'disturbing' on several counts. For many of the women in our study it produced tensions as women confronted existing and closely held identities. Contradictions were generated as the women confront their own positioning of themselves as particular sorts of women workers with the ways in which they are positioned by others, such as their colleagues, their mentor, or the institution more generally. The work of self-improvement was also disturbing for the women because it unsettled fixed conceptions of what work is like and what it might become when the women in this study analyse the assumptions that shaped the changing contexts of their work. This political work did not happen without intervention. For these women, such intervention often took the form of women colleagues, women's networks and, in some cases, a workplace educator. These relationships may enable new and 'disturbing' readings of work and of identity. What the study shows is that workplace education in universities, although framed through institutional discourses of economic imperatives, may have potential as a progressive politicising force, disturbing work in productive and life-enhancing ways as women workers confront their own and others' conceptions of what it is to be a woman and an academic.

## Work and learning in contemporary Australia

This chapter has considered three forms of regulation, each from somewhat different theoretical perspectives and drawing on different kinds of conceptual and empirical resources. Yet what emerges is a kind of montage that reveals the way social and symbolic practices, operating across various spatial scales, have had constitutive effects. The regulatory regimes that form entities–identities have been constructed differently in each case but they show many intersections – these include women, men, workplaces, workspaces, occupational groups, institutions, nation-states and global networks. As these social practices, and their forms and functions, have shifted and reconfigured, they have disturbed work and other institutional spaces and also created disturbances in people's lives, experiences and commitments.

The forms of regulation we describe are multiple and simultaneous – they do not sit in isolation but interact, and their effects are compounded. So, for a worker in a car factory in Melbourne, or a woman academic in an Australian university, the work, workspace and working identities have been actively redefined through the introduction of individual work contracts and increased casualisation of work. ICTs too – like the 'Virtual Workspace Project' in the factory, or email, web-based teaching platforms and the Internet in universities – have redefined social relations and the working day within these new virtual and real workspaces.

The demands of quality, performance and accountability that characterise workspaces have driven many to self-regulate in order to secure future employment and autonomy in work, and have led workers to seek out development opportunities to become even more attractive to their (prospective) employers. In this climate many workers continue to organise through their trade unions to counter the worst excesses of deregulation or, like the women academics described, seek solidarity through women's networks and associations. Many people have sought connections outside their workplaces through community groups and churches but these connections are strained as the demands of deregulated working life impact. A challenge then is how workers can develop and sustain solidarity with others, at work and outside work, to find connectedness and develop transformative possibilities for themselves and with others.

It is clear that every aspect of this picture is political. In part, this is because the construction of regulatory regimes crystallises particular circuits of power (Clegg 1989) that operate through resource distributions, discursive rules and disciplinary dispositions. It is also because these regulatory regimes are contradictory in their effects. They do not predictably and smoothly realise results but consistently fail in their effects. Subjects exercise agency – both individually and collectively – to seek outcomes to satisfy collective and individual goals that may deviate from regulatory norms. These effects are clearly evident in workplaces where industrial relations and technological interventions have complex consequences but they are also evident in learning – whether in the negotiation of mentor–mentored relations or in wider debates about the purposes of education. For both work and learning are characterised by difference, contradiction and open-ended formation. Work and learning entities–identities are contingent and contested, fuelled as much by narratives of future possibilities as by contemporary constraints.

## References

*The Age*, 14 June 2006, 'Spotlight exposed issue for leader'. Available at: http://www.theage.com.au/news/national/spotlight-exposed-issue-for-leader/2006/06/13/1149964534778.html (accessed 25 May 2009).

Arunachalam, S. (1999) 'Information and knowledge in the age of electronic communication: A developing country perspective', *Journal of Information Science*, 25(6): 465–479.

Australian Council of Trade Unions (2006) *Govt's Own Research Shows AWAs Remove Conditions and Cut Take-Home Pay*, ACTU Media Release, 13 June 2006. Available at: http://www.actu.asn.au/work_rights/news/1150249060_9865.html (accessed 25 May 2009).

Axford, B. and Seddon, T. (2006) 'Education, training and the citizen-consumer: Lifelong learning in a market economy', *Australian Journal of Education*, 50(2): 167–184.

Blackmore, J. and Sachs, J. (2001) 'Women leaders in the restructured university', in A. Brooks and A. Mackinnon (eds) *Gender and the Restructured University*, Buckingham: Society for Research into Higher Education and Open University Press, 45–66.

Brown, J. S. and Duguid, P. (2002) 'Local knowledge: Innovation in the networked age', *Management Learning*, 33(4): 427–437.

Castles, F. (1988) *Australian Public Policy and Economic Vulnerability*, Sydney: Allen and Unwin.

Chappell, C., Rhodes, C., Solomon, N., Tennant, M. and Yates, L. (2003) *Reconstructing the Lifelong Learner: Pedagogy and Identity in Individual, Organisational and Social Change*, London: Routledge Falmer.

Clegg, S. (1989) *Frameworks of Power*, Cambridge: Polity.

Deetz, S. (1998) 'Discursive formations, strategized subordination and self-surveillance', in A. McKinlay and K. Starkey (eds) *Foucault, Management and Organization Theory: From Panoptican to Technologies of Self*, London: Sage, 151–172.

Devos, A. (2004) 'The project of others, the project of self: Mentoring, women and the fashioning of the academic subject', *Studies in Continuing Education*, 26: 67–80.

du Gay, P. (1996) *Consumption and Identity at Work*, London: Sage.

Dussledorp Skills Forum (1998) *Australia's Youth: Risk and Reality*, Sydney: Dussledorp Skills Forum.

Dussledorp Skills Forum (1999) *Australia's Young Adults: The Deepening Divide*, Sydney: Dussledorp Skills Forum.

Farrell, L. (2006) *Making Knowledge Common: Literacy and Knowledge at Work*, New York: Peter Lang and Co.

Farrell, L. and Holkner, B. (2004) 'Points of vulnerability and presence: Knowing and learning in globally networked communities', *Discourse*, 25: 133–144.

Ferguson, K. and Seddon, T. (2006) 'Decentred education: Suggestions for framing a socio-spatial research agenda', *Critical Studies in Education*, 48(1): 111–129.

Foucault, M. (1983) 'The subject and power', in H. L. Dreyfus and P. Rabinow (eds) *Michel Foucault: Beyond Structuralism and Hermeneutics*, Chicago: University of Chicago Press, 208–226.

Foucault, M. (1988) 'Technologies of the self', in L. Martin, H. Gutman and P. H. Hutton (eds) *Technologies of the Self: A Seminar with Michel Foucault*, Amherst: University of Massachusetts Press, 16–49.

Freeland, J. (1986) *The Political Economy of Schooling*, Geelong: Deakin University.

Jackson, N. (2004) 'Introduction', in M. E. Belifore, T. A. Defoe, S. Folinsbee, J. Hunter and N. Jackson, *Reading Work Literacies in the New Workplaces*, Mahwah, New Jersey: Lawrence Erlbaum Associates, 1–15.

Massey, D. (2005) *For Space*, London: Sage.

Mills, C. W. (1971) *The Sociological Imagination*, Harmondsworth: Penguin.

Ong, A. (2006) 'Mutations in citizenship', *Theory, Culture and Society*, 23: 499–531.

Pixley, J. (1993) *Citizenship and Employment: Investigating Post-Industrial Options*, Melbourne: Cambridge University Press.

Plowman, D. (1992) *Australian Industrial Relations*, Sydney: University of NSW Press.

Roe, J. (1998) 'The Australian Way', in P. Smyth and B. Cass (eds) *Contesting the Australian Way: States, markets and Civil Society*, Melbourne: Cambridge University Press, 69–80.

Rose, N. (1989, 2nd edn 1999) *Governing the Soul: The Shaping of the Private Self*, London: Free Association Books.

Scheeres, H. and Solomon, N. (2006) 'The moving subject: women's work/or working (on) women', paper presented at the 36th Annual Standing Conference on University Teaching and Research in the Education of Adults (SCUTREA) Conference, Trinity and All Saints College, Leeds, UK, July 2006.

Seddon, T. (1993) *Context and Beyond: Reframing the Theory and Practice of Education*, London: Falmer.

Sholtz, S. and Prinsloo, M. (2001) 'New workplaces, new literacies, new identities', *Journal of Adolescent and Adult Literacy*, 44(8): 710–713.

Smyth, P. and Cass, B. (1998) *Contesting the Australian Way: States, Markets and Civil Society*, Cambridge: Cambridge University Press.

Townley, B. (1994) *Reframing Human Resource Management: Power, Ethics and the Subject at Work*, London: Sage.

Usher, R. and Solomon, N. (1999) 'Experiential learning and the shaping of subjectivity in the workplace', *Studies in the Education of Adults*, 31: 155–164.

Watson, I., Buchanan, J., Campbell, I. and Briggs, C. (2003) *Fragmented Futures: New Challenges in Working Life*, Sydney: The Federation Press.

Zuboff, S. (1988) *In the Age of the Smart Machine*, New York: Basic Books.

# Part 11

# The politics of expertise

Chapter 5

# Reconstructing US community college faculty

## Mobilising professional expertise

*Richard L. Wagoner, John S. Levin and*
*Susan Kater*

## Introduction

In this chapter we address the current and potential future conditions of community college faculty in the United States as we describe its work and propose a transforming identity. The chapter has three primary purposes. First, to give a sense of how community colleges have changed during the past 25–30 years, we offer a brief discussion of our concept of 'new world colleges'. Next, we investigate how work has been disturbed and is disturbing for community colleges as the shift to 'new world colleges' has taken place. Finally, we move to the heart of the chapter: an exploration of a transforming politics, offering possible alternatives that might allow community college faculty the means to respond proactively to the changes brought by the New Economy.

## The community college sector

There are close to 1,200 community colleges in the United States. They serve a total of 11.6 million students (6.6 million in credit-bearing courses and 5 million non-credit courses), representing nearly half of all initial post-secondary students and half of all undergraduates. Of the 1,200 community colleges, approximately 1,000 are public and, while over 40 per cent of all community college students are under 21, the average age of all community college students is 29 years, indicating that community colleges represent the sector of higher education institutions in the United States that offer access to older, returning students who may or may not be adequately prepared for post-secondary education (National Center for Educational Statistics (NCES) 2006; Phillippe and Gonzalez Sullivan 2005).

Community colleges have been a part of the American higher education system for a little more than 100 years. Originally they were conceived of as a means to offer the first two years of a baccalaureate degree. Later, community colleges also became associated with terminal, vocational training. In both cases community colleges hold a low-status position in the hierarchy of American higher education institutions. Regardless of its status, the institution has been variously defined from the 1950s to the 1980s as 'democracy's college', 'a second chance institution' and an 'open door college'. This reflects their connection to the political economy, their association with personal development and social mobility, and of being an 'entrepreneurial' institution, a multipurpose institution, a multicultural institution and a globalized institution (Levin 2001a).

Community college faculty represent a major labour force in the United States and constitute almost one-third of all post-secondary education faculty (NCES 2006). As a labour force of 354,500 (33 per cent full time and 67 per cent part time; 52.2 per cent female; 16.2 per cent non-white), community college faculty epitomize professional work in the New Economy (Carnoy 2000) and the post-bureaucratic organization. They are not only influenced but also structured in their work by new technologies; they, or the majority, bargain collectively for a restricted compensation package; they are predominantly temporary or part time; and arguably they are agents of a corporate ideology rather than autonomous professionals. As workers, they struggle to find stability and professional identity in a world that increasingly supports flexible capitalistic principles and processes (Sennett 2006).

## From community colleges to 'new world colleges'

In what follows, we draw on data, both quantitative and qualitative, collected and analysed in our previous studies on community colleges and their faculty (Levin 2001a, 2007; Levin et al. 2006; Wagoner et al. 2005). We refer readers to these studies for detailed descriptions of the data and methods we have previously employed. In essence, we collected more than 200 qualitative interviews with faculty and administrators at eight community colleges in six legal jurisdictions between 1996 and 2004. Faculty interviewed included full-timers and part-timers in a large number of programme areas and disciplines, including academic, occupational and vocational fields and librarians and counsellors as well as faculty who occupy quasi-administrative roles such as department chairs, programme heads or union executives.

In this chapter we reinterpret these data in the light of the more recent work of Sennett (2006). Briefly, he posits that the traditional iron cage of bureaucracy has been dismantled by the new capitalism and it has created three 'social deficits' within organizations: low institutional loyalty; diminishment of informal trust – knowing who you can depend upon in a crisis or under pressure – among employees; and weakening of institutional knowledge – knowing how work is accomplished in the organization within the rules as well as how to move outside the rules when a situation warrants it, closely tied to informal trust and loyalty (Sennett 2006). Additionally, two consequences arise from these social deficits for the 'moral prestige' of work: the elimination or at least serious diminution of delayed gratification and long-term strategic thinking and planning.

The scholarly literature from the 1970s to the present understands the community college as a comprehensive educational institution conceptualized as curricula, programmes and instruction and viewed as bounded by traditional notions of education and training, encapsulated in a closed and rational system. There is an absence of external connections, such as the political economy, in this system. For some, the community college was and is a junior college – a pathway to university education. For others, the community college was and is a vocational preparation institution. For still others it was and is a combination of curricular tracks – academic, vocational, remedial and developmental (Brint and Karabel 1989; Cohen and Brawer 2003; Cross 1985; Dougherty 1994; Grubb 1999).

In the face of post-industrialism and globalization, these conceptions are out-moded (Levin 2001a). During the 1980s and 1990s the institution and government policy makers became attached to a political economy resembling neoliberal ideological tenets. The institution developed along the lines of 'fast capitalism' (Gee *et al.* 1996) within a context of 'new managerialism' (Deem 1998). Community colleges adopted practices that were intended to transform the institution into a market-savvy and responsive organization, directed by a corporate executive body that inculcated the institution's missions and goals to employees. Practices that included contract training, business and industry part-nerships, distributed learning opportunities, flexible scheduling and programming, one-stop student services and the like under a business plan guided by managers and accountable to public officials characterized actual behaviours of community colleges (Alfred and Carter 1999; Levin 2002).

Concepts of instruction also altered so that 'learning' not 'teaching' became emphasized (Tagg 2003), elevating consumers (students) and demoting deliver-ers of instruction (faculty). Colleges' articulated purposes altered as well. Mission statements began to reflect a corporate identity consistent with neoliberalism and economic markets (Ayers 2005). Organizational behaviours focusing upon stu-dents altered in this direction as well (Levin 2005; Slaughter and Rhoades 2004). As Ayers (2005: 545) points out, such purposes and practices:

> (a) subordinate . . . workers/learners to employers, thereby constituting identities of servitude, and (b) displace . . . the community and faculty in planning educational programs, placing instead representatives of business and industry as the chief designers of curricula.

In this sense, the community colleges are now better termed 'new world colleges' – a combination of an institution closely associated with the New Economy and the 'brave new world' implied by that concept. New world colleges suggest on the one hand a promising image of progress and transcendence (see Shakespeare's *The Tempest*). On the other hand, it suggests a trend toward dehumanization through human engineering (see Huxley's *Brave New World* and Mintzberg 1994). At the beginning of the twenty-first century community colleges have not only multiple and possibly conflicting missions but also new alliances and a new identity. The alliances are with economic entities such as business and industry and political affil-iations with neoliberal proponents such as those elements of government and business that foster economic development and competition. Yet, they continue to carry the comprehensive curriculum, albeit an expanding one, into the twenty-first century. Thus, the context of work for community college faculty is multi-faceted, dynamic and closely connected to the political economy.

## Disturbed and disturbing work

Our research identifies four areas of community college faculty work as disturbed – technology usage, governance, part-time faculty and faculty values.

### Instructional technology

In addition to increasing the general return to education, the fast pace of technological change rapidly altered the skills required to compete in the workforce (Castells 2000). Consequently, more students enrolled to take courses periodically for specific training, behaviours especially important for community colleges as they are the institutions that provided these services. Together, these trends point to the pressures from the New Economy that obligated community colleges to educate more students in different ways, without proportionate increases in resources from the government.

The use of information technology in both instruction and in administration spread rapidly in public community colleges and this growth reflected pressures from the greater economy. Three conditions influenced the selection and implementation of information technology within community colleges: government policies, constituent demands and socio-economic demands (Roe 2002). The first condition involved an increase in government policies that provided incentives for community colleges to generate revenue, become more efficient and meet the needs of business and industry for skilled labour. With respect to the provision of a skilled workforce, community colleges were under pressure to produce employable graduates, especially in the numerous jobs that required mid-level management or technical skills (Autor et al. 1998; Levin 2002).

The second condition advancing the use of information technology included the demands by students and potential students who wanted training in specific areas and flexibility in time, location and pedagogical methods. These demands were both for greater use of technology within the classroom and increased course offerings through distance education. In addition, demographic trends in many states (especially those in the south east and south west) resulted in a significant increase in the number of high-school graduates (Hebel 2004). Given the limited availability of space at four-year institutions, considerable pressure was placed on community colleges to enrol and accommodate these additional students.

The final condition that influenced the use of technology was the expanding demands of the socio-economic environment. Of special interest was the movement within community colleges to a more managerial or business-like culture, and the focus of community colleges on the needs of business and industry rather than those of the local community (Levin 2001b). Within that context, the promise of a new instructional approach that would increase efficiency and improve workforce development was attractive. Instructionally, the integration of technology into community college curriculum had mixed effects:

> The way I run the class is I bring in a disc with highlights from the textbook plus transparencies that I brought over as jpegs from PowerPoint. I show them that just by rolling a long Word document up on a big screen behind me, and use that to talk from. That allows them to look at pictures, and gives them all the features – verbal, tactile, visual – which I think is important. Some of them sleep through class; others write like hell. I try to exploit all the ways I can to talk to them. I show them ten-minute videos for every chapter. The textbook is there in the order of things.
>
> (Part-time business faculty member,
> California community college)

Yet, less uncertain is the structuring of work and the increase in workload brought about by technology use. A full-time science faculty member at the same California college amplified not only the workload but also the impingement of work on personal, daily life:

> I have a home office. A lot of students email me at home and I respond to them from home. I tell them if they send me an email, I'll respond quickly. So, I'm available through the weekend. I check my email regularly through the weekend. I'm sort of working 40 hours, and then I'm consistently on-call since I make myself available via email.

Because the use of technology was tied to productivity and to a competitive, fast capitalistic environment directed by a managerial imperative for growth and efficiency, there was little opportunity for faculty to dissent or to reconstruct practices around a professional identity. The common bond among faculty became workload and speed of information processing. This was not a culture that was consistent with professional characteristics of ethical norms and autonomy (Brint 1994).

### Governance

Sennett (2006) suggests that educational organizations are becoming 'structurally pliable' as rigid bureaucratic structures across welfare organizations (including health care) adapt to current social and political conditions. This is particularly significant for community college governance where the very foundation of the historically rigid bureaucratic model is descriptive of the typical community college organizational structure. Beyond working inside the classroom, at many institutions faculty also participate with management in institutional governance (Kater and Levin 2005). Although governance is viewed as a mechanism for higher education's constituents to engage in institutional decision-making, this participation, and particularly that of faculty, may be furthering the interests of management in increasing the productivity of the institution's workforce (Hines 2000; Kater and Levin 2005).

Traditionally faculty have accepted the condition of higher productivity with the reward of higher salaries: 'The faculty . . . has been willing to trade that high level of productivity for better salaries' (part-time faculty member at a community college in California). But the promise of salary and benefit increases is waning under new economic imperatives. In our study, faculty, at least through their collective bargaining agreements, accepted an increasing role in managing the institution 'in lieu' of resource rewards. That is, faculty were asked to take on managerial roles through participation in governance over and above their normal teaching loads (Kater and Levin 2005).

While faculty unions assumed they were extending the rights of faculty they may have, inadvertently, agreed simply to participate in a neoliberal regime. Thus, the concept of shared governance in the community colleges may not have constituted advancement in joint decision-making so much as increased faculty work and responsibility for the management of the institution. As noted by a California community college dean, faculty participation is variable and often not linked to critical institutional decisions:

> I have a division council of 23 of my faculty and classified employees who advise me on the running of the division. We have periodic meetings in order to get their input . . . On some committees we have a [faculty union] rep and we have a [faculty] senate rep, particularly on some of the senior-level committees . . . Now, sometimes the deans aren't consulted! Because the VPs [vice presidents] are all making decisions on their own and the doors are closed.

Indeed, the expansion of work responsibilities and the enlargement of curricula affected faculty work and thus 'participation' in governance. As noted by a part-time instructor of philosophy at a California community college, their participation in governance had little authentic impact:

> Nobody has the time to make it work. Basically you have 35 per cent of the faculty being full time, and 65 per cent being part time. That 35 per cent can barely keep the curriculum up-to-date, much less do a serious job of participating in shared governance at that level. What ends up happening is that the biggest crisis at the moment gets dealt with, and everything else goes on to emerge as a crisis the next week, the next month, or next year.

The effects of expanded work responsibilities for faculty were considerable, as part-time faculty were asked for more than their employment contract specified and full-time faculty not only participated in governance but managed the curriculum in light of a growing part-time labour force.

## Part-time faculty

Although a lower stratum of professional labour, part-timers also became crucial to the strategic plans of New Economy organizations. The use of part-time employees in recurrent tasks that had traditionally been fulfilled by permanent employees was promoted as a management principle. Smith (2001) sees this stance as a 'paradigmatic shift' in the way that managers view the employment of part-time employees. This paradigm shift was evident in the increased, and increasingly institutionalized, use of part-time faculty in community colleges. Senior administrators at community colleges were willing to accept the continuing exploitation of part-time faculty – although they may not even have viewed their institution's behaviours as exploitation – if it allowed them to achieve those goals they deemed essential for their colleges (Wagoner *et al.* 2005). This exploitative use of part-timers enabled colleges to increase efficiency and productivity while simultaneously increasing the authority and control of managers.

This drive toward efficiency and control exhibited by managers affected the individual perceptions of part-time faculty. Abel (1984) and Barker (1998) have documented an important shift in the locus of control and motivation for part-time faculty. Abel argues that, until the early 1980s, motivation and control for part-time faculty was mostly intrinsic and based upon a belief in meritocracy. Barker noted that motives became considerably more extrinsic by the mid-1990s. She found that part-timers were acutely aware of the new business efficiency model and its exploitation of part-time faculty. As a result, part-timers no longer blamed themselves for lacking a full-time position, but instead indentified the unjust system as responsible, a strong indication that the nature of part-time work in community colleges changed and with it the perceptions and responses of part-timers as well. Barker (1998: 199) recognizes the unequal outcomes of a competitive system, where individual economic gain is at stake:

> The contradiction of workplace transformation in higher education is that it institutionalises privilege for one set of citizens (tenured and tenure track faculty) at a cost to others. The failure of inclusion within academe, or the success of exclusive membership, is revealed when a system of layered citizenship is constructed, made coherent, and legitimated.

Deem (1998) points out that 'new managerialism' and the New Economy business practices it fosters have led to a contradictory labour market where temporary employees exist side by side with permanent employees. Both groups serve similar functions (Smith 2001) but part-time employees are forced to negotiate this potentially exploitative market on their own; those with rare skills and abilities may be valued commodities in numerous markets, while those with common skills find themselves on the wrong side of a labour market chasm (Carnoy 2000; Castells 2000; Smith 2001). Our research on community colleges has confirmed this trend.

Community college administrators indicated that they could not afford to run programmes without the cost savings of part-time faculty. For many of these administrators their stated obligation was to their local community. One college dean from Arizona indicated: 'The mission is to serve the community . . . We couldn't be at every place for the whole community without adjunct faculty.' Several administrators went further than merely stating that part-timers allowed them to serve their communities. They indicated that colleges had no obligations to their part-time faculty. As the Arizona dean noted: 'We can expand with adjuncts, or we can reduce what we are doing with adjuncts; and we don't hurt the programmes; we don't hurt the full-time faculty.' This dean also highlighted that full-time positions were both privileged and protected by the tenuous status of part-timers. For this administrator, part-time positions had become important only for the flexibility they offer institutions, not as a means for part-time faculty to earn a living wage or receive reasonable employment benefits, and certainly not for their professional expertise.

Arguably, the economic savings made possible by part-time faculty had negative effects on instruction at community colleges. Data from the National Study of Postsecondary Faculty of 1993 and 1999 (National Center for Educational Statistics 2002) on the availability of professional development opportunities illuminate the lack of resources dedicated to part-time faculty in community colleges (Wagoner 2004). In both years, professional development opportunities were available to full-time faculty at a rate at least twice that of part-time faculty. The data also indicate that, on average, support increased for full-timers and decreased for part-timers from 1993 to 1999. This disparity is particularly important because community colleges are acclaimed as teaching institutions where quality of instruction is viewed as sacrosanct (Cohen and Brawer 2003). Part-time faculty are not all part time by choice. Indeed, the majority seek full-time employment. As a part-time business instructor from California explains:

> I want to do this, do it right, and get a reputation for doing a good job of teaching, and hopefully have the chance to move into a full-time position . . . [I]n fact there is an opening now in the Business Department, and I am applying for a full-time position as a general business instructor . . . Any time there is a faculty meeting that part-timers are invited to or a training session that I have knowledge of, I go to those. I also volunteer to write two course descriptions. I set up and started a course in International Business Management. In fact, that is one of the reasons why I came over here. I interviewed with the business department chair and one of the things he wanted to have happen was to have someone come in and start an International Business Management programme here. I came in on that basis, and part of my commitment was to volunteer my time to develop the course, write the course description and take it before the committee, the Articulation Committee.

Part-timers are willing to volunteer for additional projects that benefit the institution, but will not necessarily advance to or be guaranteed a full-time position (Smith 2001). Colleges have been able to increase efficiency – create an increased workload without increased compensation. This is in many ways part of an illegible power regime (Sennett 1998). Part-time faculty are not necessarily forced into this additional work, but do it with the notion that it will increase their standing in the college without tangible proof that it actually will. Such behaviours by the institution typify the divide between economic and education values. The tensions are evident in the work of faculty and in the ways in which community colleges are managed and governed.

### Faculty values

The press for greater productivity and efficiency by governments and business and industry, coupled with a managerial model of institutional decision-making, has called into question the professional identity of faculty and skewed their work as educators. Faculty's work as educators – teachers, developers of curriculum, counsellors, mentors, advisers of students and members on committees – is configured or framed within an economic and competitive context, even though their values may be based upon other principles and other goals, such as personal and cognitive development of students or the social advancement of society.

Our research indicates that faculty are to some extent stuck. We frame this tension as a conflict between education and training, between traditional institutional goals, such as student-centred, and economic interests, such as business and industry-centred, and as a tension between centralized, hierarchical decision-making and decentralized, democratic or shared decision-making. Furthermore, faculty, with the exception of the faculty unions, could be considered to be situated at the periphery of both institutional decision-making and institutional influence on matters of institutional action related to purpose, even though faculty work – curriculum and teaching – is the core of institutional action. Faculty reported that they were expected to generate revenues as well as assist in enrolling more students. As noted by faculty in a Washington State college:

> We are expected to solicit associations and increase enrolment in our programmes . . . Faculty are getting involved in fund raising. They feel that if a programme will continue to exist they need to get out in the community and raise money or solicit donations of equipment.

In the face of questionable administrative practices, faculty were held hostage in their efforts to stabilize organizational functioning and provide their expertise. As a faculty union president of a California college asserted:

> There is an incompetent administration [at the] district office. They have a lack of experience with collective bargaining . . . New ways have undone

shared governance: [it is] now superficial . . . The quality of teaching is [being lost]. Teaching gets lip service from administrators. Money is going to technology, not to faculty support. The computer is seen as a tutor . . . [The district is looking for] a magic pill: more technology, more distance education. It is training versus classical education. The pressures from business will define the goals. Money drives . . . They are showing how faculty are no longer necessary.

What is lost in such an environment of productivity and competition is what some view as the integrity of higher education. Thus, meaningful work becomes problematical. Faculty expertise is neglected and the usefulness of their service is demeaned. One example is the emphasis in community colleges on students as products for the economic marketplace. One part-time faculty member of a California college noted:

> The community college is the goal, the ideal, the image of a democratized higher education that would provide the humanized possibility for citizens in a highly technical, democratic society, but that is being co-opted by job training. Even if it's in the area of Humanities and Social Sciences, it's still being forced to be preparatory work to some line of career development or direction. The focus disappears from the educational experience.

## A transforming politics

So far, we have chronicled four areas of faculty experience that have transformed the US community colleges into 'new world colleges'. These changes are connected to the social deficits related to the culture of new capitalism (Sennett 1998, 2006). Because these changes, and the deficits they embody, serve to isolate individuals and diminish their ties to colleges and their missions, we argue that faculty need to explore, both deliberately and actively, alternative practices that will help unite them and tie them directly to their colleges, creating a group identity grounded in community – a community that possesses the ability to change the culture of new capitalism and its effects on the character of workers.

The potential power of this collective identity is what leads Sennett (1998) to categorize 'we' as the dangerous pronoun. It expresses a sense of community and, while it is often used to exclude outsiders of all types (for example, part-timers from full-timers, community college faculty from university faculty), it is emblematic of connections that can move beyond the control of a New Economy organization. When one group is dependent on another the result may be unrest as the dependent group comes to feel shame or a sense of uselessness about their lack of independence. This can erode both trust and commitment – values that create bonds for collective enterprises (Sennett 2006).

The concept of dependence relates to faculty. As described earlier, full-timers are certainly dependent on part-timers for their privileged positions, and the potential shame they may feel about that exploitation can make matters worse, not better. Therefore, a new professional identity must include all faculty members no matter what their status or discipline. This community of educators, however, will neither be devoid of conflict nor shallow in its sense of agreement. In this, we reject McGrath and Spear's description of community college faculty as agreeable, forming a 'practitioner's culture' as a condition to be emulated (McGrath and Spear 1991). For an authentic community to survive and develop, there should be substantive disagreements, contention that forces productive communication. As the group seeks consensus, or perhaps agrees to disagree – particularly as the various goals of community colleges may rule out 'one size fits all' faculty policies – the solidarity will be strengthened through debate. This deep community can move beyond the control of contemporary administration, unlike the facile community frequently seen in cooperative teams where conflict is suppressed (Sennett 1998: 143).

Central to the overall proposition of creating a functioning collective are the questions 'Who needs me?' and 'Who relies on me?' Sennett (2006) argues that the modern condition negates any notion of being needed in three distinct ways:

- the outcomes of one's efforts where there is no connection between risk and reward;
- the absence of trust in organizations – this, in turn, creates a situation in which there is no reason to be needed; and
- through the constant recreation of organizations where people (workers) are treated as disposable – if you are disposable you are not needed.

These 'disposable employees' in Sennett's words – those who are left behind in the flexible regime – cause fear or at least discomfort (dis-ease) in the new power elite, because of the potential they represent for organized resistance to the new order.

Change may occur because of a sensed need among the disposable workers to be valued and respected, and because 'a regime which provides human beings no deep reason to care about one another cannot long preserve its legitimacy' (Sennett 1998: 148). We posit that this is particularly the case for faculty at community colleges. To wait upon such a development, however, is not our goal. Administrators, faculty and state policy officials must construct a new workforce within 'new world colleges' which values all faculty, one where faculty believe they are working together toward shared goals that are in the best interest of society – a transforming politics.

### Creating new narratives

Given the institutional transformation manifested in 'new world colleges' and how this has disturbed the work of college faculty, how might the situation be re-imagined and reconfigured? We argue that this can be done through the creation of new work-life narratives: creating new professional associations or 'parallel institutions'; a re-imaging of job sharing; and a re-interpretation of the concepts of usefulness and craftsmanship.

### Parallel institutions and job sharing

The need for narrative arises because the fragmented, adapting organization does not allow individuals the opportunity to create a work-life narrative. Sennett suggests two possible sources for improved narrative that could have value for community college faculty. First he suggests 'parallel institutions' – a type of guild or union that offers stability and a professional home to temporary, contingent and/or part-time workers. These parallel institutions have also been described as next generation unions (Osterman *et al.* 2001). As is frequently the case with discussions such as this, there is a risk of creating a notion of the good old days in terms of stable, full-time positions of the past. Sennett reminds us that there can be problems with that as well – what he describes as the 'deadening politics of seniority and time entitlements' of unions (Sennett 1998: 117). Therefore, community college faculty cannot be mired in the past, particularly the use of part-timers propping up full-timers and protecting privileged positions that do have a reliance on seniority and time entitlements, whether in a unionized or non-unionized setting.

While they face multiple challenges, including overcoming a stigma of inefficiency and corruption attached to traditional labour unions in the United States, the new unions are conceptualized as offering 'political voice, direct participation, collective bargaining, strategic partnerships, mobility and occupational community' (Osterman *et al.* 2001: 98). These functions do not necessarily need to be performed by one organization. Multiple organizations, each focusing on a particular need, could work in cooperation to offer a complete service to workers. That is, the boundaries of such organizations could be both permeable and fuzzy, allowing for overlap of function while ensuring coverage for all members. In this sense, next generation unions are parallel organizations, aligned and working together.

While perhaps of most direct benefit to part-time and contingent employees, parallel organizations are best viewed as a home for life where the place and status of employment do not change membership in the organization. The next generation union could function as an extended network that represents and serves workers' interests 'inside firms, in local areas and labour markets, in professional communities and in political affairs' (Osterman *et al.* 2001: 98). Ideally, this type of extended network would be suited to a faculty career as individuals could remain a member even as their employment status changes – part time to full time, one institution to several. This type of model offers an essential factor: to be successful, unions need to not only meet the needs of workers but also fit the demands of an economy's structure (Osterman *et al.* 2001: 98).

For faculty, the parallel institution may also come via informal networks of colleagues – within or external to their disciplines – with whom they interact professionally on an ongoing basis. As we and others have suggested, the new organizational form for 'new world colleges' will be less bureaucratic, more fluid and will create opportunities for informal networks of professionals across functional lines within the organization. Faculty may work more regularly with student service professionals in improving student retention. No longer the solitary purview of faculty, retention issues for the new demographics of students will require diverse forms of programmes and services to match student characteristics. Faculty will begin to create narrative agencies from the specific knowledge and expertise they bring to the process of student learning and student engagement, but it will no longer be their exclusive organization.

The second method Sennett (2006) suggests to nurture narrative is job sharing. For community college faculty at 'new world colleges', the concept of job sharing is introduced through the functioning of learning communities, particularly those created through inter-related courses simultaneously taken by the same group of students. While not a pure form of job sharing, as both faculty members are expected to co-create and co-teach the classes, the concept does integrate some forms of job sharing including increased collaboration between professionals, a theoretically reduced workload as some areas of learning community classes overlap and allow for instructional sharing of responsibilities. Learning communities have proved supportive of student learning and attainment, and while they are expensive to administer and require more planning, they have the tripartite benefit of providing a parallel institution for faculty, of improving opportunities for student attainment and for creating new networks and alternative agencies for faculty. These connect with the need for a new concept of usefulness.

## The concept of usefulness

Usefulness, the antithesis of uselessness, equates to status – the recognition that, in the case of college faculty, the work they do is both valuable and legitimate. Historically, uselessness has always been a problem for workers, particularly during industrialization. Its definition has changed with new capitalism. In the rhetoric of cutting-edge organizations the ideal worker or individual is one who can work as a part of a team, change positions often and move quickly to think critically and solve new and ever-changing problems. There is, however, no notion of the quality of the solution, nor the specific expertise which it might take to solve the problem sufficiently. This new ideal (useful) worker stands in contrast to an older model: the craftsperson, one who approaches a problem or process in-depth, makes mistakes, learns from them and grows to create quality products. Sennett emphasizes that these products do not have to be material – a superior watch, for example – but can also be intellectual or interpersonal. In taking the time to focus on one process or problem and create a craftsperson's excellence, one is marked as not flexible (able to work with constantly changing team-mates while moving from one problem to the next) and one is deemed use-less. In this context, the proven ability and expertise of craftsmanship is to be avoided at all costs and one merely needs to display the potential for quality to be useful in a new capitalist organization. Usefulness, once measured by depth, is now measured by superficiality. Clearly, a concept of usefulness that values only flexibility is one that needs to be challenged.

Beyond their work as discipline-specific experts, and adapting their roles for work at 'new world colleges', faculty have the opportunity both to create inter-pretive agencies and to influence the direction – mission and goals – of the institution. This requires reframing their role into one that expands beyond the classroom. Giving time to managerial activities needs to become viewed not as an ancillary, compensated activity, but rather part of the value of faculty in 'new world colleges'. Contingent labour is less expensive and readily available and full-time faculty can recognize and counteract the potential tidal wave of reform and replacement as the current corps of faculty retire and are replaced by part-time contingent labour. If faculty are to limit themselves to classroom teaching only, they miss the opportunity to provide expertise and direction to college plans, which decreases their usefulness to the institution.

A key area where faculty currently have the ability to take a leading role and enhance their usefulness is in student assessment. An accountability measure dri-ven by regional accrediting agencies, supported by state accountability measures (in some states) and tied to funding in others, the assessment of student learning is an institutional outcome that influences institutional planning and direction at the highest levels, but has been crafted as the distinct purview of faculty. They have the responsibility for the design, measurement and evaluation of learning outcomes: 'Faculty must be convinced that they control the assessment process, and, ultimately, that they are held accountable for student learning and develop-ment' (Anderson 2004: 23).

The movement has increased communication between disciplines, has increased the work of faculty, but has been a rare opportunity for externally directed – demanded – accountability, as prescribed by faculty with the support of administration. We are suggesting that faculty seize the opportunity to reframe assessment and evaluation as an opportunity to take centre stage in institutional planning, affecting the direction of their institutions – relatively unfettered by management – instead of viewing the movement as adding to their already over-whelming workload. Our research makes clear that student progress and positive outcomes are highly valued by faculty:

> [T]he bottom line of everything we do here is student outcomes. Sometimes we get focused on 'the budget' or 'the hire' or 'the computer' and we may or may not consider why we are buying that computer or doing that hire.
>
> (Chair of faculty senate, California college)

And again:

> I've always believed in community colleges because I think the focus is on teaching. You're catching a lot of students and getting them in those first two years thinking right and disciplined, and then they move on to universities. I don't think there's a better programme going than the two plus two programme. I wouldn't want to be anywhere but a community college.
>
> (Science faculty, California college)

The accountability movement, operationalized for faculty via their responsibility for institutional assessment plans for student learning, enables faculty to have a direct influence on institutional mission and goals. As Lopez (2004: 34) argues: 'Faculty need to recognize its [assessment's] potential value . . . accept ownership and responsibility for the assessment program, and participate fully in all of its components.' We agree and encourage faculty to seize the opportunity.

## The concept of craftsmanship

Craftsmanship exists at the centre of the professional identity that we advocate. A craftsperson desires to perform and make a product well for its own sake, not for some extrinsic reward. As discussed earlier, this entails a notion of deep knowledge and/or skill, not a superficial one. This deep knowledge and skill constitute expertise, and faculty expertise is or can be measured by scholarship. Three of the four forms of scholarship suggested by Boyer (1990) are directly relevant to community college faculty and can be used to establish their authority and expertise.

The first of these three is the scholarship of integration (of knowledge), which is a multidisciplinary approach that seeks to place 'isolated facts into perspective'. While integration can be an outgrowth of one's own original research (Boyer's scholarship of discovery, generally not associated with community college faculty), integration can also be an interpretation of others' work, placing that work into larger intellectual patterns. The scholarship of integration is intellectual scholarship that synthesizes, orders and expands through thought the meaning and importance of the research of others. All community college faculty can employ integration in the course development process when they create syllabi, reading lists, lectures and class notes for courses. Instructors in vocational and technical courses could also feature integration with an emphasis on the connections of those courses to society at large.

In reflecting the service aspect of faculty work, the scholarship of application insists that service must be tied directly to one's academic speciality. Application is the creation of useful connections of knowledge generation (research) and everyday life. For faculty from traditional academic disciplines this could be an outgrowth of integration; that is, finding relevant real world connections in the curriculum based on integration. This may entail a particular type of synthesis, one that integrates knowledge in service of a particular problem in society.

Furthermore, as we have seen in some of our research, some vocational faculty view their teaching at colleges as a form of service related to their full-time professional position outside the college – 'a feather in my cap' as one part-time computer science faculty member noted. In this sense the vocational faculty synthesize knowledge gained through occupational or professional experience and training into the improvement of courses and more relevant preparation for their students. This is a salient example of how the different programmes and missions of colleges can have separate expectations, policies and practices for faculty, not a one-size-fits-all approach, thus fostering faculty identity and autonomy.

The scholarship of teaching marks the obvious heart of community college faculty practice and identity. No matter their position or programme all faculty members can create a craftsman-like professional identity through the scholarship of teaching. As always there needs to be a clear distinction between the two broad areas of teaching: content knowledge and pedagogy, or androgyny for adult learners. That is, what you are going to teach and how you are going to engage the class with that content. Faculty must be willing to achieve these three interrelated forms of scholarship as a part of their positions. Parallel organizations can function in part to nurture scholarship among all community college faculty.

The essential virtue of craftsmanship is commitment because it ameliorates the three social deficits inherent in the culture of the new capitalism that corrodes character – low institutional loyalty, diminishment of informal trust and weakening of institutional knowledge (Sennett 2006). Sennett suggests that craftsmanship could be the means of a revolution that overturns the culture of new capitalism. Within 'new world colleges', at the heart of faculty work is the art and craft of teaching: knowing what to teach, how to teach it and how to serve and develop individuals. Teaching, as the ultimate form of craftsmanship, can be the basis of parallel organizations and can be tied directly to student outcomes and assessment, offering the means to incorporate the values Sennett (2006) champions to counter the destabilizing and corrosive effects of new capitalism. Both the state and society are expected to value and grant this craft status. At the same time, we argue that faculty should control, define and refine those skills, abilities and competencies, characteristics akin to a professional identity (Brint 1994).

## Conclusion

To sum up: our research indicates that community colleges are not only instruments of government policy regarding workforce development and, therefore, subject to the influence of neoliberalism, the new global economy and the often illegible regime of power (Sennett 1998) that these forces represent, but also adopters and adapters of the policies and practices of institutions valorized by the New Economy. These include not just a flexible workforce but economic competitiveness with other institutions. In line with these conditions and circumstances, we present a portrait of community college faculty and their work, which increasingly resembles that of workers in the New Economy. More importantly, we examine ways faculty might create 'cultural anchors' for support as they craft an interpretive agency for understanding work within an increasingly fragmented organization (Sennett 2006).

Inherent in the transformation of community colleges and the work their faculty perform is a vicious cycle marking a contradiction within neoliberal education reform in which educational institutions are squeezed in ways that disrupt the symbolic and social practices of work and learning. Our view of the destabilization of the community colleges is consistent with Sennett's argument that, through increasing fragmentation of bureaucratic structures and processes consistent with the new capitalism, many professionals are left conflicted (Sennett 2006). Our research found that, on the one hand, the managerial and market imperative disconnected faculty from their prior professional identification with specialist knowledge and skills, and re-anchored them in a corporate identification in which they had little choice but to take on company needs, for example, budget and innovation. On the other hand, resource constraints (for example reduced funding, narrow specification of curricula, increasing regulation and accountability), that underpinned the managerial preoccupation with productivity and efficiency within education, undercut the quality of teaching and learning and eroded the effectiveness of education and training. We argue that these changes have resulted in a situation in which the 'products for sale' today or their proxies – status, recognition and their exchange – do not fulfil the expectations of either the economy and industry or communities and societies.

As a result, there is a crisis of legitimacy centred on the potential inability of educational institutions to serve their staffing function in the economy and their civilizing function in society. This crisis is compounded by the simultaneous erosion of knowledge guardianship committed to meritocracy and the effectiveness of learning under the mantra of efficiency. The successful negotiation of this contradiction by faculty suggests a powerful practical politics within lifelong learning and work. This social and symbolic politics requires a re-mobilization around knowledge and meritocracy, as well as professional identity and occupation, on the grounds that effective learning, which produces knowers with the practical knowledge and skills necessary for routine and non-routine work in local-global settings, is both a public good and a rational economic investment.

To be transformative, college faculty may have to embrace aspects of the culture of the new capitalism as a means to manage it. For Sennett (2006), the 'ideal' person able to prosper in our fragmented societal conditions is one who can manage short-term relationships while changing jobs, roles and spaces continually; one who can develop new skills, continually; and who can let go of the past, or at least ignore its outdated norms. We suggest that the reflection of a craftsperson in a 'new world college' more closely resembles the part-time or adjunct faculty than the full-time faculty – the employee without tenure, who creates his or her own institutional history on a daily basis, who constructs meaning from high quality scholarship that strengthens and supports student learning and who communicates and shares that craftsmanship with other faculty. These are the ways faculty reconstruct their work in the New Economy.

## References

Abel, E. K. (1984) *Terminal Degrees: The Job Crisis in Higher Education*, New York: Praeger.

Alfred, R. and Carter, P. (1999) 'New colleges for a new century: Organizational change and development in community colleges', in J. C. Smart and W. G. Tierney (eds) *Higher Education: Handbook of Theory and Research*, New York: Agathon Press, 240–283.

Anderson, J. (2004) 'An institutional commitment to assessment and accountability', in P. Hernon and R. E. Dugan (eds) *Outcomes Assessment in Higher Education: Views and Perspectives*, Westport, CT: Libraries Unlimited, 17–28.

Autor, D. H., Katz, L. F. and Kreuger, A. B. (1998) 'Computing inequality: Have computers changed the labor market?', *Quarterly Journal of Economics*, 113(4): 1169–1213.

Ayers, D. F. (2005) 'Neoliberal ideology in community college mission statements: A critical discourse analysis', *The Review of Higher Education*, 28(4): 527–549.

Barker, K. (1998) 'Toiling for piece rates and accumulating deficits: Contingent work in higher education', in K. Barker and K. Christensen (eds) *Contingent Work: American Employment Relations in Transition*, Ithaca, NY: Cornell University Press, 195–220.

Boyer, E. L. (1990) *Scholarship Reconsidered: Priorities of the Professoriate*, Princeton, NJ: Carnegie Foundation for the Advancement of Teaching.

Brint, S. (1994) *In an Age of Experts: The Changing Role of Professionals in Politics and Public Life*, Princeton: Princeton University Press.

Brint, S. and Karabel, J. (1989) *The Diverted Dream: Community Colleges and the Promise of Educational Opportunity in America, 1900–1985*, New York: Oxford University Press.

Carnoy, M. (2000) *Sustaining the New Economy: Work, Family, and Community in the Information Age*, New York: Russell Sage Foundation.

Castells, M. (2000, 2nd edn) *The Rise of the Network Society*, Malden, MA: Blackwell.

Cohen, A. and Brawer, F. (2003) *The American Community College*, San Francisco: Jossey-Bass.

Cross, K. P. (1985) 'Determining missions and priorities for the fifth generation', in W. Deegan, D. Tillery and Associates (eds) *Renewing the American Community College*, San Francisco: Jossey-Bass, 34–50.

Deem, R. (1998) 'New managerialism and higher education: The management of performances and cultures in universities in the United Kingdom' *International Studies in Sociology of Education*, 8(1): 47–70.

Dougherty, K. (1994) *The Contradictory College*, Albany: State University of New York Press.

Gee, J. P., Hull, G. and Lankshear, C. (1996) *The New Work Order: Behind the Language of the New Capitalism*, Boulder, CO: Westview Press.

Grubb, W. N. (1999) *Honored but Invisible: An Inside Look at Teaching in Community Colleges*, New York: Routledge.

Hebel, S. (2004, 2 July) 'No room in the class: As student populations explode in some states, public colleges struggle to find enough places – even for high achievers', *Chronicle of Higher Education*, 50(43): 19.

Hines, E. (2000) 'The governance of higher education', in J. Smart and W. Tierney (eds) *Higher Education: Handbook of Theory and Research*, *XV*, New York: Agathon Press, 105–155.

Kater, S. and Levin, J. (2005) 'Shared governance in community colleges in the global economy', *Community College Journal of Research and Practice*, 29(1): 1–24.

Levin, J. (2001a) *Globalizing the Community College: Strategies for Change in the Twenty-first Century*, New York: Palgrave.

Levin, J. (2001b) 'Public policy, community colleges, and the path to globalization', *Higher Education*, 42(2): 237–262.

Levin, J. (2002) 'In education and work: The globalized community college', *The Canadian Journal of Higher Education*, XXXII (2): 47–78.

Levin, J. (2005) 'The business culture of the community college: Students as consumers; students as commodities', in B. Pusser (ed.) *The Emerging Competitive Environment for Higher Education*, San Francisco: Jossey-Bass, 11–26.

Levin, J. (2007) 'Neo-liberal policies and community college faculty work', in John Smart and William Tierney (eds) *Handbook of Higher Education*, Vol. XXII, Norwell, MA: Kluwer Academic Publishers, 451–496.

Levin, J. S., Kater, S. and Wagoner, R. L. (2006) *Community College Faculty: At Work in the New Economy*, New York: Palgrave.

Lopez, C. (2004) 'A decade of assessing student learning', in P. Hernon and R. E. Dugan (eds) *Outcomes Assessment in Higher Education: Views and Perspectives*, Westport, CT: Libraries Unlimited, 29–71.

McGrath, D. and Spear, M. (1991) *The Academic Crisis of the Community College*, Albany, NY: State University of New York Press.

Mintzberg, H. (1994) *The Rise and Fall of Strategic Planning*, New York: Free Press.

National Center for Educational Statistics (NCES) (2002) *1999 National Study of Postsecondary Faculty (NSOPF: 99)*, Washington, DC: National Center for Education Statistics.

National Center for Educational Statistics (NCES) (2006) *2006 Digest of Education Statistics*. Online. Available at: http://nces.ed.gov/programs/digest/d06/ch_3.asp (accessed 15 May 2009).

Osterman, P., Kochan, T. A., Locke, R. M. and Piore, M. J. (2001) *Working in America: A Blueprint for the New Labor Market*, Cambridge, MA: MIT Press.

Phillippe, K. A. and Gonzalez Sullivan, L. (2005, 4th edn) *National Profile of Community Colleges: Trends and Statistics*, Washington, DC: American Association of Community Colleges.

Roe, C. E. (2002) *Effects of Informational Technology on Community College Faculty*, Tucson: University of Arizona.

Sennett, R. (1998) *The Corrosion of Character: The Personal Consequences of Work in the New Capitalism*, New York: W.W. Norton and Company.

Sennett, R. (2006) *The Culture of the New Capitalism*, New Haven: Yale University Press.

Slaughter, S. and Rhoades, G. (2004) *Academic Capitalism and the New Economy: Markets, State, and Higher Education*, Baltimore, MD: The Johns Hopkins University Press.

Smith, V. (2001) *Crossing the Great Divide: Worker Risk and Opportunity in the New Economy*, New York: Cornell University Press.

Tagg, J. (2003) *The Learning Paradigm College*, Bolton, MA: Anker Publishing Company.

Wagoner, R. L. (2004) *The Contradictory Faculty: Part-time Faculty at Community Colleges*, Tucson: University of Arizona.

Wagoner, R. L., Metcalfe, A. S. and Olaore, I. (2005) 'Fiscal reality and academic quality: Part-time faculty and the challenge to organizational culture at community colleges', *Community College Journal of Research and Practice*, 29: 1–2.

# Chapter 6

# German school-to-work transition programmes

## Disturbing work for educators

*Beatrix Niemeyer*

## Introduction

This chapter examines disturbances in the work of educational professionals in the field of school-to-work transition in Germany. While the perspective is on the pedagogical workers, it transcends the world of school, teaching and learning. Not only teachers but also vocational trainers, social or youth workers and other educational professionals are actively engaged in this part of the educational system, which has been in a constant process of reconfiguration during the past 30 years. The institutional and pedagogical reforms in this sector mirror the disturbing effects of changing educational demands that result from a changing labour market, and social and technical developments that have been labelled as 'flexible capitalism' by Sennett (1998).

Although the education system was not the focus of Sennett's attention, it is evident that the fundamental transformations he describes seriously challenge practical and theoretical concepts of pedagogy. Educational systems evolved in the nation states and their institutions and their actors, i.e. the persons working there as educational professionals, form the contexts and shape the contents and practices of how a society is organising its reproduction of skills and knowledge and of its systems of social relations. Education contributes to the production of social coherence since it plays a crucial role in the reproduction of societal structures: knowledge and skills as well as the relationships of its members. To refer Sennett's ideas to the field of education and pedagogy raises the basic question of how education contributes to the 'flexibilisation of character' or to the stabilisation of the ego in a flexible world.

While formal education determines spaces for collective experiences in which a collective 'we' can develop, the flexibilisation of educational systems opens new spaces. In the context of lifelong learning these are usually considered as being opportunities for individualised competence development. This approach focuses on the perspective of the single learner, cutting out the question about opportunities of collective experiences that enable individuals to identify themselves as part of the collective pronoun 'we'. But the problem is two-fold. The flexibilisation of education systems and institutions does not only affect learners and their way of learning but also deeply disturbs the work of educational professionals.

In Germany these disturbances can best be studied in the nutshell of the educational sector of transition from general school to vocational education and training (VET). In this sector the normative presuppositions of education are challenged in a specific way, established educational institutions have lost their integrative potentials and new programmes are introduced, which are especially exposed to marketisation. How this flexibilisation affects the work of the educational staff in and outside of vocational schools in Germany is explored in this chapter by telling the story of two related cases. They show how flexible capitalism is reconfiguring educational occupations. This is disturbing the work of those who educate and train future workers and citizens. Their work is doubly challenged while they are supposed to prepare and train young people for the unpredictable qualification demands of a future labour market; they work in the heart of the factory where the social fabric is woven. They need to respond to the young individuals' needs as well as their own for long-term perspectives that make possible the development of stable social relationships and biographical stories on which they can build during an unpredictable work and life course.

The analysis of the two case studies of transformations in the educational work with so-called disadvantaged young persons – those who are facing difficulties with their transition from school to vocational training and work – will serve as a basis for reflection on how the concept of vocational education, which has been an anchor point for the German idea of education and its institutionalisation, has recently been challenged. Examining the interface of work and learning, not from the perspective of work and skill formation of future workers but with a focus on professional teaching and education, intended and unintended reconceptions of pedagogical work become evident in this less structured part of the German educational system. This leads to reflections about the culturally rooted norms of education and vocation, how they are built into the system and its institutions and how they affect the (educational) agency of their actors.

The analysis of the case studies therefore focuses on reconfigurations of professional education and pre-vocational training in terms of changing work relations and changing educational aims. I start with a description of how the specific challenges posed by school-to-VET transition are culturally rooted in the German context, how this sector of the educational system is affected by reforms in educational politics and how both old and new problems challenge the educational professionals. In this context the central concepts of professional vocational education will be introduced. The following section contextualises the case studies and provides information about the methodology applied for this analysis. Then the stories of the two related cases are told, giving voice to two different professional groups, both dealing with identical educational tasks but in different institutional contexts. The focus of the interpretation is the perception of staff of change and their handling of transprofessional collaboration. This allows for conclusions to be drawn regarding the re-disturbing effects of flexibilisation in the last section of the chapter. In this final section the lessons to be learnt from the case descriptions are discussed against Sennett's critique of flexible capitalism.

## The German VET system

*Bildung* and *Beruf*, education and vocation, are central concepts. The German term *Bildung* incorporates the idea of actively forming oneself, and the passive process of being formed, as an interactive dialectical process; it also means 'coming into existence'. It is translated as education, since the term learning does not have the same complexity. Learning is rather related to institutionalised forms of education and teaching and is applied with reference to schools, while learning at the workplace within the system of vocational education is termed *Ausbildung*. This is usually translated as apprenticeship. The German term, however, expresses the subjective, holistic, dimension of the training process. This goes beyond technical qualifications and includes ideas of critical emancipative action and self-responsible engagement in work and society.

The German educational system can be considered as a ladder of institutions from the elementary level up to three types of secondary and vocational schools that lead to a vocation. It needs to be stressed here that the academic and the vocational track are equally socially acknowledged. Around 60 per cent of each age cohort entered vocational training while only 38 per cent opted for a university degree in 2006 (BMBF 2006: 3).

Vocational education and training has a high reputation. Vocationalism, in spite of all recent debates, remains an ordering principle of the German labour market and in the educational system. Social security is tightly related to the participation in the labour market, and occupational choice directly influences social positions. Vocational education and training – commonly conceptualised as dual apprenticeship with alternating periods of school and workplace training – has a central social and socialising function in Germany. At no time in history was it exclusively targeted at workplace training and technical skills but was, and is, at the same time directed at the enhancement of social participation and has always stressed its educating function.

Theories of vocational education and training pointed to the double intention of training and education for a vocation, aiming at the development of technical *and* general skills and knowledge. In Kerschensteiner's concept for a vocational school we find the idea of educating citizens through vocational training (Kerschensteiner 1901). In the German post-war theories of vocational education and training the idea of emancipation through vocational training was prominent. In these debates the claims of the working subject against the demands of the capitalist labour market were stressed. Lately, this has been expressed in the idea of shaping competence for a vocational biography (Hendrich 2002).

The appreciation of vocational skills and learning at the workplace goes back to the traditional craftsmen apprenticeship model, which had a high integrative potential with the apprentice sharing the work practice of his master and slowly becoming an expert in his vocation through learning in practice. With the general establishment of vocational schools at the beginning of the twentieth century the principle of vocationalism shaped their structure, since classes and curricula were organised according to vocations. This tripartite division of educational labour, with general schools delegating the preparation for the world of work to the vocational track – and vocational schools concentrating on the theoretical foundation of technical qualifications and in-company training for vocational skills – has had a strongly gendered dimension. It is a dominant feature for a vocational biography of the male breadwinner entering a lifetime profession through a dual system apprenticeship.

## Flexibilisation of the German vocational education and training system

The field of vocational education and training is jointly ruled by the economy, in the form of chambers of commerce and industry, and the state, embodied by the regional ministries of education who are responsible for the vocational schools. Reconfigurations towards flexibilisation can be identified in the structural reforms of vocational schools. These are imposed at regional levels and enable vocational schools to take part in the education market – that is, to buy and sell education programmes.

Vocational schools are now conceptualised as 'regional centres of education'. They have their own budgets, managing and selling a part of their learning offers, with the school director being responsible for hiring teachers – but not to fire them, since teachers are appointed by the ministry of education with a lifelong secured working contract. This concept appears quite innovative in a country with a state-guaranteed right for free education for all. At the moment it only applies for model schools and is mainly aimed at further education programmes, but some of these schools discovered the field of transition into vocational education, which so far has been covered by private institutes as an additional market.

The German educational system is highly structured and has a strong selective function, leading to the social status of individuals appearing as a family heritage that can hardly be changed through education. The outcomes of the PISA study have pointed out these selective effects and they have also been criticised by recent OECD reports. At the age of ten, at the end of elementary school, pupils are distributed to three different types of secondary schools:

- The '*Hauptschule*', literally translated as main school. After five years the school-leaving certificate is considered to be the minimum entrance standard for a vocational apprenticeship. It used to be the normal pathway towards vocational education in the post-war period, when labour was easily to be found, regardless of school qualifications. However, it has recently lost much of its reputation and attractiveness.
- The middle school ('*Realschule*') has taken over the function of preparation for the vocational track from the main school.
- The '*Gymnasium*' prepares students for the academic track, and the final exam '*Abitur*' after nine more years of schooling, allows entry into university.

More than 90 per cent of an age cohort complete secondary education but about two-thirds of them do this by following the vocational track (Konsortium Bildungsbericht 2006: 72). These figures express the persisting ideal of vocational education in Germany – studying at a university has long been an elitist concept, while master craftsmen, with their technical skills acquired through vocational education, still have a high reputation.

The normative ideal of social and vocational integration is built on the idea of ten years of schooling followed by three years of apprenticeship in the dual system alternating between workplace training in a company eligible for training, secured by a work contract, and with a fixed salary and one or two days per week in a vocational school. But this normative ideal of the German dual system is under challenge with a constant and growing lack of training places. Since the 1980s there has been an increasing imbalance between the economic realities and the educational assumptions that underpin the German dual system.

## The impact of German reunification

The lack of training places has become even more severe with the reunification of Germany in 1989. The educational and economic structures of West-Germany were transplanted into the East, thereby destroying work and training places there on a large scale.

In the Eastern regions in the years following reunification a large number of training places have been offered by state-funded organisations that lacked links to the labour market and had little labour market orientation. This has occurred in a period when the labour market itself was rapidly and deeply restructuring, there was large-scale unemployment in the East, and workers were forced to move to the West and South of Germany. This problem still has not been solved. Youth unemployment rates in the Eastern part of the country still are much higher than in the Western part.

## New transition-to-work programmes

In many regions of Germany, especially for young people with social or individual disadvantages, it has become extremely difficult to pass on from school directly to vocational apprenticeships. Therefore, additional programmes have been implemented to help bridge the gap between school and work (cf. Evans and Niemeyer 2004). A variety of programmes and models have been introduced to substitute training places, to avoid drop-out from training, and to ease transition from school. Basically, there are two options: either to continue school in a special class of a vocational school or to participate in a programme for vocational orientation organised outside of school, which can be run by welfare organisations, the churches, the chambers of commerce or other non-governmental organisations or by private enterprises. These programmes offer vocational orientation through work-based learning with regular internships in companies as well as social support.

Since the early 1980s they have flourished in the open space between general and vocational education and have developed a broad range of innovative learning approaches, such as individual support, competence assessment, counselling and case management. The staff usually comprises a multiprofessional group of trainers and social workers, often hired on short-term contracts, since the organisations directly depend on funding from the employment agency. This agency is the administrative body of the compulsory unemployment insurance and had held the monopoly for vocational guidance, the distribution of unemployment benefits and the employment service for matching job seekers and vacancies until it was restructured in 2002.

These programmes outside of school are subject to employment and welfare policies, and experience the neoliberal reforms in these sectors. Furthermore, marketisation has been introduced to the mechanisms of financial support. Each organisation offering an out-of-school programme for vocational orientation has to apply for funding at the local labour agency, for each programme on an annual basis. Educational quality standards must be met within an economical budget. The question to be answered by each programme provider is therefore: how much education can we afford to provide?

If long-term funding is avoided, long-term perspectives can hardly be developed. The effects of a changing labour market, such as time pressure at the workplace, reduced time and reduced space for learners and learning, generally growing qualification demands, as well as inflexible regulations of the established vocational education system, show in the figures of unemployed young people. Educational programmes, aimed at easing the transition from school to vocational education and training, are supposed to cure these deficits (Niemeyer 2002; see also Biermann *et al.* 1999; Galuske 1998).

At the same time, vocational schools increase their special classes for pre-vocational training outside their regular programme. Recently they have also begun experimenting with integrated workplace training in collaboration with local companies, thereby designing learning spaces beyond the classroom. While these additional educational offers of vocational schools react to the shortcomings of the apprenticeship market and the missing link between general schools and the job market, they disturb the concept of the vocational schools themselves. These classes run counter to the principle of structuring classes according to vocational fields, since the pupils do not have a vocation but are desperately looking for one. Teaching in theses classes is often disturbing for the teachers, who have a lifelong workplace security, but recognise that their students may not be so lucky. It also disturbs their work and their understanding of good practice:

- Pupils are often considered to be difficult. They do not fit the norms of a (future) skilled worker. The principal target of vocational education is put into question, since vocational and social integration for these young people does not work as an automatic track via a dual system apprenticeship.

- To motivate or remotivate for a vocational career, 'new cultures' of learning have to be developed that build on work-based learning experiences in authentic, meaningful learning contexts.
- Teamwork and cross-institutional collaboration is encouraged but this takes place outside the classroom and leaves the teacher's interactions with the young people as still a lonely classroom task.
- Because the established ordering framework of the apprenticeship system is not available to young people in these programmes, additional tasks arise for the staff from the organisational changes. For example, regional networks must be developed with the local economy as well as with the labour agency, welfare organisations and other institutions of social support.

The tension between employability and qualification of skilled workers, between job placement and vocational education, runs as a subtext through the funding guidelines (Niemeyer 2008). It can also be heard in the interviews with the professional educators.

In 2005, for the first time, the number of those who participated in transition programmes exceeded those who started a 'normal' apprenticeship (Konsortium Bildungsbericht 2006: 73). Although school-to-work transition has been a growing challenge to the established formal education, the widespread use of transition programmes was referred to as a 'transition system' for the first time in 2006 in the report on education in Germany by an independent group of researchers. This marked a proper shift in the discourse, since it showed that transition programmes had become a stable addition to general and vocational schooling. Until then the representatives of the dual system held up the idea of direct entrance, and transition programmes were themselves considered to be a transitory phenomenon.

Today the normative assumptions of a lifelong stable employment of a male breadwinner are outdated and the long and culturally deeply rooted traditions of established formal education and training are under challenge from the inside. They are also corroding from the outside through a – slow – flexibilisation of the school structures and a rapid change of welfare and employment policies. These press towards work placement and an enhancement of employability while having a tendency to neglect the traditional contents of education, including the emancipatory and the biographical shaping of competences.

## Evaluation processes revisited: the ethodological challenge

There are three reasons to focus research on the teaching, education and training in the field of transition from school to vocational education and training for disadvantaged young persons:

1   This is the most flexible part of the German educational system, since it has developed partly outside the established and secured structures of formal education and has thus been exposed to marketisation.

2   Problems with transition from school to vocational education and training signify shortcomings of the established structures when they point out the hurdles and barriers individuals are facing in their transition process. At the same time, they also allow study of the potentials of a flexibilisation of these structures.
3   Testing the idea of training pupils to have 'flexible characters' in this context raises questions about social inequalities and exclusion, along with the development of self-responsibility in precarious working conditions.

To trace the effects of flexibilisation in educational professions two cases of further training for vocational school teachers, trainers and social workers, who are engaged with improving the transition from school to vocational education and training, are used. The presentation of the cases builds on a close observation of two training programmes carried out in two different institutions at different periods of time and followed over a period of three years. One programme was jointly organised by three private institutes; the other was situated in a large vocational school. In both cases counselling, accompanying reform processes and evaluation were part of an action research project. The methods applied were close observation of practice, regular reflective meetings with key persons and the steering groups, and interviews with practitioners from all levels and with selected young persons.

While the aim of this evaluation was the improvement of educational methods and instruments in practice, the data collected is here re-interpreted with respect to the arguments of Sennett. Thus, the qualitative data can be used to gain insight into the changes in educational practice that accompany the flexibilisation of the educational system in Germany. Both cases can be told as a common story.

## Reconfigurations I: Reframing pre-vocational training

The first case is a common further training programme of three years for the educational staff of three training institutes specialising in vocational orientation for young school-leavers with severe learning problems. In this programme the young persons were working with trainers, social workers and vocational teachers for a period of one year, during which they were supposed to acquire a school-leaving certificate and find a place for a three-year apprenticeship. While trainers and social workers were employed by the institute, vocational teachers came from the regional vocational schools. This programme aimed to qualify all members of staff to follow a common educational approach towards the young participants of programmes that would empower their self-responsibility and self-awareness and enhance self-directed forms of learning in any vocational and social field.

Why was this further training project put into practice? The first reason was that the local labour agency explicitly required a more action-oriented individualised approach for the learning support. These ideas were linked to the expectation of improving the conditions of learning and the learning competences of the young people by constructing an atmosphere and organisational culture that promoted self-responsibility and respected the personalities of learners and their differences in learning. It also aimed to provide the staff with a strategy to cope with the everyday challenges, not to become frustrated in the pedagogical jungle, and to help them to be more content with their work.

The everyday practice in the workshops of these institutes was to be re-constructed in a way that forced the young persons to take responsibility for their actions. For example, this implied allowing them to work in their own way, but risked things going wrong, work products being spoiled and materials being wasted. However, this also carried the possibility that the consequences of technical faults would became evident to the young people in training. This presupposed a clearly structured social setting, clearly determined rules and clearly formulated learning aims as a stable social framework in which the young participants could position themselves. By acting self-responsibly they would themselves help to keep this social framework in place. In practice, very often the educational staff felt responsible for keeping up the rules and caring for the solution of practical problems at the workplace as well as in the social contexts.

One example of a different approach to education and a more participant-oriented strategy of support was the introduction of individual support plans and contracts. During a solution-oriented counselling session, the youth worker or trainer and the young person would agree on a realistic set of steps towards the solution of a learning problem and sign a contract on this agreement. An example might be 'I will do my homework everyday next week' or 'I will get up on time at least three mornings next week'.

While attending the further training sessions and observing team meetings, a lot of material was gathered about the process of change in the educational attitude of staff. Most obvious was the change in language. The change in the vocabulary with respect to the description of the educational practice was most striking. Problems and solutions were described by different words and thereby commonly re-interpreted. The most pronounced changes were:

- low achievers became learners;
- young people were no longer supported but enabled;
- mistakes were considered as chances for learning;
- selfishness or egoism was re-interpreted as the ability 'to care for oneself';
- trainers and youth workers were renamed as counsellors for learning; and
- the labour agency, the provider of financial support, the sponsor turned into client, to whom the preparation of young persons for vocational education and training was sold as a service product.

The idea of education was thus re-negotiated in the work practice of the educational staff; the communication focused on the common improvement of the learning culture in the three participating institutes. The corresponding processes also affected the organisational level: the relations of trainers and youth workers changed, participation in decision-making was claimed and a participating culture of decision-taking was implemented.

These processes, however, often disturbed lifelong habits, established relations and hierarchies in teams. They produced resistance against the unknown and, sometimes, the reluctance to subordinate professional paradigms under pedagogical needs. Conflicts with professional standards came up. For example, a product should be perfect according to professional standards and values. But to have it produced by learners now included the risk of mistakes and failures. With an established parental approach, the adult trainer wanted to help by stepping in, doing things better, improving, thereby devaluing the practice of the learners.

Still, the common perception of this further-training project was positive and affirming. The staff agreed new definitions of educational aims, found proposed activities helpful and were willing to make an extra effort. Participation in the project was seen as a personal chance. This common learning process also produced a new kind of 'we'. It enabled the transprofessional community of trainers and social workers to identify their collective aims and to value their practice. This common project can be regarded as a collective process of re-disturbance. It provided an opportunity to learn to integrate the disturbing shortcomings of the educational system producing disadvantaged young people on a large scale with the ideas of education by offering the space to re-train educative practice. In this collective learning process a new 'we' could be developed across professional paradigms.

## Reconfigurations II: Changing the framework

Following this further-training project, one of the three institutes managed to get funding for a new building. The new learning culture was now to be supported by the architecture. Transparency and flexibility were principles taken up in the construction of the new building. The learning and working sites were grouped around an open space where three computers with internet access allowed constant access to any information needed to solve problems with learning or working. The internal walls were made of glass but had curtains which could be drawn if undisturbed learning was required. Most impressive was the flexibilisation of the workspace for teachers and trainers. Instead of their own offices or classrooms they now had individual desks for their tools and teaching materials, files, work sheets and personal belongings. These desks were mounted on wheels so that they could be moved through the building. Teaching and training activities could now take place anywhere.

After two more years the labour agency changed the funding regulations. These included a strong promotion of in-company work experiences and therefore the time which students could spend at the training institute was reduced to a minimum. The well-trained staff found themselves in almost empty rooms with so few boys and girls to train that the whole institute's further existence was in danger.

## Reconfigurations III: Disturbed teaching

The second case was situated at a vocational school which was profiting from this change in the funding regulations. The number of classes for unemployed young increased; special classes for disadvantaged and unemployed youth were established with the financial support of the local employment agency at the regional vocational school.

The newly adopted business-like structures enabled the school in the study to buy additional educational resources, including hiring additional staff at a lower salary than a teacher would normally receive – and on short-term contracts. A 'learning centre' was implemented on the initiative of a small group of teachers who were mainly engaged in classes for unemployed young people. Three persons who had work experience in the educational field, but did not hold degrees, were employed and a special room was reserved where pupils suffering from social or psychological problems, violating classroom rules, showing too many difficulties with learning, and so on, could spend a short or longer period of time out of the classroom if they were disturbing lessons.

This centre was designed to serve as relief for the teachers and offered additional social and pedagogical support for the pupils. It opened a new space for learning for both teachers and pupils. However, this was disturbing to the established concept of the school and challenged the work identity of teachers. Here again a collective and transprofessional learning process started, although not consciously intended and without anyone to steer the process. The majority of the teachers were reluctant to use this new 'learning centre' when it was first introduced. Three modes of reaction could be observed:

- a peaceful co-existence without taking real notice and avoiding getting in touch with the new colleagues;
- a form of labour division between teachers concentrating on classroom instruction and the staff of the learning centre taking the responsibility for the social pedagogical support and, later on, also for the 'external affairs' of organising the collaboration with the local labour market; and
- a collaboration of both teachers and educators, exchanging background information about the pupils and joining in regular reflective meetings, developing common educational concepts over time.

During the following year, a division of labour developed. The learning centre served as a mediator for the local labour and apprenticeship market. Workplace experience was built into the curricula as a regular element for pre-vocational classes and the task of the 'new' staff was to counsel and coach this part of the learning programme. In the beginning, the implementation of this additional educational offer at the vocational school was disturbing in many ways. The new staff were struggling to find their roles in the school hierarchy and to adapt to the established learning cultures and to get acceptance from the teachers. The self-concept of teachers as 'single actors' was disturbed as well. They had first to learn that it was acceptable to ask for assistance and to admit that they had problems in the classroom. It was confusing for some of the young students, too, who were not sure if being sent out of the classroom represented support or punishment.

## Transprofessional collaboration

Both cases described above can be read as examples of transprofessional collaboration: in the private institutes different professional groups were collaborating in the pre-vocational training of the young; in the vocational school new professions were put aside by the established group of teachers. The common institutional frame in the first case supported the formation of a common identity and the development of a common educational approach to integrating training and education. At the vocational school, however, the appearance of a new type of educational professional challenged the identity of teachers as well as the idea of good teaching which so far had been limited to classrooms. On another level the changes also questioned the clearly defined access rules for working at a school which secured income and social status of teachers.

It also challenged the concept of education. Teachers could no longer interpret teaching as the production of knowledge but had to acknowledge that social learning and workplace training also play an important role in the process of becoming an adult. The school case is an example of how rigid and long-term structures of a school become flexibilised, leading to new types of work organisation and new types of divisions of labour, including new hierarchies. Those teachers who were open to this innovation could gain more flexibility in their work and get support from other employees. They managed to organise regular reflective meetings as well as ways of team-teaching. Here again it could be observed that a new type of a transprofessional 'we' could develop, building on the common educational aim of improving school-to-work transition for disadvantaged young persons.

It is interesting that both cases built on the importance of work-based learning. This shows the persistent idea of the German concept of vocation and at the same time it documents an adaptation to the imperative of employability and the way it is imposed through labour, education and welfare policy.

## Disturbing lessons

By following the changes in the practice of educational professionals we can ask questions about how the changes brought by 'flexible capitalism' affect education and training. Sennett's deconstruction of the flexible capitalist society (2000, 2007) demonstrates that in a short-term world of fluid values and mobile individuals those features of character that link people together and produce a stable concept of self are threatened (Sennett 1998: 31). This threat, Sennett (2007: 10) argues, results from:

- reduced opportunities to experience or show commitment;
- short-term relationships in the working as well as in the private area; and,
- changing modes of acknowledgement and appreciation.

Sennett points to the social dimension of these changes, when he comes to the conclusion 'that a regime which provides human beings no deep reasons to care about one another cannot long preserve its legitimacy' (Sennett 1998: 148). He argues that flexible capitalism needs flexible characters and shows the consequences of the economic development of the construction of social relationships, hence for the social construction of society.

While Sennett is pointing to the effects that transformations in the economy and the organisation and distribution of labour have on the human character, his concepts also challenge the theory and practice of education. What should be the scope of formal education in a flexible world of changing values and drifting individuals? Where are the limits of institutionalised education? The growing group of young persons in Germany who fall into the gap between general school and work points to the limits of their integrative potential and provides evidence of the missing link between general schools and the job market. The new approaches go beyond general education and the formation of technical skills, adding social pedagogical support as well as an extended workplace experience to their curricula. Educational theories and institutes have been conceptualised as building on stable social relationships and long-term biographical planning within stable institutional structures. The demand for flexibility, as it is expressed in the concept of life-long learning, thus questions some of the basics of education. How could education for flexibility be put into practice? Does life-long, self-directed learning of individualised self-employers need education at all? Will teaching become an outdated profession?

The lessons to be learnt from these German stories do not suggest that teaching will become an outdated profession. They show how the concept of teaching is re-interpreted and how the practice of education and the community of educational professionals are broadened. Both cases tell a story of how flexible conditions, resulting from a gradual marketisation of education, disturbed educational professionals who were highly challenged by the task of educating and training young disadvantaged persons who had reduced chances of entering the labour market through the established apprenticeship track. The case studies also tell a story of how established educational structures, norms and practices lost their integrative potential – that is, their educating potential – and how it can be re-discovered in new forms of transprofessional collaboration in the new space created by a broadened institutional framework, allowing the formation of new types of collective identities.

According to Sennett, to succeed in this flexible world an ideal person needs to direct his or her learning strategies towards potential competences rather than towards the idea of masterly expertise. They need to be ready to change their habits repeatedly. He points out how these features of a flexible character contradict people's need for a long-term biographical story, pride and dignity in vocational skills and knowledge and personal experience.

In Germany, this has been experienced by the educational staff in a specific way. The fact that the established track of vocational and social integration in Germany is becoming outdated challenged their professional identity – good teaching was no longer enough, nor was proper training. The interviews are full of examples of how this disturbance of the idea of expertise and education was negotiated: they talk about a different approach to the young participants, no top-down relationships but rather a collaboration. They also talk about trust in the young person's capabilities, about allowing them their own experience and about the chances they want to offer:

> It is really liberating for the young not to be directed from above, but really to be taken seriously, to have more space to try themselves out, to say: I want to do something and I may try it out myself, without the fear to fail. . . . Action-oriented learning, that's the term which describes it: they act, right or wrong, but they act in any way. They do something and then they find a way. If I notice that they do something wrong, I guide them in another direction. They learn while they are doing.
>
> (Trainer, metal department)

The changing perspective of learning was expressed by a discourse on learning processes in which terms like education or pedagogic (*Erziehung und Bildung*) lost their significance and were replaced by terms such as competence development and self-learning abilities. At the same time pupils, teachers or schools, as actors and institutions of education, were replaced by terms such as learners, learning environments, learning contexts, managers or moderators or counsellors of learning processes. The new talk – the new vocabularies – that had to be learnt by the staff in the first case evoked a new way of thinking about their everyday practice. Their educational expertise, so far rarely reflected upon and largely experience-based, was re-interpreted. New methods of education were introduced, for example individual support plans or learning contracts.

To sign a contract to commit yourself to improve your behaviour or to develop specific skills or behaviours transfers the responsibility for the learning success from the teacher to the pupil, from the expert to the newcomer, from the adult to the youngster. At first sight this seems to de-skill education, since failure is now the student's fault. However, it remains the teacher's task and responsibility to enable the student to succeed. And so it was experienced by the educational professionals of the institutes. They did not feel their expertise was in question. The new approaches to learning, the new 'tools' in the educational practice, contrasted with the established habits and concepts referring to care, parenting and tight leading, but were experienced as improvement and liberation.

Consequently, the majority of staff highly appreciated this further training programme. They felt that they could develop their professional expertise and that it was a specific way to acknowledge their work. They did not give up their responsibility for the educational process but re-interpreted and enacted their educational task as counselling, accompanying and preventing their pupils from failing. The lesson they learnt was that a parenting, over-caring approach, which can be found in many fields of social and youth work, and the dominance of technical skills and technical standards, limits the learning potentials of the young, while 'new learning cultures' open potentials for self-responsible personality development. This was liberating rather than disturbing for them. This change in language reflects the tendency to transfer social and educational responsibility from the corresponding societal institutions to the learning individuals themselves but this does not mean that the institutions lost their significance and function.

The new conception of the educational relationship may affect the adoption of business-like attitudes. There is a danger that they could lead to a lack of commitment in the relationship between adults and young and a growing marketisation and contractualisation of structures and relationships. The educational relationship could be changed by market structures and instruments introduced from the economic world. While on paper participation and partnership are highlighted, in practice partners may become business partners or contractors. The formerly criticised space of protection could become a free space. New approaches to learning open up both ways. Since young persons under the actual conditions do not even have a chance to develop into a '*Arbeitskraftunternehmer*', a modern flexible and mobile self-employer, in the end the introduction of market mechanisms to this field of the educational system remains on the surface or becomes an educational means in itself. It does not make too much sense to adopt market-like structures and mechanisms to a field that needs commitment to social responsibility to ensure the framework conditions in which individual self-responsibility can develop. To the staff participating in the further-training project this seemed to be self-evident. The 'danger' of the infiltration of market mechanisms into education had not been reflected at all. As the interviews show, the new vocabulary had been integrated with the old idea of education. The concept of care and responsibility was not given up in this training process, which might as well be read as a process of teaching the educational staff to respect the disadvantages of the young with whom they were working. While the educational practice was reconceptualised, its educative function was not in question. Long-term commitment was rather endangered by market pressures from the outside – by the unstable funding conditions.

Another lesson can be learnt about the effects of structural reforms when turning to the example of the vocational school. While the German educational system, its schools and the profession of teachers may be regarded as especially traditional, representing long-term stable relationships that provide workplace security, values and norms, structural reforms have started to introduce market principles into the vocational schools organisation – at least to a degree. They disturbed the established long-term security which strongly influences German teachers' job decisions. They are appointed as civil servants or officials with life-long contracts and secure retirement pensions.

However, this flexibilisation of structures has also given room for innovations in teaching culture. In the observed case discussed above it has considerably helped to improve staff working conditions by employing additional people and thereby enlarging the educational expertise – for those who could profit from it. At the same time new forms of inequality were introduced, since the learning centre staff were hired on short-term contracts and with very low pay. An inter-nal hierarchy between the 'real' teachers and the 'helpers' was kept up and impeded collaboration and acceptance. Still, in this case the opening of space has given room for those teachers who were especially engaged and under pressure while working with the most difficult young people and who were physically experiencing the limits of school teaching. For them this new space offered an opportunity to re-discover their agency beyond the established role of teacher. They could move and think beyond the classroom. In this space new forms of education and training could emerge in a common transprofessional working and learning process.

These reconfigurations have seemingly changed professional identities and broadened the professional experiences and expertise but they have challenged them less than expected. The change to the framework conditions could not do away with the personal interrelationship between the expert and the novice, the adult and the young person. New spaces and new perspectives help to rethink the tensions which are typical of professional education and support to actively shape them.

The two cases paint a picture of how flexibilisation cautiously affects the field of education in Germany and how ambiguous the effects are. Who is actu-ally disturbed by these processes? Teachers find their practice under challenge and need to change the traditional learning cultures they had as single actors in a closed classroom. Social or youth workers, who are employed to support school-to-work transition in private institutes, respond much easier to flexible concepts of learning, counselling, and so on. Young people, who have rarely experienced respect or found room for self-directed, autonomous decisions and had mainly had de-motivating experiences with school-based learning, sometimes still may be disturbed when they are exposed to the challenge of efficiency.

Obviously, research and researchers are disturbed as well. The reproduction of a society cannot be reduced to the reproduction of knowledge and skills. It must also include the reproduction of social relations. The question of where and how the ability for long-term social relationships, commitment and trust could be developed has not yet been answered. But autonomy, emancipation and self-responsibility, the core concepts of critical educational theory, might better be developed in a flexible educational system than in rigid, disciplining and selective structures. Still, reforms are very often put into practice in a rather pragmatic way. There is not much space for critical reflective thinking through all the tacit dimensions and consequences of the changes in methods and systems of education and the effects they have for professional action.

The story told above has opened a window for reflection about the effects of flexible capitalism on education. A profound analysis of the processes is, however, still lacking and there is certainly also a need to find out how educational reforms influence access to education and affect social inclusion and justice. One of the big challenges will be to find methods of investigating and researching the small differences between care and paternalism, respect and ignorance, and acceptance and indifference.

## References

Biermann, H., Bonz, B. and Rützel, J. (eds) (1999) *Beiträge zur Didaktik der Berufsbildung Benachteiligter*, Stuttgart: Holland & Josenhans.

Bundesagentur für Arbeit: Neues Fachkonzept, 12.1.2004.

Bundesministerium für Bildung und Forschung (BMBF) (2006) *Berufsbildungsbericht*, Bonn.

Evans, K. and Niemeyer, B. (eds) (2004) *Reconnection – Countering Social Exclusion through Situated Learning*, Dordrecht, NL: Kluwer.

Galuske, M. (1998) 'Jugend ohne Arbeit. Das Dilemma der Jugendberufshilfe', *Zeitschrift für Erziehungswissenschaft*, 1: 4–98.

Hendrich, W. (2002) 'Implizites Wissen für erwerbsbiographische Gestaltungskompetenz. Zur Begründung notwendiger berufspädagogischer Neuorientierungen', unpublished habilitation thesis, Flensburg.

Kampmeier, A., Niemeyer, B., Petersen, R. and Stannius, M. (2008) *(Das) Miteinander Fördern. Theoretische und praktische Lösungsansätze für eine professionelle Benachteiligtenförderung*, Bielefeld: W. Bertelsmann Verlag.

Kerschensteiner, G. (1901) *Staatsbürgerliche Erziehung der deutschen Jugend, Gekrönte Preisschrift*, Erfurt: Villaret.

Konsortium Bildungsberichterstattung (2006) *Bildung in Deutschland*, Bielefeld: Bertelsmann.

Niemeyer, B. (2002) 'Begrenzte Auswahl – Berufliche Orientierung von Jugendlichen mit schlechten Startchancen', in J. Schudy (ed.) *Berufsorientierung in der Schule. Grundlagen und Praxisbeispiele*, Bad Heilbrunn: Klinkhardt, 207–220.

Sennett, R. (1998) *Der flexible Mensch*, Berlin: Berliner Taschenbuch Verlag.

Sennett, R. (2000) *Respekt im Zeitalter der Ungleichheit*, Berlin: Berliner Taschenbuch Verlag.

Sennett, R. (2007) *Die Kultur des neuen Kapitalismus*, Berlin: Berliner Taschenbuch Verlag.

# Chapter 7

# Paraprofessional development in the UK

## Ambivalences and contradictions

*Chris Kubiak*

Since 1979 when the Conservative government took office, the UK Health and Social Care (HSC) sector has undergone a radical redesign. When New Labour came to power in 1997 it did not return to the long-standing model of centralised command and control which had been dismantled under the Conservative government but rather introduced an era of almost hyperactive intervention and redesign (Appleby and Coote 2002). Grounded in neoliberal ideology, the welfare sector has been revised and revisioned along a number of recurring themes. Mooney and Law (2007) present a thorough analysis describing an increasing concern with efficiency and effectiveness in both administration and clinical practice, coupling a drive for cash savings with increasing levels of intervention in professional practice. Service users have been reconceptualised as customers and services reconfigured around their needs, bringing increased monitoring, review and audit as well as a considerable blurring of the traditional occupational and professional boundaries.

The neoliberal turn, with its continual pursuit of an ever-more efficient, value-for-money service, also introduced the use of Taylorist techniques (Bolton 2004) that provided the space for a redistribution of the division of labour. This reform has been characterised by a reshaping of occupational roles as well as complex systems of regrading and reclassification (Mooney and Law 2007). Staff are called upon to be more flexible about role definition with drives to shift out of traditional boundaries (Dawson *et al.* 2007; Department of Health (DH) 2001; Department of Health, Social Services and Public Safety 2008).

In this chapter, working life in such 'liquid times' is analysed in terms of learning and identity. The requirement for workers to move with various waves of change has long been associated with drives for lifelong learning and reskilling, an agenda of some ambivalence. The need for flexibility defines a learning agenda coupling the creation of malleable human capital, capable of adapting to the current agenda, with one focused on achieving self-actualisation or building human potential. Moreover, the need to move with centrally determined best practice, as is often the case under clinical governance, is set against hard-won experience, knowledge and skill (Jacobs 2004). 'Moving with the times' introduces tensions around what it means to be competent or to have a vocation.

Such conditions also have implications for identity. The implications of the push for constant change were captured by Sennett (1998) in his compassionate analysis of the corrosion of character in which he argued that the working conditions of flexible capitalism corrode the individual's attempts to develop a narrative of identity and life history. His concern is that practitioners do not strive to be just another pair of labouring hands but desire to develop careers, professional identities or the skills of craft work.

This raises the question of how human beings maintain their vocation and develop a narrative of identity in such fluid times. Such forces do not have a uniform impact on workers but are mediated by their own agency and the social conditions in their workplace. This question leads me to consider how individuals are shaped by such times as well as the way in which they develop the agency needed to shape their circumstances for them to earn a decent salary, do a good job or earn esteem and status from their colleagues. In this chapter this concern is taken up in relation to a group collectively referred to as paraprofessionals in health and social care. Exploring the way in which the role and skill demands on this group have changed, this chapter considers the ambivalence surrounding these workers' development.

## Reshaping the paraprofessional workforce

One aspect of the reshaping of HSC has involved changes in the role of the HSC paraprofessional – the assistant to nurses or allied health professionals, the care worker for those with mental health problems or learning disabilities – a group referred to here as support workers. The development of this group has been presented as a cost effective method of addressing the problem of under-resourced, over-subscribed services (see, for example, Keeney et al. 2005). The reshaping of the role has taken different forms. In some quarters, new paraprofessional roles have been created – such as support, time and recovery workers in mental health. Others have been subject to the same occupational boundary blurring that has been running across the workforce as a whole. For example, in some quarters, the uni-professional practitioner has become a multi-professional generic rehabilitation worker with skills from nursing, occupational therapy and physiotherapy (Knight et al. 2004; Rolfe et al. 1999).

Most controversially, support workers are performing tasks previously exclusive to professionals (Ashby et al. 2003; Atwal et al. 2006; DH 2006; Mackey 2004; Rainbird et al. 1999; Spilsbury and Meyer 2004; Sutton et al. 2004). Certainly, this development reflects the demands of an over-subscribed, under-resourced sector. In addition, it also marks a shift in the division of labour in which the registered professional increasingly withdraws from client engagement into paperwork, reports and audits, leaving another tranche of staff, the paraprofessionals to do the basic frontline work (see, for example, Kennedy and Kennedy 2007).

In other parts of the sector, the demands made of support workers have had a different emphasis. Users' needs are seen as increasingly complex (Fleming and

Taylor 2007; Rainbird *et al.* 1999). Service users are seen in diversified terms, conceptualised as active and competent subjects with services increasingly commodified and with direct delivery to families and children (Cameron and Moss 2007). Moreover, policy emphasises goals of autonomy, empowerment and choice (see, for example, the NHS and Community Care Act 1990). Service users themselves are no longer seen as passive recipients of care but as active citizens calling in their rights for quality and personalisation (Cameron and Boddy 2006).

Consequently, low levels of skills are no longer sufficient. The priority given to holistic care means that the discrete tasks of caring (for example, washing or feeding) are not merely instrumental ones to be delegated to the unqualified but are part of developing and deepening the relationship with the client and creating opportunities for supporting that person's development, autonomy and empowerment (Moss *et al.* 2006). In addition, the HSC landscape has become one marked by high public expectations, a keener focus on professional standards, social welfare legislation and a litigious culture dampened by risk management procedures (Fleming and Taylor 2007). Similarly, there are plans for support worker registration across HSC (DH 2006; General Social Care Council 2007).

## Paraprofessional learning and development

The recognition that the frontline care offered by paraprofessionals requires complex skills and knowledge focuses attention on the need for ongoing training and development. While the development of support staff may be necessary or even supported in policy statements, the socio-cultural dynamics of the workplace may reflect considerable ambivalence constraining their growth. Billett's (2004) notion of co-participation provides insight into the way in which such ambivalence may impact on development. Working from a socio-cultural perspective, Billett presents 'affordances for learning' as a product of both the opportunities and activities available in the workplace and the individual's capacity to construe and take such opportunities. In other words, the socio-cultural nature of the workplace will shape the nature of practice and its development.

So at the most basic level of analysis, HSC's resource difficulties provide a source of ambivalence around the service vision and actual opportunities for development. For example, the National Health Service (NHS) commitment to lifelong learning is paradoxically undermined by the inability of human resource managers to plan for anything longer than a year (McBride *et al.* 2004). In practice settings, heavy workloads, lack of resources for change and lack of management back-up can inhibit changes to practice following study (Forrester-Jones and Hatzidimitriadou 2006). Access and interaction with skilled others is a significant source of learning, though support workers may find that supervision or support is lacking due to professional colleagues' workloads (Coffey 2004), lack of training in supervision (Coffey 2004; Ellis and Connell 2001) or simply inadequate staffing levels (Stokes and Warden 2004).

Affordances for learning are also associated with workplace norms, values and practices which not only structure activity but are also often concerned with the continuity and reproduction of practice (Billett 2001). As such, making changes in practice can mean that learning is a contested process. Thus, opportunities to participate in activities and access support and guidance may be unevenly distributed across participants on the basis of factors such as race, gender, worker or employment status or perceived value (Billett 2004). Care workers can occupy a marginalised position in the workplace (Miers *et al.* 2005) and issues of status or hierarchy may challenge development opportunities. The lack of standardised, consistent training for health care assistants can impact upon or reflect the perceived value given to their role (Keeney *et al.* 2005). More effort may be put into enabling qualified staff to access training while opportunities are withheld from other groups (Munro *et al.* 2000).

In addition, the reconceptualisation of support worker roles is a reflection of the professionalisation of this workforce. This shift has the potential to disrupt well-established occupational hierarchies and understandings of who does what work and how it is rewarded. The acquisition of qualifications and skills has the potential to alter collegial perceptions of the status of the worker (Munro *et al.* 2000) and thus impact on power relations and hierarchies. For example, Keeney *et al.* (2005) found that, after completing their National Vocational Qualification (NVQ), health care assistants perceived little difference between their work and that of qualified nurses. They became reluctant to assume basic duties, arguing that these should be taken on by non-qualified staff.

Thus, support worker learning opportunities can impact on their 'professional' colleagues' role and work. The extension of paraprofessional roles into professional work is worth exploring to illustrate the particular dynamics of workplaces in health and social care. There is an argument that training support workers to perform certain tasks frees professionals to perform more complex work closer to the core of their profession (Baldwin *et al.* 2003; Coffey 2004). In contrast, the extended roles of support workers have been seen as encroaching on professional roles (Atwal *et al.* 2006; Coffey 2004; Mackey 2004; Nicholson 1996; Rainbird *et al.* 1999; Rolfe *et al.* 1999). The extension of support worker roles has been described as a process of 'nibbling away' the more routine tasks of professionals, further fragmenting their role and cheapening the rate for the job (Law and Mooney 2007). While role extension may be interpreted by support workers as a development opportunity, their professional colleagues may view it as a threat (Spilsbury and Meyer 2004). Certainly, journal articles with titles such as 'The health care assistant: Usurper of nursing?' (Edwards 1997) or 'Are we giving away nursing?' (Nicholson 1996) convey the tone of these issues.

Examples abound. The attitudes of colleagues can influence the support workers' opportunities to enact a particular role or change their practice (Rolfe *et al.* 1999; Spilsbury and Meyer 2004). NVQs have been resisted by employers as they highlight the previously unacknowledged aspects of auxiliaries' work that overlap with the professional staff (Thornley 2000). A highly skilled and trained occupational therapy support worker may blur the professional–non-professional boundary, invalidating any necessity for formal education and diminishing professional roles (Mackey 2004).

Support workers themselves may be ambivalent about particular opportunities for learning or role development. Some may be satisfied with their current role and level of responsibility (Hancock *et al.* 2005), while others may associate training with work intensification (Rainbird *et al.* 1999). Some may be reluctant to engage in training because of the lack of financial reward at the end of it (Ellis and Connell 2001; Hancock *et al.* 2005; Rolfe *et al.* 1999). Support workers may have negative attitudes to development opportunities that extend their role, feeling that particular tasks should be provided by professionals (Hancock *et al.* 2005). Interviews by Rolfe *et al.* (1999) with support workers who were moving from profession-specific roles to generic roles identifies tensions around these workers' sense that the shift was equated with relegation and loss of the status that they attached to the individual professional groups.

What is proposed in this short review is that paraprofessional practice and development can operate in a space of ambivalence. The notion of ambivalence connects with the concept of contradictions as historically accumulating structural tensions within and between activity systems (Engeström 2004). Indeed, it can be argued that the ambivalence around paraprofessional development is a reflection of the tension between the way in which work practice is called upon to change and well-established organisational social orders and habits. Engeström (2004) presents an optimistic framing of contradictions, however, by arguing that while they create disturbances they also give rise to change and innovative solutions within systems.

## The case of support workers' learning

To explore the ambivalence surrounding role and development, this section draws from a subset of data from a PhD in progress focused on understanding support worker learning. Thirteen participants working in learning disability, mental health or district nursing services were involved in the study. The mental health and learning disability workers were involved in caring work supporting people in the activities of daily life. Often taking a developmental focus, they worked with their clients to understand and support them to achieve their goals, for example to live in their own home, to care for themselves, to have a job, to have friendships. The health care assistant in the district nursing service performed a range of nursing tasks ranging from taking electrocardiogram readings, taking blood or changing dressings. Workers ranged in experience from a few months in the role to over ten years' work history. Some of those with long histories of work described experiencing role extension or contraction. Others recounted tales of requirements for increasingly sophisticated work with clients.

Six workers were observed in practice in tasks such as working with clients, attending meetings, preparing meals or planning sessions. Those in the mental health and district nursing service participated in interviews only. In 2008 each participant was interviewed four times. The first interview consisted of a biographical interview tracing their history from first entry into the field and an exploration of their role and setting. The following two interviews carried out at monthly intervals explored critical incidents in the worker's practice as well as follow-up questions drawn from the previous interviews. The fourth interview combined the discussion of a participant profile prepared out of the data and a further critical incident interview. This profile interview was not simply respondent validation. It was a final stage in data collection and the first step in analysis in which the participant discussed at a deeper level some of the themes in their development and practice and contributed to an interpretation of the data. These themes are used to organise the discussion below.

## Practice as the presentation of self

The place of self in the participants' work was a theme running through the dataset. Participants' accounts of their life histories often referred to quite intentional attempts to find work that held some personal meaning for them. They sought work that allowed them to be who they wanted to be and where they could use and develop their personal qualities as carers. While this drive was partly an issue of job satisfaction it was also related to something more fundamental to effective practice. That is, understanding the service user and supporting even the simplest activity involves the formation of trusting and sometimes intimate relationships. These relationships provide the basis for the emotional work and intricate negotiations that form the basis of supporting someone's needs or facilitating their development. In carrying out relationship work, the carers' main tools were themselves and their own personality.

Thus, the workers' emphasis on the expression of their personal qualities reflected the way in which these were exploited to further their work with clients. For example, working with genuine enthusiasm and interest in a shared activity with a client rather than going through the motions is part of connecting with and motivating clients – creating an authentically human encounter. While work did involve much emotional labour with various degrees of deep or surface acting (see Hochschild 1983), the participants presented themselves as 'being me' or 'doing what comes natural'. Moreover, participants proudly emphasised the distinctive nature of how they worked and discussed their personal style or the unique nature of the relationships formed with service users. Indeed, being able to express this distinctiveness was considered a development task in itself or a mark of mastering their role.

However, as personal as practice seemed at the time, it was ultimately co-configured within the team and the wider organisation. Services would exert considerable formal effort ensuring that practice operated along defined lines. Newcomers engaged in induction courses, shadowing, mentoring and intensive supervision to ensure that they understood the way things were done 'around here'. Experienced workers would not only receive training around issues to ensure compliance with policy or particular practices, but much of their activity was negotiated within the team. The approach taken with a client arose out of team discussions, negotiated interpretations of behaviour and agreed ways of operating within service resource constraints and policy. Workers also maintained agency here, actively modelling themselves on their colleagues while trying to create a distinctiveness to their practice that reflected their values and sense of self.

## Being visible and invisible

The interviews suggested that practice is constructed in the interface between social structuring and individual agency. One dimension of workers' workplace experience clustered around a theme of being visible or invisible in the workplace. To be visible was to have one's capabilities, talents, interests, goals and contributions recognised as valid. To be recognised could have a profound impact on a worker. Certainly, recognition brought an emotional pay-off – pleasure at being acknowledged as competent, accepted or valued. It also allowed continuities with the past – skills developed in previous roles had a place in the current organisation. For example, the ex-teacher is able to use skills in instructional design to plan work with a client. More than this, one's uniqueness – the tools necessary in relationship work – would be enhanced and strengthened. The interviews suggest that this was not simply a matter of the transfer of skills and knowledge from one setting to another but the establishment of oneself in an organisation. Indeed, in the interviews, having one's capabilities made visible through appraisal, supervision or casual conversation could be a turning point in creating a role the worker felt comfortable with.

To be recognised or visible would expand the workers' scope for action. Being 'talent spotted' by colleagues or associates provided opportunities for different practices, new challenges or role progression. For example, career development could be predicated on a manager encouraging a worker to apply for a new role, being allowed to 'act up' to fill in for a senior or to join a team in an innovative project. Similarly, managers who notice aspirations or capabilities for a particular role or activity may provide opportunities for different sorts of participation such as attendance at professional meetings, more complex work or further training. Such involvements support worker learning.

Certainly, the interviews revealed many examples of being made visible. At the same time, workers in the study reported that they could also be rendered invisible. 'Invisibilisation' could take many forms. Support workers may not be counted in accounts of staffing levels. For example, professional colleagues would complain about understaffing, arguing that 'there's only me on' (PZ) and failing to count the health care assistants on the shift. Similarly, in team discussions, support worker opinions may be discounted by registered colleagues. Support workers accepted discounting with the blankness of, for example, 'they're the social worker . . . that's just the way it is' (PD). For example, one interviewee, who like a few other workers in the study had once held a professional role but had allowed her registration to lapse, describes how her opinions were sidelined in clinical discussions. With obvious frustration, she relates this to how 'sticky' registered staff are about their roles. She also linked this experience of making the transition into a new team with a different sort of hierarchical structure in which she had a different role and no one knew her:

> Sometimes I forget myself that I'm there is a hierarchy and that I am a [support] worker; I forget that because I've always worked in . . . that I forget that I actually am not in a position where I can actually engage so openly in a clinical discussion.
>
> (PM)

This is partly an issue about the low positional power of these workers. As 'unqualified' they may appear to have opinions that count for less in contrast to the registered social workers or nurses. The frustration here is complex. Workers respected the professionals' training and knowledge but noted that many had irregular contact with clients. In contrast, the support workers felt that they not only had considerable experience and knowledge but also possessed a detailed understanding of their clients, drawn from regular and long-term contact with them. They had 'frontline authority' and this should stand for something.

However, discussions with workers revealed that discounting was not simply a matter of professional protectionism. Many teams did operate in a collaborative fashion where everyone's opinion mattered. However, some colleagues were just seen as 'difficult' people who would try to write you off. However, this conclusion cannot be treated as separate from power. In conflicts about duties or opinions, the professional staff, unlike the support workers, can draw down their positional power to get the final say.

'Invisibilisation' can create self-doubt or fears that one is not in the right job. It can also impose self-constraint. For example, one worker described the way that the social care orientation she developed in her previous post did not always have a place in the medically oriented teams. Even though she was studying at degree level and read around the topic so that she went into team meetings well informed, her invisibilisation appeared self-imposed:

> . . . reading around and read about the referral process, read a few things and I'm saying 'maybe I'm going overboard' because I think I have this thing about I'm not qualified so I sell myself short of how far I can go within, because what is the point of going in so far and be knocked back

because I don't have some of the requirements, so why am I wasting my time doing all these things?

(PC)

## Grading practices

Workers were surrounded by a complex technology of role specifications and skill profiles tied to salary levels. Issues of grading, role definition and job title were not simply matters of salary but were also related to their scope for action and team respect. Within this technology, workers recognised the blurring of roles with those of professional staff as they take up duties that were once in the professional domain or conversely lose tasks they once held. Support workers doing identical jobs noticed that some were on higher gradings. This inconsistency is discordant in a system that placed all in their 'right place' and leaves workers feeling unrecognised and undervalued, perplexed by the discrepancy.

Workers picking up the tasks once carried out by nurses or social workers can feel ambivalent about their role. Certainly, such work presents learning opportunities and increased challenges but raises questions about appropriate titles or working in a role as 'cheap labour'. Being cheap labour does matter. Feeding one's family, going on holidays or saving for the future is difficult on a low wage. In 2008 when the interviews were carried out, the growing threat of recession held a special fear for workers on low pay. Similarly, the UK government's changes to taxation levels for lower-wage earners felt like a direct hit on them and their families. Such fears and frustrations were expressed in bald terms. For example, one worker discussed 'having to buy cheaper bread'. Some wondered if they could afford to continue in their role.

However, grading and role definition was not simply a matter of salary. It too was related to the process of invisibilisation. One worker astutely pointed out that, when workers fill in gaps for others, an accurate picture of service needs and resources are concealed. Workers are then not recruited for those positions. For others it was about identity and place in the team. Titles mark skills, expertise and authority and, without these, what the worker brings and offers can be lost:

I have these skills and I come here and I'm deskilled, and I'm beginning to feel that most of the skills that I have are not being utilised and I'm beginning to lose those skills, and because I have that fear of losing those skills I'm always going on. I think I find myself going on about wanting to do this and this, because I have that expertise, and sometimes I just think – am I in the right place?

(PB)

Mechanisms rendering workers invisible varied. For services where need outstripped resourcing, supervision and staff appraisal easily slipped off the schedule.

Workers understood why this happened and often assumed a no-blame attitude to overworked senior colleagues. Even so, they remained aware that the lack of formal appraisal detached them from the organisational mechanisms that could recognise and reward skill:

> No they do, they do know how we work, they do know that we put a lot of effort into it, and they give us the praise for it, they just don't give us the appraisal! If I had had an appraisal done a couple of years ago, I wouldn't be still on a band two, do you know what I mean? It would have been sorted by now.
>
> (PA)

One aspect of being made invisible relates to the ever-changing nature of HSC service. Services shift, policies change and workers can lose responsibilities and the tasks they once had. For example, one worker who had lost responsibility for delivering medication 'felt like that I had buttered myself a slice of bread, and somebody snatched it out of my hand' (PA). A hard-earned responsibility, one that reflected hard-won skills and experience, was just taken away:

> Well, here I was doing a responsible job and doing a very good job at the same time. They came along and they changed the rules. We weren't allowed to be handling medication . . . I felt so bad about it that I actually ended up in tears over it because I thought, 'What is going on here? Is this what it's come to?' I've worked hard all my life and I have always put 100 per cent into it, do you know what I mean, and I've always got results.
>
> (PA)

Similarly, another worker notes that a sudden change in the system redefining roles, associated grades and salary had duties taken away in a single swoop:

> Yeah, they've taken my skills, they've taken my, some of my skills. And I do not get the same respect within the team. The team members have changed and the newer people come in, they see me as my role as support worker and they don't know, or they don't care, about what's gone on in the past, what role I've had. . . . Why won't they do that? Why won't they listen to me? And that was the frustrating thing.
>
> (PB)

## Agency building through learning

The interviews suggested that experiences of both visibility and invisibility may occur in the same workplace or to the same worker. Support workers were not powerless. They exercised agency in resisting invisibilisation or promoting their visibility. Indeed, such acts expanded their capacity to act and, as such, were often associated with learning activity itself.

Most typically, workers engaged others to enhance their agency. They built their understandings of the situation and bolstered their support through discussions with colleagues. It was important to gather alternative perspectives and realise 'it's not just me' (PJ). Some participants confronted discounting colleagues face-on or had quiet conversations with managers to explore how to deal with the situation or even restructure shift rotas.

For others, study was a way of minimising the possibility of invisibilisation. Workers would find affirmation through study. For example, one worker found her 'social care' orientation at odds with the medical approach of her team. However, through her study, she found others (academics and fellow students) who not only shared her values but also her understandings of clients and approaches. Such solidarity provided reassurance and validated her approach, strengthening her capacity to represent her perspective to the team. In addition, her study not only made her ambition to enter a professional role visible but it also marked her commitment. Recognising this commitment, her manager begun to facilitate access to training and professional meetings that extended her role into the professional domain associated with studies.

In addition, study was not only developmental but the formal qualification marks expertise already possessed. For example, one worker explained that she was being encouraged to enrol in nursing training as she was doing much of the work of a trained nurse:

> He also feels that the amount of work or things that they expect me to do here, they put upon me, um, and if I'm doing that already or supporting his qualified staff then why the hell don't I go and get recognised for it?
>
> (PI)

Similarly, workers recognised that having a professional qualification provided a licence to speak on things that they knew about client needs:

> I've had colleagues say 'Oh, you can be listened to'; I don't believe that. If I'm qualified and I have my degree and I have my qualification, that is where that I feel that I have the authority to make a difference. I'd have authority to fight this person's corner because I would have all the skills and the values that I'm supposed to meet in terms of . . . I'm supposed to use in terms of meeting that client's needs.
>
> (PC)

However, the emphasis above was placed on what were seen as professional qualifications. Not all qualifications carried the same weight. Vocational qualifications themselves were devalued. For example, National Vocational Qualifications credentialise the skills workers have in their specific area of work. Workers claimed that these did not carry the same status: 'I don't think they really see it as a qualification' (PZ).

So in the quest for authority, better money or more opportunities, some workers held aspirations to study for professional qualifications. However, their role presented a double cul de sac. The role could lack opportunities to progress into more senior positions and their salaries were such that many could not afford to fund study themselves. They needed workplace support for further training but may lack the occupational status necessary to attract that support. In other words, their aspirations and capabilities need to be recognised in order to win the support for study they need. When this support is not available, workers may read this as a statement from management about a lack of skills and potential in itself. The effect was demoralising – leaving workers feeling that their ambitions had no place in this workplace and that they had little choice but to reach for the jobs pages.

## Politics of paraprofessional practice and development

The study of support workers' learning showed that this group is driven by, draws from and works through personal qualities, ambitions and interests. These personal qualities are tools that must be engaged with commitment and genuine concern in order to do the relationship-based work of caring and person-centred development work – what Wosket (1999) refers to as the 'therapeutic use of self'. Indeed, one of the learning tasks for the worker is to develop a distinctive or personal style in the work. One's personhood must be engaged in care work and is bound up with a strong sense of meaning and identity as a practitioner in a particular workplace.

The workplace structures the worker's enactment of their vocation for practice. They are both shaped by, and shape, their workplace and, as such, their scope for action lies in the interpenetration of social structure and agency. Within this relationship, affordances for action may be predicated on one's visibility or invisibility. To be visible is to have expanded opportunities for action and, as such, is closely related to opportunities for learning and the pursuit of self (see Billett 2008). Moreover, finding one's place in the battleground of the HSC team, where members are in competition with each other as they jostle for recognition and attempt to carve out role boundaries (Finlay 2000), relies on the recognition that accumulated experience and skill counts for something. The worker is valued by the workplace and has status as someone useful (Sennett 2006).

When one is rendered invisible, the value of experience, development and aspirations are negated. This deprives workers of the possibility that their knowledge and experience have the same value as that possessed by other workers. This 'invisibilisation' confronts and corrodes workers' occupational identities, sense of self as a skilled worker and accumulation of experience. Invisibilisation is bound up in the construction of 'otherness' (Johnson *et al.* 2004). Certainly, it challenges the value of training and experience – what does accumulated knowledge, skill and experience built through years of experience, team discussion of service users and problems, confrontation of challenges and training count for if it no longer has a place in the workforce? Such experiences could leave workers feeling de-skilled and having low status.

When training for support workers is such a priority, such forces can undermine policy and service goals in the United Kingdom. Workers can therefore operate in a space of ambivalence, an unconstructive misalignment between what their role needs to be and how it is configured in their organisation. Feelings of frustration, anger and sadness result when practice requires the worker's heart, life experience and commitment but, at the same time, such 'resources' are treated casually by others in the workplace. Moreover, workers may exert self-constraint as they are reluctant to learn more in order to contribute beyond their place.

Broad sweeps of policy change knock cherished aspects of personal capabilities and responsibilities off the map while the turnover of staff in an under-resourced service can mean that your colleagues no longer know who you are. Systemic 'structural invisibilisation' is intertwined with the agency of those in the team. Personality clashes or the lack of acknowledgement of 'frontline authority' are bound up with the use of power for veto or the supremacy of academic professional knowledge.

The effects of these forces are not uniform, predetermined or non-negotiable but present as a swirl of ambivalences in that workplaces can both render visible and invisible. While the social agency of the workplace exerts a powerful effect, such forces are not passively accepted by the workers themselves but challenged. Indeed, it is the way in which workers exercise agency in order to negotiate the tension between visibility and invisibility that demands highlighting. What Sennett (1998) refers to as 'the politics of we' emerge in the small acts described by the participants. To assert their place in the team and resist invisibilisation, workers engaged their colleagues and lobbied their managers to seek reassurance, gain perspective, talk problems through and find ways forward in relation to these difficulties. These involve marshalling the power arising from an increased understanding and an expanded scope for action.

While invisibilisation appeared to have a relationship with learning, it appeared to be a paradoxical one. Certainly, it appears that, by negating the value of experience, invisibilisation has the potential to undermine the motivation to develop further. Certainly, the worker who expressed reluctance to study literature that pushed her 'beyond her place' is one such example, as is the worker who found herself wondering about the value of her years of training and development.

Yet at the same time, invisibilisation does not have uniform effects on the value of study and training. Some workers presented study as a means to overcome invisibilisation. Study or qualification is not simply a way of building job security but marks out expertise and skill. In addition, by making ambition visible through study, it can facilitate access to different learning experiences. Education plays another role. These workers, like those elsewhere at a similar level (see Henriksson's chapter), use education as a means to form a professional identity. It creates another form of 'we-ness' as students join a 'discourse community' (see

Northedge 2003) of like-minded thinkers sharing values, conceptual tools and approaches to practice. Thus study itself is an act that can marshal power and authority.

The tensions of visibility and invisibility should not be viewed in simple black and white terms. To pick up from Engeström's (2004) framing of contradictions established at the beginning of this chapter, such situations are disturbing but they represent forces that have the potential to catalyse system-wide change. In his use of Bateson's (1972) characterisation of level-three learning, he argues that contexts presenting contradictory demands can lead individuals and groups to question and deviate from established norms as well as construct alternative ways of working. I argue that such contradictions not only reflect the changes in how this group are seen but are also forces for further change such as increased learning opportunities. Indeed, Thornley's (2000) reference to the 'Quiet Revolution' in the role of the non-registered health care assistant and nursing auxiliary suggests that much has changed already but advocates the need for a fundamental reappraisal of the real skills and experience of this group, and of their potential.

## References

Appleby, J. and Coote, A. (2002) *Five Year Health Check: A Review of Government Health Policy 1997–2002*, London: King's Fund.

Ashby, M., Bowman, S., Bray, K., Campbell, J., Campbell, K., Leaver, G., Pilcher, T., Pratt, P., Plowright, C. and Stewart, L. (2003) 'Position statement on the role of health care assistants who are involved in direct patient care activities within critical care areas', *Nursing in Critical Care*, 8: 3–12.

Atwal, A., Tattersall, K., Caldwell, K. and Craik, C. (2006) 'Multidisciplinary perceptions of the role of nurses and healthcare assistants in rehabilitation of older adults in acute health care', *Journal of Clinical Nursing*, 15(1): 1418–1425.

Baldwin, J., Roberts, J. D., Fitzpatrick, J. I., While, A. and Cowan, D. T. (2003) 'The role of the support worker in nursing homes: A consideration of key issues', *Journal of Nursing Management*, 11: 410–420.

Bateson, G. (1972) *Steps to an Ecology of Mind*, New York: Ballantine Books.

Billett, S. (2001) 'Learning throughout working life: Activities and interdependencies', *Studies in Continuing Education*, 23(1): 19–35.

Billett, S. (2004) 'Co-participation at work: learning through work and throughout working lives', *Studies in the Education of Adults*, 36(2): 190–205.

Billett, S. (2008) 'Learning throughout working life: A relational interdependence between personal and social agency', *British Journal of Educational Studies*, 56(1): 39–58.

Bolton, S. (2004) 'A simple matter of control? NHS hospital nurses and new management', *Journal of Management Studies*, 41(2): 317–333.

Cameron, C. and Boddy, J. (2006) 'Knowledge and education for care workers: What do they need to know?' In J. Boddy, C. Cameron and P. Moss (eds) *Care Work: Present and Future*, London: Routledge, 50–70.

Cameron, C. and Moss, P. (2007) *Care Work in Europe: Current Understandings and Future Directions*, London: Routledge.

Coffey, A. (2004) 'Perceptions of training for care attendants employed in the care of older people', *Journal of Nursing Management*, 12: 322–328.

Dawson, S., Slote Morris, Z., Erickson, W., Lister, G., Altringer, B., Garside, P. and Craig, M. (2007) *Engaging with Care: A Vision for the Health and Care Workforce of England*, London: The Nuffield Trust.

DH. Department of Health (2001) *A Health Service for All Talents: Developing the NHS Workforce.* Available at: http://www.dh.gov.uk/en/Publications andstatistics/Publications/PublicationsPolicyAndGuidance/DH_4003182?IdcSer vice=GET_ FILE&dID=15951&Rendition=Web (accessed 6 November 2008).

DH. Department of Health (2006) *The Regulation of the Non-Medical Healthcare Professions: A Review by the Department of Health*, Leeds: Department of Health.

Department of Health, Social Services and Public Safety (2008) *Priorities for Action.* Available at: http://www.dhsspsni.gov.uk/pfa0809.pdf (accessed 10 November 2008).

Edwards, M. (1997) 'The health care assistant: Usurper of nursing?', *British Journal of Community Nursing*, 2(10): 490–494.

Ellis, B. and Connell, N. A. D. (2001) 'Factors determining the current use of physiotherapy assistants: Views on their future role in the south and west UK region', *Physiotherapy*, 87(2): 73–82.

Engeström, Y. (2004) 'The new generation of expertise: Seven theses', in H. Rainbird, A. Fuller and A. Munro (eds) *Workplace Learning in Context*, London: Routledge, 145–165.

Finlay, L. (2000) 'The OT role: Meanings and motives in an uncertain world', *British Journal of Therapy and Rehabilitation*, 7(3): 124–128.

Fleming, G. and Taylor, B. (2007) 'Battle on the home care front: Perceptions of home care workers of factors influencing staff retention in Northern Ireland', *Health and Social Care in the Community*, 15(1): 67–76.

Forrester-Jones, R. and Hatzidimitriadou, E. (2006) 'Learning in the real world? Exploring widening participation student views concerning the "fit" between knowledge learnt and work practices', *Assessment & Evaluation in Higher Education*, 31(6): 611–624.

General Social Care Council (2007) *The Social Care Register Explained.* Available at: http://www.gscc.org.uk/The+Social+Care+Register/The+Social+Care+Register+ explained (accessed 20 April 2007).

Hancock, H., Campbell, S., Ramprogus, V. and Kilgour, J. (2005) 'Role development in health care assistants: The impact of education on practice', *Journal of Evaluation in Clinical Practice*, 11: 489–498.

Hochschild, A. (1983) *The Managed Heart: The Commercialization of Feeling*, Berkeley: University of California Press.

Jacobs, K. (2004) 'Accountability and clinical governance in nursing', in S. Tilley and R. Watson (eds) *Accountability in Nursing and Midwifery*, Oxford: Blackwell Science, 21–37.

Johnson, J., Botorff, J. and Browne, A. (2004) 'Othering and being othered in the context of health care services', *Health Communication*, 16(2): 253–271.

Keeney, S., Hasson, F. and McKenna, H. (2005) 'Health care assistants: The views of managers of health care agencies on training and employment', *Journal of Nursing Management*, 13(1): 83–92.

Kennedy, P. and Kennedy, C. (2007) 'Control and resistance at the ward-face: Contesting the nursing labour process', in G. Mooney and A. Law (eds) *New Labour/Hard Labour? Restructuring and Resistance Inside the Welfare Industry*, Bristol: Policy Press, 93–119.

Knight, C., Larner, S. and Waters, K. (2004) 'Evaluation of the role of the rehabilitation assistant', *International Journal of Therapy & Rehabilitation*, 11(7): 311–317.

Law, A. and Mooney, G. (2007) 'A "Third Way"? Industrial relations under New Labour', in G. Mooney and A. Law (eds) *New Labour/Hard Labour? Restructuring and Resistance Inside the Welfare Industry*, Bristol: Policy Press, 53–74.

Mackey, H. (2004) 'An extended role for support workers: The views of occupational therapists', *International Journal of Therapy & Rehabilitation*, 11(6): 259–266.

McBride, A., Mustchin, S., Hyde, P., Antonacopoulou, E., Cox, A. and Walshe, K. (2004) *Mapping the Progress of Skills Escalator Activity: Early Results from a Survey of Learning Account and NVQ Managers in Strategic Health Authorities*, Manchester: Manchester School of Management.

Miers, M., Coles, J., Girot, E. and Wilkinson, G. (2005) 'Empowering learners: An exploration of mediating learning for care workers', *Learning in Health and Social Care*, 4(4): 180–191.

Mooney, G. and Law, A. (2007) 'New Labour, "modernisation" and welfare worker resistance', in G. Mooney and A. Law (eds) *New Labour/Hard Labour? Restructuring and Resistance Inside the Welfare Industry*, Bristol: Policy Press, 1–22.

Moss, P., Boddy, J. and Cameron, C. (2006) 'Care work, present and future: Introduction' in J. Boddy, C. Cameron and P. Moss (eds) *Care Work, Present and Future*, London: Routledge, 3–17.

Munro, A., Holly, L. and Rainbird, H. (2000) '"My ladies aren't interested in learning": Managers, supervisors and the social context of learning', *International Review of Education*, 46(6): 515–528.

Nicholson, T. (1996) 'Are we giving away nursing?', *Accident and Emergency Nursing*, 4(4): 205–207.

Northedge, A. (2003) 'Rethinking teaching in the context of diversity', *Teaching in Higher Education*, 8(1): 17–32.

Rainbird, H., Munro, A., Holly, L. and Leisten, R. (1999) *The Future of Work in the Public Sector: Learning and Workplace Inequality*, Centre for Research in Employment, Work and Training, Northampton: University College Northampton.

Rolfe, G., Jackson, N., Gardner, L., Jasper, M. and Gale, A. (1999) 'Developing the role of the generic healthcare support worker: Phase 1 of an action research study', *International Journal of Nursing Studies*, 36(4): 323–334.

Sennett, R. (1998) *The Corrosion of Character: The Personal Consequences of Work in the New Capitalism*, London: Norton.

Sennett, R. (2006) *The Culture of the New Capitalism*, New Haven: Yale University Press.

Spilsbury, K. and Meyer, J. (2004) 'Use, misuse and non-use of health care assistants: Understanding the work of health care assistants in a hospital setting', *Journal of Nursing Management*, 12: 411–418.

Stokes, J. and Warden, A. (2004) 'The changing role of the healthcare assistant', *Nursing Standard*, 18(5): 33–37.

Sutton, J., Valentine, J. and Rayment, K. (2004) 'Staff views on the extended role of health care assistants in the critical care unit', *Intensive and Critical Care Nursing*, 20(5): 249–256.

Thornley, C. (2000) 'A question of competence? Re-evaluating the roles of the nursing auxiliary and health care assistant in the NHS', *Journal of Clinical Nursing*, 9: 451–458.

Wosket, V. (1999) *The Therapeutic Use of Self: Counselling Practice, Research and Supervision*, London: Routledge.

# Chapter 8

# Finnish redefinitions of the 'social' in social work

## An eroding ethical discourse?

*Päivi Niiranen-Linkama*

In this chapter I look at the construction of professional expertise of social work in Finland in the context of global and local changes at many levels of society, education and work. I examine the meanings, definitions and redefinitions of the 'social' in social work education in upper secondary vocational education and training, referred to here as the polytechnics. The key idea here is to presuppose the 'social' as a changing concept in society. The underlying hypothesis is that of Wagner's (2001): when a society changes then the concept of 'social' will also change. My interest principally focuses on how the older welfare state discourse of the 'social' is being disturbed and how a new discourse is being created within the educational and occupational orders of social work in the polytechnics. As Henriksson (2008) argues, globalisation and welfare state change reconfigure welfare service occupations and education, thus challenging professional identities and belongings. I take a closer look at how the Finnish vocational teachers, professionals and students of social work define the 'social' in their work and how the variety of these meanings are connected to the changes in welfare service institutions and the practices of social work.

As a background for my theme I briefly portray the development of social work education in Finland. This point of view interlinks my research to the writings of the international research network Vocational Education and Training (VET). As discussed in this network, the economisation of education means that in vocational education it is necessary to effectively produce key qualifications: social competences and expertise (Lindgren and Heikkinen 2004). But paradoxically, can this promotion of social competences in fact mean the erosion of the meanings of the 'social' as we traditionally understand it in social work? Modern work organisations and political agendas often view the social competences only as a means of producing social capital and economic growth. The social dimension or 'sociability' in the life politics of individuals can function in the same way; people engage in their individual well-being. I argue here that in a contemporary welfare state context, the 'social' evolves as a discourse of efficient modern education and knowledge production, while the deeper meaning of the 'social' – for example those meanings that associate the concept with identity and ethical values – disappears.

I am interested in the construction of hegemonic discourses and legitimisation of the social dimension when talking about expertise in social work. The identification of hegemonic discourses in interviews is one point of analysis of how professionals use power in their talk and how they (or somebody else) try to modify their professionalism in the changing situations in society (see Foucault 1978/2000). An additional question that arises from this view is whether it is possible that the 'social' has different meanings in different occupational contexts, in different generations and in different times? My interest in hegemonic discourses thus involves looking at who is the one speaking about social, whose voice is heard, and in which position is one speaking?

## Social work education in Finland

While the current structure of education in social work was formulated in the 1990s, social welfare and social work education has a long history in Finland. Social work started as an element within deaconess training (1867) and continued under such occupational degrees as a 'social educator' (1918) and a 'child protect worker' (1928). The training for social welfare workers began in the university college in 1942 during the Second World War. At the university level, social work education started in 1970, when the first associate professorship was established in social welfare. Since 2001 social work has become a major subject in six Finnish universities (Opetusministeriö 2007).

An education reform of the 1980s was a landmark for the present changes in vocational education and created the basis of a new type of generic qualification called practical nurse, a basic degree in social and health care. In 1993, practical nurse education was founded by integrating seven occupational degrees in health care and three in social care (see Henriksson, this volume). This three-year curriculum comprises 120 credit units which include joint studies (2/3) and an option for a specific professional area (1/3), for instance for child care and elderly care (Vocational Education and Training Act 630/1998). This reform was implemented according to the policy principles and ideals of a generic competence and the labour market needs of flexibility (Vuorensyrjä et al. 2006: 286–287).

Since the 1990s, vocational education and training in Finland has comprised two hierarchical levels. The upper-secondary level includes basic-level degrees such as a practical nurse. In the polytechnics, it is possible to complete a Bachelor-level degree in social work and nursing. A degree taken at this level is a higher education qualification and therefore the polytechnics are often called universities of applied sciences (see Filander, this volume). In accordance with the policy principles, implemented since the 1990s, opportunities for step-by-step education have been created. This means, for instance, that students are able to move from one education level to another, and they move from the upper-secondary level to the polytechnics and further, from the polytechnics to the universities. A variety of options are also available for social work professionals: they can also enter the university and earn a Master's degree in social work. In the vocational education track there are two educational pathways. The recruits can start with the practical nurse degree and then move upwards and continue their studies and become qualified as a Bachelor in social work. The recruits may also enter the polytechnic directly.

At the polytechnics, the Bachelor of Social Services degree started experimentally in 1992 and has been regularised since 1995. At present there are 22 institutions offering social work qualifications at the polytechnics (Opetusministeriö 2007: 21). Social work education consists of 210 credits and usually takes three and a half years to complete. The main areas of specialisation are social work and social pedagogy. However, the spectrum of studies is often wider, comprising, for instance, rehabilitation and early childhood education. There are also optional studies to be chosen in the final stage of education. In addition to the Bachelor's degree, a two-year Master's degree (300 credits) is available at the polytechnics, which necessitates a three-year work experience. These study programmes in the polytechnics are, however, more work- and labour market-oriented than the research-oriented ones at the universities. As planned, a Master's degree should also open up the pathway to doctoral studies. The tensions related to the implementation of the dual model in social work education also mean that the two higher education tracks, the universities and the polytechnics, also offer different ranks of qualifications and hierarchical positions in working life, thus creating professional disputes on social work knowledge and expertise (see Julkunen 2004; Opetusministeriö 2007: 27–28).

My interest in this theme of social work expertise is linked to the changes in education policy but also stems from my personal history in social work. I have experienced the transformations of the education system outlined above as a social work professional, a vocational teacher and a PhD researcher. The aim of social work education is primarily to promote social security at the societal level and participation and well-being of individuals, families and communities. But my lived experiences and 'intuitive knowledge' (Niiranen-Linkama 2005: 70) of the existence of the hegemonic 'social' have not always covered these aspects. Something important to me has often been missing in the hegemonic discourses on the social dimension in social work. This disturbance allured and forced me to study the various meanings of the social, often taken for granted in professional education and work practices.

The contested profile of social work education and the nature of future competences and expertise are the core challenges of education policy and expertise. From the point of view of the contemporary Finnish social work education, one key question is how to lower the gaps between different educational levels, especially between the universities and the polytechnics. The Finnish dual model in higher education thus comprises a great deal of tension. There is a vivid discussion going on about how to properly fit together and organise vocational education according to the needs of the citizens, educational aims and the needs of research and the labour market (see Opetusministeriö 2007).

The restructuring of the public sector has an impact on education. The labour market needs workers with flexible qualifications and low salary. In the history of social work education there has been some discussion about its professional and societal tasks and the meanings of the social dimension in society. This discussion has usually addressed education and educational systems (Vuorensyrjä et al. 2006). Only a few studies have focused on the social organisation of professional work and the construction of welfare and social citizenship (see Satka 1995).

## The contested meanings of the 'social' in social work

My intention here is to elaborate how the basic assumptions of the 'social' have been changing during my career. Client work in different surroundings has been and is the heart of social work and most of the students start working in this field after graduation. Nowadays students also move on to other types of qualifications, for instance to work as various types of experts, entrepreneurs and developers of organisations and communities. Although the theory base of social work at the polytechnics is multidisciplinary, there is also a great deal of knowledge which is deeply rooted in social work practice and social work research.

The core theme I have chosen here derives from my doctoral dissertation on social work expertise (see Niiranen-Linkama 2005) where I examined the concept of the social from two different perspectives. First, I looked at the social dimension as an element of negotiation in changing social work expertise in the context of the restructuring of the public sector and the reconfiguration of welfare service occupations. As Julkunen (2001) states, this tradition includes the ideas of social cohesion, universal social rights and equality. The concept of the social implies these perspectives and meanings which are also strongly embedded in the professional ethos and practices of welfare service occupations such as social work. But the discontinuity of this tradition is also obvious. In a time of neoliberalism and 'soft capitalism', this Finnish tradition of 'a good life for everyone' has yet to be broken. Restructuring of service organisations in accordance with the measures of New Public Management such as cost-efficiency, quality assessment and the market ethos have challenged the traditional meanings of the 'social'. The heart of social work practice and expertise is under new interpretations and struggles for meaning. My aim here is therefore to focus on the discontinuities and continuities of the discourses on the social dimension in social work. At the same time I am also reflecting on and promoting professional practice of public sector social work which is more aware of its ethical legacy, 'the incomparable value of human beings' (Niiranen-Linkama 2005: 71).

Second, my interest focuses on individual social work actors. When considering the concept of the 'social' in the context of a personal account, I reflect upon the 'social' through the lens of individual values and professional identity. Hall (1999) writes about 'broken identities' and divides the concepts of identity into three categories: Cartesian, sociological and post-modern identity. Cartesian identity is based on individual ethos and subjectivity which is being broken down. The same is also happening to the sociological identity – which was based on the dialogue between society and culture. The post-modern world has no permanent structural principles, so maybe there is no place for a stable identity, he continues. Identity in this sense thus refers to the changing actor positions and indistinct boundaries. My questions here include: What do 'broken identities' mean when thinking about professional practice and identity in social work in the era of New Public Management for the individual actors? What kinds of discourses of the social are created and how do they construct discontinuities of professional identities? As Heikkinen and Henriksson (2001) argue, professional identity could be understood as a sense of ethical awareness and respect of self and others. It is about belonging to the societal and cultural community and responding to other people's needs. How do these meanings of professional identity and dignity fit with the new educational and occupational orders of New Public Management, marketisation and 'soft capitalism'?

## Research material and methodology

The main research material, collected between 1998 and 2001, consists of interviews with five polytechnic teachers (born in the 1940s, 1950s and 1960s), five students (born in the 1960s and 1970s) and five employees (born in the 1950s, 1960s and 1970s). All the interviewees (N = 15) were women of different ages, educational backgrounds and work experience. The teachers participating in the study had a broad background in social and behavioural sciences or a cross-disciplinary background. Students had either recently started their education or were finishing their degrees. The employees interviewed worked in various types of positions in social care, child care and in arts and crafts-related work.

The definitions of the 'social' are here highlighted from three perspectives: the subjective, practical and epistemic positions. Subjective positions refer to the individual understandings of professional identity, beliefs and values. The practical position in turn refers to the contested meanings of professional practices and associated relationships. Finally, the epistemic position highlights the knowledge aspects of the social in social work.

The interviews were analysed using critical discourse analysis. Fairclough (1992) uses the concept of discourse when speaking about language as social practice. There are three basic elements in discourses. First, discourses construct our social identity or subjectivity or types of self, the researcher included. Second, discourses construct our social relationships. Third, our knowledge and beliefs are constructed through discourses. In accordance with this idea, the research material is divided into three positions that are constructed from these three elements. The subject position is constructed from the talk of the individual interviewed and her personal and professional identity and values.

In my analysis I look at discourses on three different levels: as a text (speech, talk), as a discursive practice (the mode of speaking and the identifying of different positions) and as a socio-cultural practice (situational, institutional and societal level – see Fairclough 1992). This categorisation makes it possible to find discourses of socio-cultural and discursive practices and to discover the connections between these practices. My intention here is to analyse the interview data either on one level or on all the levels at the same time.

## The empirical case

### The transformation of social values

In the interviews with the teachers the roots of the 'collective social' were identified. In the teachers' talk the study identified the 'roots' of social citizenship and the features of the normative tradition of the welfare state. There was a concern for maintaining the 'social' as a core value of welfare services and society – teachers, students and employees shared the same concern. In many studies a teacher is seen as an ideal citizen (Syrjäläinen 1995; Värri 2002). The position of teachers as well as employees and students between traditional 'super-values' and neoliberal values is demanding and full of tension. This ambiguous position can lead to uncertainty about one's competence and identity.

> Example 1: 'You know love for your fellow man isn't quite enough, nor is the need to help other people . . . that is quite risky somehow . . . and it is reflected in a kind of respect in society . . . what is seen as important in this society of ours . . . is it economic growth and success in that field or is it people and above all those not-so-fortunate people? Also, priorities are evident when dealing with money so that the handicapped and those suffering from mental disorders get the least amount of the common resources, and is it possible to think about a kind of productive view in society, meaning who to invest money in and who not? . . . For example, for me one big issue is the EU, or this unification, meaning what comes out of it. Also how stable is the Finnish welfare state and how long society will give money to these services, or shall we have some other model in the future?
>
> (Teacher 2, work experience in the social care field one year, teaching nine years)
>
> Example 2: '. . . And second, of course, there is the lack of appreciation for the whole field, when it cannot be carried out by the market forces, or the market forces cannot take the social care field forward, but instead it is basic work done for the well-being of mankind. It is important, but not possible, to count in terms of money.'
>
> (Teacher 1, work experience in the social care field five years, teaching 13 years)
>
> Example 3: 'Also, the students we are educating now will be operating in a different society, as far as a discussion of values is concerned, than we are now . . . How can I even teach them or how shall I teach them to be strong enough so they can participate in the discussion of values? And of course, on

the other hand, the social care field remains on the whole a problematic area, and is so strongly based on discussion about values.'

(Teacher 3, work experience in the social care field
13 years, teaching 11 years)

In the above examples the teachers' positions can be interpreted as operating strongly on the subjective level, but also on the work practice level. The teachers talk about the discontinuity of the value of the 'social' in society in relation to their work. In the study, these discourses were labelled as discourses of referential values because teachers and employees often only indirectly referred to 'those values'. They never talked about the values directly or analytically. Referring to Julkunen (2004) I may interpret that as indicating a symptom of discontinuity in the traditional value base of welfare service occupations. In the examples above the social contra-economic issues and the ethos of the market can clearly be seen. These results are easily connected to the ideas of Sennett (1998) and they indicate that the old order of the welfare state has broken down and the new order of economic reasoning is evolving.

### Marginalising of professional identity

In the interview data there seemed to be shared, universal meanings of the 'social' among the teachers and the employees, but more individually oriented values for the social among the students. Student discourses on the 'social' were more personal and, surprisingly, students reflected upon their values in the context of their own life-politics. The emerging discourse on expertise and education in social work, especially among younger professionals, seemed to have a very individual orientation.

In the next example the very ideal and universal human values of the social dimension in social work were mentioned as the basis of professional practice – charity and the value of the human being.

Example 4: 'Yes, personally I feel at least that the kind of people who apply for this work, and I speak only of myself, should have certain types of values, or their set of values is of a certain kind, just human values and charity and helping your neighbours and that kind of thing . . . it really seems that these belong together . . . That you appreciate somebody irrespective of whether they are handicapped or children, or alcoholics or whatever . . . That you appreciate a human being as such, and not according to their deeds or qualities, but in the way that a human being is always valuable, whatever he or she is like.'

(Student 8, young student, work experience
in the social care field one year)

In the following example the student talked about the classic virtues of social work such as equality and social justice. In addition to this shared professional ethos, she argued that her own values and intentions are also important in work.

Example 5: 'What do I find important in social work? Well, at least I think I should be fair and just and I should treat everybody in the same way. You also need to work with yourself, to think about your own values and aims at work, and you shouldn't let your own opinions, whatever prejudices you have about something, for instance if you take gypsies as an example, even if you had bad experiences with them, you wouldn't let that influence your work. You know, some kind of justice, at least. How shall I succeed . . . ?'

(Student 7, young student, no work experience in the social care field)

Students reflect upon the values related to the 'social' on a subjective level and their talk sounds quite idealistic, as is often the case with young professionals entering the field of welfare service work. In this study, the students also seemed to value their work and their talk also reflected their strong professional identities. In another study, the opposite emerged. An assessment of social work education in Finland in 2004 found that students did not have very strong professional identities (Murto *et al.* 2004: 53). Instead, they had many difficulties in getting their education and qualifications accepted in the labour market.

On a subjective level there was another kind of talk on social work as a professional practice identified in terms of burnout, tiredness and a sense of marginalisation. Teachers were more likely to touch upon these topics than the other groups interviewed. This may reflect the different positions of the interviewees. The teachers shared a more realistic experience of working life than the students and so their talk better reflected the escalating demands of working life and the labour market. These tensions are illustrated in the following example:

Example 6: 'Yes, a clear threat is the so-called economic cutbacks, so that there are less resources than before to do this job, meaning that there is no money, no staff and, still, the workload is growing all the time. You know you have to work more than before with fewer resources . . . what will happen to the workers then? . . . For me a big threat at the moment seems to be burnout and tiredness at work and therefore it is quite an ethical problem, too . . . through which you can also become aware of the responsibility for the customers and where your own resources face their limits . . . Or the threat of whether there will be employees who will actually work with people in social care in the future . . . And it is quite problematic for people to stick to this work, due to the pressures of the work, which is certainly so hard that people are constantly thinking about how they can escape from this situation.'

(Teacher 2)

The discursive practice illustrated above can be interpreted as a style of marginalised talk. It reflects the changing role of the public sector employment and welfare services. There are not enough personnel resources and money to maintain all the welfare services and pay salaries to the skilled workers. This leads to fatigue and frustration with their work. There is an evident link to Sennett (1998: 10) here – teachers experience a deep uncertainty of self and a strong sense of an increasing control of their work which they cannot either handle or disagree with. In this situation optional career plans for the future are made and skilled professionals begin to move to other kinds of jobs. The traditionally secure public sector industrial relations and employment safety are being disturbed.

### Struggles for occupational boundaries

How are the new discourses related to social work expertise and education? In my data, the modern expertise on an institutional level was constructed by underlining personal expertise and by drawing boundaries between related educational, occupational and professional fields. I interpret this partly as a discursive practice legitimating social work expertise. The following examples highlight the ongoing struggles for professional expertise in working life. They show how the teachers and employees negotiate the role of social work in society and how they talk about the changing division of labour associated with the related fields.

> Example 7: 'What takes a huge amount of resources in the social care field is the fight for your own value and the right to have your own personal area . . . so that you can somehow keep the health care field behind the fence so that it doesn't use your own resources . . . And it is a terrible pity! But somehow I see that you have to maintain it . . . You know, it is a question of change and people's right for participation and social sharing and this is extremely important for me. I find it very problematic and I also think it is a pity, because if there was a kind of tolerant, mutual respect instead of this eternal fight, an awful lot of resources would be available for a lot of things.'
>
> (Teacher 3)

> Example 8: 'It is really difficult to say when private services begin to increase, perhaps what I'm worried about is that there will be lots and lots of private services in the social care field . . . but you should be able to offer the customer quality service. The customer should get what he or she is paying for. I'm worried about continuity, in the future; when these small firms are mushrooming so rapidly, will they really be capable of offering continuity to the customer?'
>
> (Employee 5, work experience in the social
> care field five years)

Also in this study, the young students had an experience of being 'nomads' in the labour market (Field 2001). Their position was paradoxical. On the one hand, they shared idealistic values of the social dimension in social work; on the other hand, their lived experiences in the labour market were quite hard.

> Example 9: 'You know the situation will certainly improve, of course now that we also have an occupational title so that other people know what we

really are. When it was suggested that we use the occupational label "sosionomi" [Bachelor of Social Sciences/P.N-L], we couldn't use it because it was already used as a title within the university. It seemed in a way that people think we were somehow treading on other people's toes. It has been said that we could work as kindergarten teachers, but soon kindergarten teachers boycotted that and we don't even get those jobs any longer. So it somehow feels that we are treading on quite a few toes here. You know our education is so broad that the supervisors for the handicapped also think that we are trying to replace them and they will be nothing. Also, problems arise because the kindergarten teachers think that we don't have a university education, but they had to go to university for many years, and then if we tread on their toes, then this system won't work.'

(Student 5, young student, no work
experience in the social care field)

The student in the example above felt that nobody in the labour market was interested in their competence and qualifications. The students have to seek their positions on their own and they were left alone to do so. Even though this is not always the case, this discussion highlights the reconfigurations of labour. As the young student observes, the old order of work has changed and there is uncertainty, confusion and struggle between work positions. Is that a feature of a new agenda in working life – professions and workers trying to keep their positions in the struggle against an unknown future?

### Organisational developers or client workers?

One interesting theme in the interviews was the changing occupational role of teachers and social work practitioners as developers in work organisations. Nearly every teacher and many employees made comments on this topic. Social work in organisational settings was even found to be the most important part of contemporary social work in practice, whereas some interviewees criticised this role transformation. Some found that there was not enough time for client work in service settings and student counselling in educational settings because organisational development work destroyed the 'real' work which the social work professional is educated for.

Example 10: 'In the future society they will also need ordinary workers, so-called basic workers. Will the qualification of a practical nurse be enough to satisfy that need? You know, I sometimes think that people graduating from the polytechnics will get jobs for which they are over-educated in some way. In fact, in working life we need the so-called developers of the work and we also need those who stay and work with the people and focus on that. We need some kind of . . . an intermediate level . . . professionals who could just concentrate on education and educational work and work with the people and somebody else could take care of development at the organisational level. Combining these efficiently at the polytechnic level and in the degree may distort what is most important in this job. Is it the people or the organisations?'

(Teacher 2)

Example 11: 'Okay, in quite the same way, which way do you start when looking at the polytechnics? I see the education as somehow supporting the work, so that the students should acquire skills that will help them to organise their work and develop it. That is to say, there should be some other level than just working with the customers. In other words, there should be levels to influence and to develop.'

(Teacher 3)

Many work tasks related to organisational development seemed to be imposed from the outside – from government, the markets and the funding sector. These tasks were not emerging from within the work itself. The meaning and value of education at the polytechnics also appears to be coming under question. It seems that this new educational track has not yet found its place in working life. The rhetorical question of one of the interviewed teachers epitomises the professional dilemma of the meaning of the social dimension in contemporary social work expertise the best: 'What is important in this work – is it the people or the organisations?'

### Participation as a new professional promise

At the institutional level, 'participation' was found to be a significant part of a discourse on the 'social' in social work. The call for participation can be interpreted as a kind of hegemonic discourse because all the interviewees, regardless of their position, talked about the aims and ideas of citizen participation and participatory work practices. Teachers and employees in particular shared the same discourse, but the students also seemed to reproduce similar issues in their talk. However, the students talked in a more concrete way – they talked about helping clients practically in their everyday settings.

Example 12: 'I cannot work by sitting at a desk and thinking about what is wrong with you, but instead we could do ordinary things that the family could also do without me. In that way you will get to the things that are worth dealing with and possible to tackle. Things that the parents are tired of and they have no means of handling. Then I can offer alternatives which we can think about later on.'

(Employee 1, work experience in the social care field 21 years)

Example 13: 'You know, in the new working methods one basic element is having people participate in a more active way. And quite honestly, enhancing people's chances to influence their situation, increasing their awareness by participating in their own lives . . . Morality and perhaps in some way creativity and awareness are emerging . . . There will be a need for organisational skills, ability in that area.'

(Teacher 2)

Example 14: 'There won't be a person sitting behind a desk who knows everything and who tells you how to organise your life – in a very caricaturish way – but it's floating in the air at the moment that we'll start leading that person's everyday life and we'll see what changes are going on.'

(Teacher 4, work experience in the social care field<br>five years, teaching three years)

The above examples talk about the broken structure of public social services and the emergence of a new ideal of democratic and equal culture in social work practices. The teachers seemed to use this rhetoric of participation and voiced their worries about how to be able to 'govern' it. Perhaps they adopted this position because of their work as implementers of policy. All the interviewees shared the importance of everyday life and its quality as the crucial value of the social dimension from the citizen perspective. But the quality of everyday life meant that people themselves had responsibility for their own lives and that they were able to make their own decisions. In the next examples the students emphasise the important meanings of local networks and regional settings for social work practice. These comments also capture the way the students see their role as equal in relation to their clients.

Example 15: 'I see very clearly that this work gives people possibilities to take responsibility and decide for themselves what is best for them. Nobody can say what's best for you, it's up to you.'

(Student 3, adult education, work experience<br>in the social care field 14 years)

Example 16: 'I suppose that in the future we will do more community work, work with communities, not with special age groups. Our work orientation should be wider and include the whole family and community and region. It is more natural in that way, not making a distinction between children or alcoholics.'

(Student 8)

## What the study shows

At the beginning of this chapter I asked what is disturbing in the discourse on the 'social' in social work. It seemed that the traditional values and meanings of the 'social' have become referential simultaneously, along with the institutional fragmentation of the welfare services. It also seemed that, when the normative tradition of the welfare state has weakened and been reconfigured, the hegemonic discourses of the 'social' evolve accordingly. In addition to this inquiry on the core meanings of the 'social', I asked how the new discourses around social work are created in educational and occupational fields. When looking at the construction of contemporary expertise as a discursive practice, the interviewees seemed to have difficulties in creating new positions in relation to the fields of education, occupations and the labour market. In a modern society one has to build a space and position of one's own using exclusive strategies by struggling and using symbolic and professional power in work organisations.

In the interviews it also seemed obvious that the processes of constructing the 'proper academic discipline' of social work and excluding other fields were occurring simultaneously. This meant that, for instance, it was necessary for the interviewees to make distinctions about whom to include as a 'real professional' and whom to exclude as a misfit who did not belong to 'us'. On the one hand, I see that this discourse reflects the ongoing institutional changes and the contested educational and occupational order that embrace a variety of different educational levels, pathways and ranks in social work. On the other hand, I found that young students coming from the polytechnics were placed in challenging positions due to the changes in work organisations – nobody wanted their competence or knowledge. The teachers in the polytechnics also faced new challenges. They were placed in the position of organisational developers, but at the same time they were trying to legitimise their position as social work experts in rapidly changing work environments, in different professional settings within a strained economy.

The discourse of participation in social work may be part of the new hegemonic occupational discourse. When the basis for the 'social' as a core value in everyday work becomes unclear, rhetorical talk about participation may indicate that there is somebody who still cares. And when the public social services are curtailed, the talk about participation at least sounds good irrespective of whether there is any practical basis for it or not. The discourse of participation can also create a collective base of professional identity in times of uncertainty. It may promote anchorage and belonging/togetherness, commitment and trust in the context of disturbed work. By identifying the discourse of referential values in this study, I see a sign of the disappearing value of the 'social', but it can also mean a kind of common and shared value which is evolving. You do not need to mention those self-evident values because people know them already.

The interview talk about participation could also be interpreted as a reflection of the ongoing societal changes, as a discourse about the increasing role of non-governmental service providers entering welfare service provision. The so-called third sector partners, such as non-profit voluntary organisations and organisations of citizens, are welcome partners in the new welfare-mix model introduced in the contemporary era of New Public Management. But in these data the rhetorical nature of talk and the issue of 'governing' participation say more about the ethos of participation than about the real organisational changes in social work service structures. What is somewhat surprising is that there was not much talk about the concrete issues of how to transform social work practices in the direction of supporting citizen participation in everyday life in communities. However, my study indicates the emergence of a discourse that suggests a kind of new moral order that includes a promise of participation in social work.

One question in the study was how hegemonic discourses develop and in which positions they are constructed and by whom. It seems that the teachers were most able and the students least able to produce a hegemonic discourse. The position of employees was described as 'those who make things happen'. There may be different strategies and orders to 'govern' the changing nature of expertise. Perhaps the younger generation of students differs from the older, the employees and the teachers, in their making of these orders. The students' positions were more flexible, not so much focused on working life positions. Possibly the young students more authentically reflect the situation in work because they do not have as many counter-arguments or resistance to change as the others. What is their future – and, by extension, ours – in working life? Should we become flexible nomads, to use Field's (2001) term? Will we have more individual and tailor-made services based on local communities? How are these communities and the well-being of citizens being strengthened? What is the role of public and private sector service providers in this process? Can they create strong networks and do they have sufficient resources for the benefit of all? What does this mean for the 'social' in social work and for the social work knowledge and education in the future?

At the beginning of this chapter I outlined Finnish social work education and the dual model of higher education in Finland. It seemed that Finnish social work education is undergoing a process of restructuring and change. It may no longer be possible to fit the traditional three-rank model of education into the contemporary working life and its needs for flexibility and employability. The Finnish educational and occupational orders in working life are influenced by large-scale changes, whose direction is quite unforeseeable. These processes will change the way individuals navigate their professional careers in the context of individual life-politics, but also how individuals create their professional identities and ethical meanings for themselves and their work in society.

## References

Fairclough, N. (1992) *Discourse and Social Change*, Cambridge: Polity Press.

Field, J. (2001) *Lifelong Learning and the New Educational Order*, Stoke on Trent: Trentham Books.

Foucault, M. (1978/2000) 'Governmentality', in J. D. Faubion (ed.) *Essential Works of Foucault 1954–1984*, vol. 3, London: Penguin Books, 201–222.

Hall, S. (1999) *Identiteetti*, Tampere: Vastapaino.

Heikkinen, A. and Henriksson, L. (2001) 'Ammatillisen kasvun ajat ja paikat', in A. H. Anttila and A. Suoranta (eds) *Ammattia oppimassa*, Väki Voimakas 14, Vantaa: Työväen historian ja perinteen tutkimuksen seura, 206–263.

Henriksson, L. (2008) 'Reconfiguring Finnish welfare service workforce: Inequalities and identity', *Equal Opportunities International*, 27(1): 49–63.

Julkunen, R. (2001) *Suunnanmuutos. 1990-luvun sosiaalipoliittinen reformi Suomessa*, Tampere: Vastapaino.

Julkunen, R. (2004) 'Hyvinvointipalvelujen uusi politiikka', in L. Henriksson and S. Wrede (eds) *Hyvinvointityön ammatit*, Helsinki: Gaudeamus, 235–242.

Lindgren, A. and Heikkinen, A. (eds) (2004) *Social Competences in Vocational and Continuing Education*, Bern: Peter Lang.

Murto, L., Rautniemi, L., Fredriksson, K., Ikonen, S., Mäntysaari, M., Niemi, L., Paldanius, K., Parkkinen, T., Tulva, T., Ylönen, F. and Saari, S. (2004) 'Eettisyyttä, elastisuutta ja elämää', *Korkeakoulujen arviointineuvoston julkaisuja*, 5, Helsinki.

Niiranen-Linkama, P. (2005) 'Sosiaalisen transformaatio sosiaalialan asiantuntijuuden diskurssissa', *Jyväskylä Studies in Education, Psychology and Social Research*, 272, University of Jyväskylä.

Opetusministeriö (2007) 'Sosiaalialan korkeakoulutuksen suunta', *Opetusministeriön työryhmämuistioita ja selvityksiä*, 43, Helsinki.

Satka, M. (1995) 'Making social citizenship: Conceptual practices from the Finnish Poor Law to professional social work', *Publications of Social and Political Sciences and Philosophy*, University of Jyväskylä.

Sennett, R. (1998) *The Corrosion of Character: The Personal Consequences of Work in the New Capitalism*, New York: W.W. Norton.

Syrjäläinen, E. (1995) 'Eikö opettaja saisi opettaa? Koulun kehittämisen paradoksi ja opettajan työuupumus', *Tampereen yliopiston opettajainkoulutuslaitoksen julkaisuja. Reports from the Department of Teacher Education in Tampere University*, A 25, University of Tampere.

Värri, V.-M. (2002) 'Kasvatus ja "ajan henki" – tulkintoja psykokapitalismin armottomuudesta', *Aikuiskasvatus*, 22(2): 92–100.

Vuorensyrjä, M., Borgman, M., Kemppainen, T., Mäntysaari, M. and Pohjola, A. (2006) 'Sosiaalialan osaajat 2015', Sosiaalialan osaamis-, työvoima- ja koulutustarpeiden ennakointihanke (SOTENNA): loppuraportti. *Sosiaalityön julkaisusarja*, 4. Jyväskylä: Jyväskylän yliopisto.

Wagner, P. (2001) *A History and Theory of the Social Sciences: Not All that is Solid Melts into Air*, London: Sage.

# Chapter 9

# Adult literacy teaching in Australia

## Rethinking occupational knowledge

*Sue Shore*

This chapter explores the effects of rapid changes in adult literacy provision when a new culture of competency-based workplace training was introduced into Australian workplaces during a period of major industrial reform in the 1990s. Adult literacy provision can be identified by funding source (Commonwealth/state government and industry/community), location (schools, universities, vocational education and training institutes, workplaces and community centres), the curriculum framework in use and at times the industrial/university qualifications of the teacher. These parameters help to define an occupation – adult literacy work – and the knowledge base associated with that work. However, as I show below, these boundaries are anything but definitive.

In Australia, the provision of vocational education and training is something of a patchwork. The Australian Government has overall responsibility for tertiary provision, including teacher training at degree level. State governments are generally responsible for vocational education and training institutes and colleges. State governments also have responsibility for curriculum provision in schools, including a growing number of vocational training courses provided in upper secondary schools, but not the training of the teachers who teach at this level. In addition, there are many training partnerships that operate between publicly funded technical and further education (TAFE) institutes and industry, and between industry and private training providers. These provide accredited workplace training. Finally, there are the community-based programmes that provide support through English for new arrivals and preparatory programmes to access employment and training. These are often local government responsibilities, although funding generally comes from Australian/state government and donor sources.

Adult literacy teaching occurs in different forms across these sites. The discussion in this chapter does not address the specificities of numeracy and English language teaching. Rather, the focus is on how the coordination of changes to knowledge and practice required of adult literacy workers during the 1990s disturbed existing conceptions of adult literacy teaching, and so also the role of university programmes and academics involved in shaping adult literacy occupational knowledge. The implications of these disturbances are still being experienced today.

The chapter has four parts. First, I locate South Australian adult literacy provision of the 1990s in the wider context of a national literacy field that was asserting its role in national training reform. From the mid-1970s representations of adult literacy provision depicted a responsive and passionate social movement with ill-defined boundaries. During the 1990s these descriptions were replaced with tightly prescribed Australian and state government-funded programs delivering competency-based curricula. This section traces this shift in terms of a struggle over adult literacy workers' occupational knowledge.

Next, using a methodological approach that understands memory and experience as socially constructed, multi-vocal, textually mediated and enmeshed in interventionist discourses of the modern state (Smith 1999; Yeatman 1990), I revisit my work as an early career academic engaged in bringing to the surface the contested meanings of adult literacy teaching. The accounts of academic work offered in the next two sections link occupational knowledge as a site of struggle within university sites that provide opportunities to 'mobilise contradictions' (Yeatman 1990: 161) inherent in the shifts in adult literacy provision noted above. I discuss the changes to knowledge and practice required of 'adult literacy' workers and how they disturbed my work, developing the accounts in relation to two issues: recognition of prior learning and support for practitioner research networks. These accounts show how I mobilised contradictions in processes that produced 'official' accounts of occupational knowledge. The work described in these two sections was not 'other' to vocational work.

Rather, it was an engagement with texts, organisations and workers that understood 'fitting in' with training reform as a transforming politics necessary in generating occupational knowledge that was truly a reflection of the complex mix of practices mobilised by adult literacy workers.

The final section reflects on this story of the coordination of occupational knowledge in a field characterised by multiple delivery sites. I argue that there is a continuing need to track the decisions that created hard and fast boundaries between sectors, vocational qualifications and forms of knowledge and understanding.

## Occupational knowledge: then and now

Potted histories are always partial. The following account positions my work as an adult education academic and adult literacy researcher during the 1990s in relation to my occupational history as a community educator during the 1970s and 1980s. Government-funded literacy programmes were in their infancy in the 1970s and relied heavily on volunteer tutoring: a situation which is still current for most community programmes delivered in South Australia. Across Australia in the 1970s and 1980s, the patterns of employment and provision looked different, depending on the state in which one lived (see, for example, Lo Bianco and Wickert 2001). In common with others who entered the field (Moyse 2005: 3), I also 'fell' into adult literacy work, first as a volunteer and then paid tutor and coordinator of volunteers. This was a common point of entry alongside 'remedial' teachers, community activists and women seeking to return to the workforce after periods caring for children. Teaching qualifications for employment varied. So qualifications gained for the schooling sector or a generalist university degree (in my case a science degree) were often balanced by 'life experience' and capacity to understand the distinctive learning contexts associated with second chance learners.

During the late 1980s and throughout the 1990s changes in the organisation and experience of work, as well as changes within workplaces, emphasised the nexus between adult literacy practices, vocational training and workplace learning. I do not want to underplay the substantial changes that took place during this period, culturally, economically, socially and politically. In South Australia, for example, a broadly based social movement, located in 'outbuildings' of TAFE campuses and some community and neighbourhood houses, was reconfigured as a profession integral to the training reform agenda sweeping the country. Rather, my focus is on how, over a little more than two decades from the late 1970s to the early 2000s, the work of adult literacy educators was re-organised almost beyond recognition. Insights from the 'New Literacy Studies' (Barton *et al.* 2000) had challenged the view of literacy as an autonomous set of skills, gained in school and applied to work and life. A second major influence was the problematic, yet powerfully argued, connections between literacy, learning and earning. Australia participated in an international survey investigating literacy and the economy (Australian Bureau of Statistics 1997), but it was the local reporting of the economic costs of 'illiteracy' and the barriers presented for training reform that galvanised industry groups to action. A third influence was the necessary alignment of adult literacy occupational knowledge with parallel processes of qualifications development within the vocational sector. At national and state levels, these and other developments mobilised an ever-shifting alliance of practitioners, academics, public servants, community workers and unionists seeking a policy commitment to adult literacy. This manifested as the 'Australian Language and Literacy Policy' (Department of Employment, Education and Training 1991), a national signpost for state and Australian government responses to literacy problems that were, by the early 1990s, well recognised. The 'National Collaborative Adult English Language and Literacy Strategy' (Adult Literacy Information Office 1993) provided the national policy context to secure state government commitments. At this time, there were no clearly defined occupational pathways, professional competencies or nationally agreed qualifications benchmarks for adult literacy workers. Few universities provided specialised language literacy and numeracy teaching qualifications and the research knowledge about practice was thinly documented and often imported from other countries. What was written often took a 'national' view reflecting developments in the vocational sector more broadly as Australia attempted to build a 'national' training system. As such, the locally situated ways in which an adult literacy agenda evolved across the 1990s was absorbed into national priorities for training reform and national narratives of policy change.

Prior to the 1990 reforms, there was no national agreement on what constituted adult language literacy and numeracy competence for learners, nor were there any national agreements about assessment and reporting practices. Curriculum content was often devised in response to a broad range of work, family and community responsibilities. Assessments were often purpose-based, for example to gain a driving licence. Now there were a range of initiatives (see Lo Bianco and Wickert 2001). A significant change at the time involved the shift from a curriculum delivered by teachers with a fair degree of autonomy to a competency-based curriculum with space for pedagogical negotiation, albeit coordinated via the language of elements, units and performance criteria. Coordination of learning and reporting via nationally consistent texts (see for example Coates et al. 1995 and Cope et al. 1994) was accompanied by parallel coordination of the 'occupational knowledge' required to teach adult literacy.

While governments required evidence that those delivering literacy provision were qualified, adult literacy activists also had a vested interest in contributing to the distinctive occupational knowledge that constituted adult literacy work. A profusion of projects on occupational knowledge were funded across the 1990s and into the early 2000s. Scheeres et al. (1993) generated practitioner competencies evident from extensive consultations with 'experienced' basic education practitioners. Wyatt et al. (1997) produced a national strategy for the implementation of professional development. This was never actioned because, in common with a number of projects commissioned in the same funding round, it became redundant when Australia experienced a change from a Labour to Liberal Government at the national level in May 1996.

In the vocational education and training sector, meanwhile, a vocational Certificate IV in Assessment and Workplace Training (hereafter referred to as the Certificate IV AWT) was developed to address an urgent workforce skills gap prompted by increased training activity. Development of the Certificate IV AWT was necessarily protracted as it involved identification of generic competencies for vocational trainers as well as substantial sign off from states and territories. The Certificate IV AWT (and subsequent revisions and upgrades – Certificate IV in Training and Assessment, Diploma in Training and Assessment) quickly became a 'de facto' qualification for vocational trainers and established the benchmark for development of adult literacy occupational knowledge. During this period, discussion of qualifications repeatedly looped back to the national training system and the push for national, portable, competency-based qualifications for all workers – including adult literacy workers. The vocabularies of these debates paid detailed attention to two competing notions of competence. One was the 'integrated' conception where the 'aim [was] to identify areas of professional practice in which it is essential to demonstrate competence and then analyse these in terms of the knowledge, skills and attitudes needed by a practitioner' (Scheeres *et al.* 1993: 5). The other was based on identification of tasks and sub-tasks commonly agreed as the competency 'master discourse' informing accredited qualifications in the vocational training system.

Smith (1999) offers a way of understanding the shifts described above as 'extralocal' textual processes that coordinate, order and integrate local occupational knowledge. What this complex of extralocal practices achieved was a way of speaking about local occupational knowledge that anchored it firmly in the understandings and practices of task-based competence valorised by the vocational sector. This explains the capacity of the Certificate IV AWT to generate 'the same order' for speaking about adult literacy occupational knowledge across 'widely different settings of talk or writing' (Smith 1999: 159), including in university settings where it was not conceptualised or delivered. Nevertheless Smith (1999: 158) also argues that 'people enter into practices ordered by the texts . . . and are *active* participants in its relations' (emphasis added). Educators participate in, rather than simply comply with, the extralocal coordination of occupational relations.

From the mid-1990s and with the development of the Certificate IV AWT, the message was clear. Adult literacy provision was critical for training reform, yet any debate about adult literacy occupational knowledge had to be articulated according to the vocational master discourse of competence. Consultations on occupational knowledge stretched over the late 1990s and into the 2000s, with sign-off on an actual adult literacy qualification (Certificate IV in Language, Literacy and Numeracy in Training and Assessment) hampered by the pace and scope of change and the complexities associated with agreement on content across plural delivery sites and state jurisdictions.

During this period the introduction of vocational qualifications for adult literacy workers was portrayed as a necessary yet problematic move. They counter-balanced the previous university sector dominance of occupational knowledge (Thompson and Chan Lee 2001) by providing accessible qualifications for a range of workers. At the same time they anchored occupational competence in the textual practices of lists, tasks and discrete performance criteria and required features and formats of *vocational* documents.

Wider debates about occupational knowledge were assigned secondary status to the quality assurance considerations of a national system. As Yeatman (1990: 173) argues, this strategy 'restrict[s] the scope and development of the *politics of discourse*' (emphasis added), where politics gestures to more than contestations about a social justice/economic imperative binary. In these circumstances, the politics of discourse asserts the importance of spaces to mobilise 'alternative meaning[s]' (Yeatman 1990: 155) and to surface *negotiations* associated with understanding and making meaning of occupational knowledge. From this perspective the ability to negotiate understandings of competence is in itself an important professional quality rarely acknowledged in the process of achieving arbitrary closure around professional standards.

The Certificate IV AWT (and then, subsequent adult literacy qualifications such as the Certificate IV Language, Literacy and Numeracy) mobilised boundaries around official and marginal occupational knowledges, based on the premise that demonstration of fragments of occupational knowledge would in time build professional competence.

Other professional development continued to be available including specific adult literacy courses in undergraduate programmes and specialised postgraduate qualifications in language and literacy. Delivered within the higher education sector these programmes, unlike those delivered through TAFE or other vocational education providers, were not required to construct all new learning via documents that identified specific competency-based units broken down into discrete tasks and a bewildering array of 'range statements' associated with the contexts in which competence might be demonstrated. But the higher education sector was simultaneously experiencing major restructuring that presented other challenges. Education faculties across the country were 'downsizing'. Academic labour was scrutinised via a series of higher education reviews of teaching, research and service outcomes. A new fee structure for university enrolment made it difficult for universities to speedily allocate targeted places for adult literacy workers and for workers in a highly casualised sector to take up university study. Just as Australian workplaces were coming to see the need for skilled adult literacy workers, the scope of preparation and range of opportunities to engage with universities diminished.

Short accounts of changes in policy directions, such as the above, often gloss over the realities of how national priorities are negotiated locally. Nevertheless, some enduring themes can be recognised: literacy was essential for training reform; there was a need for a skilled adult literacy workforce able to meet the increasing demand for on-the-job literacy training, stand-alone preparatory courses and integrated approaches where literacy workers would team-teach with an industry trainer whose occupational knowledge may well be in plumbing, carpentry, hospitality or business studies. What can also be discerned is a 'politics of inclusion and exclusion' (Yeatman 1990: 155) – of what knowledge becomes valued and what de-valued – in negotiating what counts as occupational knowledge.

I experienced the discursive contradictions of these challenges at two levels: as an adult education academic responsible for undergraduate programmes and as an adult literacy researcher with vested interests in the development of a 'matrix' of activities to promote professional development and renewal (Shore and Zannettino 2002: 49), that recognised the distinctive occupational knowledge required in diverse sites and across one's career. Such an approach requires substantial cross-sectoral collaboration, given the limited chance of any single organisation being able to deliver on such a broad range of goals. In the following section I describe how I responded to these experiences of disturbed academic work by mobilising two forms of university work to explore alternative understandings of occupational knowledge not easily accessed via vocational competency statements.

## Working the discursive contradictions

So far in this chapter I have briefly sketched the ways in which changes to occupational knowledge were coordinated via a range of activities: government intervention, sponsored research projects, stakeholder activism and everyday practices required to enact a national training system. I have also noted that these more visible activities were accompanied by a parallel set of less visible 'coordinating and organising practices' that anchored understandings of occupational knowledge in prior concepts of efficiency and effectiveness representative of the master discourse of task-based notions of competency. These organising practices disturbed the ways I, as a university academic, could engage in debates about what counted as occupational knowledge for adult literacy workers. Spaces that recognised the 'dialogical' character of texts (Yeatman 1990: 165) – yes, even vocational texts – could be created even though this was difficult given the conditions of the time. In this and the following section I outline two ways in which I used a university space to debate adult literacy occupational knowledge.

Since 1989 I have taught in an adult education undergraduate programme that acknowledges the philosophical *and* pedagogical importance of prior learning. Specific sections of the programme identified where prior occupational knowledge would be recognised. This generated two specific practices: articulation and credit transfer. Articulation involved formal arrangements between sectors where whole programmes from one sector (vocational education and training or university) provided entry into and credit for substantial study within a programme offered by another sector. Credit transfer involved recognition of credentialed and uncredentialed learning. In assessing claims for credit, one had to come to terms with the notion of an 'equivalent'. Assessing equivalence was further confounded by notions of competence (and hence equivalence) within the different sectors. When granted credit, students would be awarded 'equivalent' full units of study, and would not therefore be required to complete assessment, nor would they be required to pay fees for that course. However, despite extensive processes and cross-sectoral support for the basic idea, adult literacy work, as an emerging occupation, often confounded the procedures for credit transfer.

An example helps to contextualise the challenges involved. Within the undergraduate programme in the university in which I was working, three courses were classified as 'individual studies'. These units recognise the distinctive character of many Australian adult education undergraduate degrees – preservice by design but inservice in nature. Students often had an existing vocational qualification and may well have been teaching for a number of years. 'Individual Studies 1, 2 & 3' (three courses) represented the educational content they were most likely to deliver within the vocational sector, so enrolled students used these courses to acquire content knowledge. It was, therefore, a relatively easy matter to recognise existing vocational qualifications (plumbing; business studies; computing) as equivalent to content knowledge gained in many undergraduate programmes.

Other courses designated as 'specialist studies' provided opportunities to update content knowledge by undertaking 'new' learning. There was no one-to-one alignment between hours spent on learning or objectives achieved. Rather, the recognition was granted on the basis of a commitment to accumulated occupational knowledge. Adult literacy workers and other students could therefore apply for recognition of existing occupational knowledge in two areas of the programme: individual studies where official expertise was recognised and specialist studies where more recent industry knowledge and expertise was expected.

As I reflect on applications across the late 1990s and early 2000s, I remember that men (as they mostly were) who applied for individual studies with a plumbing, carpentry or electrical qualification had little trouble gaining credit plus three courses towards their qualification, minus three invoices for the fees for each course. On the other hand, adult literacy workers (mostly women) had no legitimate occupational knowledge to present. In the community sector their work was often unpaid or intermittent, undervalued and invisible in relation to ascendant discourses of work, employment and training. Adult literacy workers employed in government-funded programmes may have had more secure employment, but still had to make a case for legitimate occupational knowledge rather than simply 'attach a copy of the vocational certificate' to their application. Even when plans for adult literacy qualifications were introduced, there were substantial delays as final roll-out was caught up in the extralocal coordination associated with vocational qualifications: regular cycles of review, state government sign-off and articulation with ever-changing industry priorities.

While review and revision seemed to depict the permanent state of the Certificate IV AWT, its material presence marked a definitive turning-point in how adult literacy occupational knowledge could be constituted. The textual practices required to produce an official version of vocational training materials were evident in the style guides that dictated how vocational qualifications were to be written and how they were to be assessed. In a move reflecting Smith's argument of textually mediated discourse in action, Thompson and Chan Lee (2001: 4) spell out the contradictions associated with merging learning across the different approaches underpinning vocational and professional development courses:

> The whole genesis was different: the historical context, the training context, the audiences, the purposes and consequently the discourse and text structure. Perhaps more important than these factors, however, were the differences in the approach to learning and teaching which underpinned the [Certificate IV AWT] and [professional] courses.

As a result, when adult literacy workers developed applications for credit within my university programme, they often drew on vocational understandings of competence as a reference point for their claims. Applications listed everyday work activities as if literacy programmes existed in isolation from the broader vocational system. Professional competence was often presented as a *fait accompli*: participation in teaching was by default evidence of learning and competence. Applicants did not articulate the links between the *quality* and *level* of prior learning and the required course objectives in the application. At times applicants provided evidence that they had met organisational goals: submission of a successful programme tender; completion of a programme; assessment of a learning cohort; and so on. However, few provided evidence of the tensions between the compliance requirements of their organisations, the varied needs of literacy learners and the insights from literature that assisted them to *negotiate* tensions inherent in those actualities (Smith 1999; Yeatman 1990).

As the number of applications across the programme increased, I saw how credit transfer might open up possibilities for recognition of occupational knowledge, as it simultaneously restricted recognition of adult literacy workers' occupational knowledge unless it could be verified through a legitimate practice of vocational certification. In the next section I outline a second response to the simultaneous challenges of opportunity and erasure of plurality of occupational knowledge brought about as Australian educators constructed occupational knowledge.

## Negotiating pragmatics and plurality

In describing my own work I have noted how a range of activities and government-sponsored projects concerning adult literacy occupational knowledge were subordinated to the ideological codes and discursive rules of competence and its formatting requirements. At a time when substantial literacy problems were identified in the population, and understandings of what literacy was – and how it was implicated in work practices – were expanding (see Barton *et al.* 2000), the role of universities in negotiating these openings was curtailed in two ways. First, severe restructuring and changes to workloads limited the opportunities for academics to engage in cross-sectoral change. Second, the development of vocational qualifications marked a definitive shift towards a notion of competence that valorised fragmented units of tightly circumscribed *practice*. There was no room for the messiness of doubt in these documents.

One of the features of work in this field that these issues highlight is that, while university programmes were not the only sites for engaging with struggles over what counted as professional knowledge, they where central to those struggles. During the 1990s, within the adult literacy field in particular, there was explicit recognition of a legacy of unqualified practitioners, a thin and poorly accessed research base and poor infrastructure given the enormity of the task at hand (Lo Bianco and Wickert 2001). At the same time, however, tertiary educators were repeatedly bombarded by textually mediated conversations (Smith 1999) coordinating their everyday practices into the competency-based discourses of vocational education and training practice. Policy statements, pamphlets about workplace literacy, websites, conference keynotes, locally organised workshops, forums convened by peak agencies and a vast array of other publications and speaking practices all circulated a core message – also relayed through the qualifications debate – legitimate occupational knowledge needed to be aligned with the quality assurance and competency-based requirements of the vocational sector.

With the demise of the national strategy and national capacity to coordinate state government commitments, commentators noted ever-diminishing funds for delivery of professional development, dramatic decline in postgraduate adult literacy enrolments (Castleton and McDonald 2002; Mackay *et al.* 2006) and diminished funding for state-based services providing specialist adult literacy expertise to agencies and individual educators (Hazell 2002). They also noted the rise of 'workforce development' (often interpreted as improved efficiencies to achieve national training goals) as a primary focus of professional development activity.

A series of Australian government and donor-funded practitioner research networks (Shore and Butler 2006) provided me with an opportunity to become involved, in a slightly different way, in debates about the contested meaning of adult literacy occupational knowledge. In South Australia these began from the various contexts in which educators practised and the questions and challenges they experienced on a day-to-day basis. This 'competence in context' focus was a way of bringing to the surface and interrogating local knowledge *in situ* and thus recognising the plurality of contexts in which adult literacy teaching took place.

In evaluations of the networks, participants expressed their key learning as changes to practice and changes in the knowledge base that informed decisions about provision. Developing a wider knowledge base about provision had two dimensions: it clarified what people were intuitively aware of and enabled them to articulate more explicitly the kind of knowledge built from close contact with a group of learners in a learning setting. On the other hand, they reported that they had also developed a wider knowledge base about provision because the discussions included people from contexts other than their own. People from community houses and manufacturing, as well as private consultants, used plurality as a way of understanding their work without diluting their focus on the distinctive occupational knowledge required for their contexts. Here was a space with the potential to generate 'a politics of lateral connections, of permeable boundaries between contexts, and of the multiplication of relevant contexts' (Yeatman 1990: 157).

The diversity of provision gave participants the opportunity to interrupt the hard and fast boundaries generated by working in a particular site (a workplace or a community centre) or delivering a particular curriculum. Growing out of this were discussions that had no immediate place in a competency-based curriculum but were clearly central to how adult literacy workers and learners participated in work. Educators associated with the South Australian research network argued that these discussions helped them make sense of those aspects of their work that often made them feel 'out of synch' with the new training culture. They talked about the 'clothing literacies' they adopted to 'fit in' in their respective industry, policy or educational context: black suits for policy work, pragmatic clothes for the factory floor, not overly dressy when working in situations of extreme disadvantage. These discussions revealed the dissonance between employment options and employment offers available to literacy learners whose own clothing literacies worked against them in many job interviews. In this way occupational knowledge was recognised as both day-to-day work at a site of delivery and as a site of struggle. Beginning with different accounts of occupational knowledge enabled us to trace connections that were simply not recognised, not even articulated, via the textually mediated discourses of competence embedded in the occupational qualifications finally developed and released in the early 2000s.

However, the sheer labour involved combined with other academic demands meant that much of my academic engagement was knitted into individuals' efforts to engage with and understand the dimensions of occupational knowledge. This limited my options to develop adult literacy specialist subjects within the undergraduate programme in which I taught and hence restricted the options for the development of more structured engagement of occupational knowledge within undergraduate programmes.

## Learning from then and now: what of the future?

Recognising and defining the distinctive knowledge associated with adult literacy teaching and aligning this knowledge within and alongside industry-oriented vocational qualifications has remained important as adult literacy workers contribute in substantial ways to the vocational system and negotiate for legitimate occupational recognition within a textually mediated vocational training system. Smith argues that these negotiations are not simply ordained via official extra-local texts and enacted locally. Rather, awareness and competent occupational knowledge emerges in its doing, in its actuality. This has substantial implications for the Australian vocational sector where evidence of change is afoot at the national level. Australia recently experienced a major change in political leadership. In November 2007 the Rudd Labour Government took office. Details of further substantial changes to the Australian vocational education and training sector have since been announced and there are clear indications that literacy provision will be a critical part of future national reforms. New changes are flagged for adult literacy occupational knowledge, in the form of updated and upgraded vocational qualifications (see for example Innovation and Business Skills Australia 2009).

The scope of national cross-sectoral reform is also quite sweeping across the vocational and university sectors. The Minister for Education, Employment and Workplace Relations, Julia Gillard (2009: 5), has indicated this will involve new ways of thinking about cross-sectoral collaboration. 'This is not about bolting on new policies to an already complex system. It is about fundamentally rethinking separate systems and institutions to create better connected learning for millions of individual students.'

In the past, cross-sectoral and multi-agency work drew on broader notions of adult literacy work to legitimise different interests (industry, educator, university and community) and value different dimensions of that work. However, the development of vocational qualifications in this field has done more than establish a 'de facto' qualification as an entry point for debates about occupational knowledge.

Underpinning values embedded in the qualification now permeate all conversations about occupational knowledge and professional competence. This diminishes the ways in which various interest groups can engage in a politics of discourse that connects to broader discipline-based traditions that provide ways of understanding the world beyond the ubiquitous anchors to workplace practices and economic productivity. Smith and Yeatman remind us, though, that these opportunities for negotiation and struggle are not completely erased. We are always there in them, engaging in the actualities of occupational knowledge. Being alert to the productive nature of these actualities, their politics and their extralocal ways of being organised will continue to be confronting but productive work for both those training adult literacy workers and those working in this multi-layered occupational domain.

## References

Adult Literacy Information Office (1993) *The National Collaborative Adult English Language and Literacy Strategy*, Sydney: Adult Literacy Information Office.

Australian Bureau of Statistics (1997) *Aspects of Literacy: Assessed Skill Levels, Australia 1996*, Canberra: Australian Bureau of Statistics.

Barton, D., Hamilton, M. and Ivanic, R. (2000) *Situated Literacies*, London: Routledge.

Castleton, G. and McDonald, M. (2002) *A Decade of Literacy: Policy, Programs and Perspectives*, Melbourne: Language Australia.

Coates, S., Fitzpatrick, L., McKenna, A. and Makin, A. (1995) *National Reporting System: A Mechanism for Reporting Outcomes of Adult English Language, Literacy and Numeracy Programs*, Melbourne: Department of Employment, Education and Training.

Cope, B., Kalantzis, M., Luke, A., McCormack, R., Morgan, B., Slade, D., Solomon, N. and Veal, N. (1994) *The National Framework of English Language, Literacy and Numeracy Competence*, Melbourne and Canberra: Australian Committee for Training Curriculum.

Department of Employment, Education and Training (1991) *Australia's Language: the Australian Language and Literacy Policy*, Canberra: Australian Government Publishing Service.

Gillard, J. (2009) Speech by the Hon. Julia Gillard MP, Deputy Prime Minister, Minister for Education. Minister for Employment and Workplace Relations. Minister for Social Inclusion. The Big Skills Conference, Darling Harbour, Sydney.

Hazell, P. (2002) *And Then There Was One: The Case of Resources Support in Victoria*, Melbourne: Language Australia.

Innovation and Business Skills Australia (2009) *Developing a Vocational Graduate Certificate and Vocational Graduate Diploma in Language, Literacy and Numeracy (LL&N)*. Available at: http://www.ibsa.org.au/news-and-projects/news/tabid/112/articleType/ArticleView/articleId/17/categoryId/2/Developing-a-Vocational-Graduate-Certificate-and-Vocational-Graduate-Diploma-in-Language-Literacy-and-Numeracy-LLN.aspx (accessed 26 September 2009).

Lo Bianco, J. and Wickert, R. (eds) (2001) *Australian Policy Activism in Language and Literacy*, Melbourne: Language Australia.

Mackay, S., Burgoyne, U. and Warwick, D. (2006) *Current and Future Professional Development Needs of the Language, Literacy and Numeracy Workforce: Support Document*, Adelaide: National Centre for Vocational Education Research.

Moyse, B. (2005) 'Discussion on Literacy SA: Teacher qualifications debate', *Literacy Matters*, Summer: 2–4.

Scheeres, H., Gonczi, A., Hager, P. and Morley-Warner, T. (1993) *The Adult Basic Education Profession and Competence: Promoting Best Practice*, Sydney: University of Technology, Sydney.

Shore, S. and Zannettino, L. (2002) 'Professional development in Australian literacy and numeracy provision', in Adult Literacy and Numeracy Australian Research Consortium (ed.) *Lessons from the Past, Insights for the Future: Discussion Papers on Adult Literacy and Numeracy Policy Research and Provision*, Melbourne: Language Australia, 36–53.

Shore, S. and Butler, E. (2006) *Global/local Conversations around Work and Life*. Available at: http://www.unisa.edu.au/hawkeinstitute/cslplc/research/global.asp (accessed 23 May 2009).

Smith, D. E. (1999) *Writing the Social: Critique, Theory and Investigations*, Toronto: University of Toronto Press.

Thompson, M. and Chan Lee, W.-Y. (2001) *Know the Trade, Not Only the Tricks of the Trade: Volume I*, Canberra and Adelaide: Adult Literacy Section, Department of Education, Training and Youth Affairs and Adelaide Institute of TAFE.

Wyatt, D., Janek, D., Mullins, G. and Shore, S. (1997) *A Professional Development Implementation Strategy for the Adult Literacy, English as a Second Language and Numeracy Fields: An Adult Literacy National Project*, Canberra: Department of Employment, Education and Training and Youth Affairs.

Yeatman, A. (1990) *Bureaucrats, Technocrats, Femocrats: Essays on the Contemporary Australian State*, Sydney: Allen and Unwin.

# Part III

# Navigating work-learning careers

# Chapter 10

# An Australian worker navigating precarious work and fluid subjectivity

*John Pardy*

With the restructuring of the Australian economy in the 1990s, the role of education in preparing people for employment has shifted. Employment in services has now outpaced manufacturing as Australia has moved away from protectionism in response to new global economic arrangements. New production practices such as out-sourcing, off-shoring, privatisation and contracted labour hire reshaped Australian industries and employment has now become more precarious. With these far-reaching economic changes, the connections between learning and employment are being reconfigured.

This chapter explores the individual consequences of these changes. It tracks the ways in which one person, Frank, used education to gain more control in his life in the face of such changes. Change in industry and production processes have recreated relationships of engagement in work and subsequently affect the uses of education as a life strategy. As labour is deployed differently – on a less permanent, more temporary and contractual basis – education becomes an important resource in dealing with such change. Learning becomes a life strategy that supports flexibility at the level of subjectivity enabling individuals to accommodate change on a routine basis.

I begin by introducing Frank and his worlds of work and education. Then, using the concepts of identity and subjectivity, I show how subjects navigate change by effecting a fluid subjectivity. Frank's story provides a case study of fluid subjectivity in which he uses education as a resource to build a self with the freedom to move through and endure uncertain employment contexts and episodic work.

Frank's employment history and learning trajectory provides a thorough case study of the differing subjective dimensions associated with the flexibility now required in employment and education. The story of Frank's education and employment experiences are drawn from a larger research project conducted in 2005 that explored the ways in which people used attendance at vocational education training colleges in Melbourne, Australia, to build a workable life. The project examined how the deployment of vocational education was a subjective strategy for the respondents to make their lives workable.

A workable life was understood and expressed by the respondents as a capacity for social participation that was not limited to the educational dividend of accessing employment. Workability involved an orientation to the world that was mindful, creative and self-determining. Frank's story highlights the subjective dimensions of a mindful, creative and self-determining instinct that involved the movement from a manually informed learning to a learning that re-equipped him for more precarious times. Throughout his learning trajectory, Frank's subjectivity shifts to place his capacities to accommodate uncertainty and insecurity in employment on a new footing.

## Changing worlds of work and education

Frank, who self-identifies as a Maltese-Australian, grew up in the semi-industrial working-class northern suburbs of Melbourne. He had a typical education experience determined by his class context and urban location. Frank attended a secondary technical school and, at 17 years of age, was indentured as a fitting and machining apprentice. In the early 1980s the separate stream of secondary technical schooling in Australia provided a well-worn pathway into trades training and employment.

Securing an apprenticeship provided Frank with a measure of security and made him feel easier about his secondary schooling. As far as he was concerned, schooling was intrinsically connected to employment and getting a job. In the mid-1980s, his apprenticeship made for a smoother transition between school and employment: 'School was a breeze after that . . . You didn't have worries about getting a job because you already had one' (Frank).

Yet within 20 years of beginning his 'working life', Frank has travelled through many education and labour market changes. His journey marks the shift from fixity in the form of a seemingly stable and 'lifelong employment' option to a fluidity that demands adaptability and reskilling to cope with sudden and unpredicted changes in the workplace and the labour market. His identity as a tradesperson, once a valued way of being, was made redundant as the manufacturing industries were restructured in response to global changes. Destabilised in tune with the sector itself, Frank's own sense of himself was brought into question. Both work and learning experiences provide Frank with knowledge and identity resources to form a subjectivity with more freedom to move. Frank's education experiences contribute to a sense of self with a semblance of autonomy.

## Trajectories of education reform

Policy decisions in the late 1980s and early 1990s meant that, for Frank, it became easier to deploy education as a life strategy. There were two critical moments of policy reform. These accompanied the rise in education participation to mass levels in both post-compulsory (years 11 and 12) and tertiary education. The first related to the Victorian government policy decision to mainstream secondary technical education on the grounds that comprehensive schooling, with a broader common curriculum, would be more inclusive and equitable and would better equip young Australians in the senior secondary years of schooling for the new worlds of employment. The second policy moment was a set of reforms that promulgated a nationally consistent approach to vocational education and training provision in Australia.

The decision to close Victorian secondary technical schools was justified in terms of opening up opportunities for people to forge career transitions and learning pathways. This agenda was directly connected to changing social contexts and occupational patterns, which demanded new ways of knowing, working and living in a world undergoing changes associated with globalisation and the information and communication technology revolution. It was thought that for an 'information age' a streamed and separate technical education would not provide the breadth of skills and knowledge needed by individuals to ensure sustained employability. The 'Ministerial Review of Postcompulsory Schooling' (Blackburn 1985) argued that

> existing high and technical schools should be amalgamated to give all students access to a more comprehensive curriculum and to broaden the opportunities of students in technical schools. The workforce structure to which technical schools originally related no longer exists.
>
> (Blackburn 1985, Report volume 1: 51)

This reform was intended to redress distinctions about ways of knowing that directly affected people's 'ways of belonging' socially and economically. In the report Blackburn argued that

> the early division of prospective workers with hand or brain represented by the technical/high split and in the structures of post-secondary educational provision has framed a concept of general education which excludes the history and experience of significant sectors of the population, and separates theory from practice and from its application. These twin forms of exclusion – social and intellectual – must be addressed in a new concept of general education.
>
> (Discussion paper 1985: 25)

The effect was to re-define the notion of 'general education' in a more inclusive way. The dismantling of a separately streamed secondary technical schooling was intended to circumvent the hierarchical mental and manual division of learning embedded in the prior split between technical and general education in schools. This step rested on the view that sustained employment for individuals was more dependent upon access to ongoing education and learning opportunities. Individuals would bear greater personal responsibility for ensuring their own livelihood by developing and crafting for themselves the necessary skills and talents that will deliver employability.

In the 1990s these developments were pressed further through national reforms of Vocational Education and Training (VET). The Australian Commonwealth government policy reforms known as the 'National Training Reform Agenda' created a training market whose outputs were qualified and competent employees. The new policy architecture established the 'Australian Qualifications Framework' together with competency-based VET qualifications that were nationally portable with an overarching quality assurance regime known as the national training framework. The currency in this market is nationally endorsed industry qualifications. The commercialisation of VET provision instrumentalised teaching and learning in line with the local contours of employment and with employer and industry requirements. The national policy reforms emphasised credentialism through qualification frameworks at the expense of capability development through syllabi and curriculum frameworks.

Industry restructuring and education and training reforms, together with increased participation in education, have seen the intensification in struggles for employment and a livelihood. More people now than ever use education and the pursuit of qualifications as a response to changes in patterns of employment and to effect sustainable labour market participation. Education, in this context, has become a positional good that can assist people in their attempts to secure a place for themselves in a labour market that is precarious in its refusal to universally guarantee a right to work.

Both the Blackburn report and the 'National Training Reform Agenda' have sought to realign technical and vocational education and training provision, albeit in different ways, to equip individuals to deal with these new contexts. The 'National Training Reform Agenda' was an administrative intervention that sought to harmonise and discipline vocational education and training through qualification frameworks. Using qualification frameworks as proxy curricula occurs at the expense of capability development enunciated through syllabi and curriculum frameworks. The 'National Training Reform Agenda' authorised employability and labour market participation and movement through the (national) portability of qualifications. The Blackburn report argued for a reconsidered notion of 'general education' as a form of learning that would enable individuals to develop skills and knowledge that could be applied in these new and uncertain times.

Technical and vocational learning in Australia was now set betwixt and between policy tensions that on the one hand sought a broader longer-term learning not informed by a mental-manual split and, on the other, offered up a short-term technicist approach inherent to a narrow credentialism. By 2009, though, the currency of credentials and qualifications had weakened as a consequence of the increased participation in tertiary education where more people have qualifications. Using Bourdieu's sociology, Brown and Hesketh (2004) maintain that 'personal capital' impacts greatly upon an individual's employability. According to Brown and Hesketh (2004: 38):

> . . . the concept of personal capital is required to understand how some winners in the education system maintain a winning streak in the job market, while other credential holders lose out. In terms of the middle classes

the management of individual employability is largely a question of how similar cultural resources are translated into personal capital in different ways. And this cannot be achieved without a nuanced understanding of self-identity.

Education has long been a social and economic resource used by individuals to improve their lot. In the present context of precarious employment the struggle for a livelihood has not only become harder, it has become more personal. In some instances education can be enabling but different sorts of education can hold people 'back' or keep them in 'their place'. Employment and educational trajectories in precarious times are characterised by meeting obstacles and attending to changes and disruptions personally. Bauman (2001: 212) argues: 'To work in the world (as distinct from being "worked out and about" by it) one needs to know how the world works.'

## Subjectivity and identity

The resources required by individuals to not only endure but to navigate precarious work contexts are a knowledgeability connected to the self and to the world, a fluid subjectivity. This fluid subjectivity is constructed in and around multiple identities that are not impermanent and are sometimes contradictory and ambivalent. The issues of subjectivity are central to thinking through the role of education and the opportunities for work and employment. Contemporary patterns and arrangements of employment have been recalibrated by the changes in the conditions of capital accumulation and profit creation associated with globalisation. There has been much research into identity, education and employment, especially with regard to socialisation and the vocational induction into occupations (Chappell 2003). The interactions between education, work and subjectivity centre on actions and experiences of belonging and becoming.

In thinking about identity, education and work, the shifting patterns of identity and the larger issues of subjectivity are revealed. Hall *et al.* (1992: 275) argue that 'old identities which stabilized the social world for so long are in decline, giving rise to new identities and fragmenting the modern individual as a unified subject'.

The modern subject in the individualist and precarious sociality that characterises contemporary society brings into focus ways in which subjectivity is formed. Societies are not stable or fixed entities but rather are by definition unstable due to rapid and permanent ongoing changes. Bauman (2001: 20) theorises this epochal change as 'liquid modernity', maintaining: '"Fluid" modernity is the epoch of disengagement, elusiveness, facile escape and hopeless chase. In "liquid" modernity, it is the most elusive, those free to move without notice, who rule.'

There seems to be no road back to a nostalgic past of predictability, safety or security. There are no longer jobs-for-life or any subject positions for that matter that persist unchanged through time and space. The place of education in supporting individuals to recognise and manage themselves through this precariousness is one that emphasises skills and knowledge for the making of selves and understanding the world. Becoming a subject in a context of precariousness requires learning different techniques and deploying education as a strategy to ameliorate the detrimental effects of uncertainty.

How individuals are formed in and against discursive practices are stories of becoming. Subjectivities are formed and defined within and through economic and cultural changes associated with flexible capitalism involving adaptation and the relinquishing of prior anchors of self-definition (identities). Subjectivity illustrates the ways in which individuals are subjects of, and subjects to, history, knowledge and practices. And it is changes in history, knowledge and practices that affect identities anew and underscore broader conceptions of what is entailed in becoming a subject. According to Hall *et al.* (1992: 275), 'the identities which composed the social landscapes "out there", and which ensured our subjective conformity with the objective "needs" of the culture, are breaking up as a result of structural and institutional changes'.

Prior education traditions premised upon mental and manual divisions in learning were dismantled by the mainstreaming secondary technical schooling in Australia. In many instances these distinctions have now been replaced by an occupationally bound credentialism where now there are qualified or unqualified subjects.

Subjectivity is concerned not so much with the making and remaking of identities but, rather, with the making of selves and what constitutes a self in a fluid social context where rapid changes destabilise fixed and solid identities. When an identity is rendered useless or outdated and made redundant there are affective consequences felt and experienced at the level of the 'self'. The social, emotional and psychological impact of having or not having employment affects the 'self' and is well documented.

Subjectivity as a conceptual tool signals larger epistemic changes that restructure ways of being and ways of knowing. Contemporary sociology not only theorises society but also involves an implicit or tacit theorisation of subjectivity. Theories of subjectivity rely on psychological renderings of the individual. In Bauman's sociology (2004: 16), for example, he maintains:

> In a society of individuals everyone 'must' be an individual; in this respect, at least, members of such a society are anything but individual, different or unique. . . . In the question of individuality, there is no individual choice. No dilemma 'to be or not to be' here.

Individuals can and do imagine themselves as different and unique, but their choices are not so much unarbitrated agentic actions as they are markers of individuals under pressure. Individuals in flexible capitalism are required to represent and express certain subjective dispositions by relying on psychical dimensions to do so. Bauman puts it rather bluntly: 'to be or not to be' is no longer the imperative. How to 'be' is the vexing question and an everyday quandary for individuals who attempt to craft a livelihood for themselves using education. The flexibility required of subjects in this globalised era is premised on learning, unlearning and relearning for ever-changing employment contexts.

Employment histories and learning trajectories are frequently understood in terms of an individual's occupation, career and particular work and learning pathways. Given this, subjectivity has now become the focus of, and determinant of, sustainable labour market participation. Following on from Sennett's (1998) etymological exploration of careers as carriageways, such careers and employment pathways are today beset by intermittent disruptions, roadblocks and unforeseen detours. The experience of a lifelong career has come under increasing pressure in a context wherein 'workers are asked to behave nimbly, to be open to change on short notice, to take risks continually, to become ever less dependent on regulations and formal procedures' (Sennett 1998: 9).

Individuals need to be subjects who can rely on their own wits when considering and negotiating employment options and work choices. With the demise of the job-for-life scenario, and the advent of employment as precarious, subjectivity becomes premised upon an agility that is able to maintain integrity and dignity. Having a job now rests firmly on the adaptability of an individual to 'fit into' and 'yield to' the changing contours of occupational categories and precarious employment patterns. This includes the subjective capabilities involved in navigating and traversing current and emerging work ethics and employment cultures.

## Crafting a self through education

For Frank, the subject of my case study, trade apprenticeship was a job. Having a job meant a smooth transition to a livelihood as a certified tradesman. Like many working-class people, Frank's education was informed by a curriculum that mapped out an employment pathway to a trade occupation. For Frank that pathway was shaped through a schooling carried out in a streamed secondary technical school. Frank spent three years indentured as a fitting and machining apprentice before becoming a certified tradesman. As well as achieving trade certification Frank also completed a Diploma in Engineering. As a project engineer, Frank worked in the staff side of the factory that was separated from the factory floor:

> The factory at work is really the shop floor on this side, a great big firewall down the middle, and on this side all the staff offices. The head engineer at our work, the guy I used to spend a lot of time with, was from England, and he just seemed so worldly, and I presumed [he had] an education. And the other engineer was from Oxford in England. I don't know and then with the marketers that I used to associate with they just seemed to be . . . there was a difference. You could tell the educated people and the people that weren't educated. And because I came from the shop floor, it was really pronounced  . . .

Frank's work in the staff side of the factory exposed him to thinking about himself in relation to knowledge, education and other people. Frank came to know himself as a tradesman as his technical and trade education enabled him to develop his technical expertise in metals fabrication and in engineering. Through his employment in the manufacturing industry, Frank was triggered into thinking about himself intersubjectively through the social interactions that made up the employee relations in the factory. Categorising the 'staff' as educated and the 'workers' on the factory floor as not educated provides a stark contrast in Frank's conceptualisation of the divisions between manual and mental labour as represented by the factory staff and the shop floor workers.

Frank had not expected or even anticipated that industry restructuring would affect the manufacturing and production processes in the factory where he was employed. The changes Frank encountered were understood not only in terms of organisational restructuring in the company but were experienced at a personal level. The changes in relationships between workers affected the human bonds in the factory that had a history and broader social and economic significance:

> That was at a time when enterprise bargaining was going through. . . . They persuaded my colleague to go on to the trainee engineering and I didn't want to go because I was too involved with the union. I still had a lot of friends and contacts with the shop floor who were all union and so I still had a lot of camaraderie with them. It's hard to explain.

As a result of the restructuring everything seemed to be coming undone for Frank in the workplace where he had completed his apprenticeship and continued to work. Restructuring meant that employment terms and conditions were subject to new imperatives as were the relationships between employer, employees (staff) and among fellow workers. The changes associated with this restructuring resulted in new patterns of loyalty within the factory, patterns that Frank had once taken for granted as fixed and permanent. These changes to the organisation of production ushered in changes to the way people related to each other in the factory.

Restructuring meant that the imperative and responsibility for the economic bottom line was being redistributed through the factory. Frank, as an active union member at the factory, and with relationships with employees at all levels, witnessed and experienced the impacts of these changes on multiple fronts. Industry restructuring at a macro-economic level in Australia in the late 1980s had micro-economic employment consequences and impacts for Frank in that he felt impelled to rethink the importance of employment in his life:

> There was a lot of restructuring and rationalisation going through the company. And what happened then, they sold the company to an American conglomerate. So there was a lot of pressure to actually go on to staff. Part of the rationalisation was that every six months they'd take voluntary retrenchments. There was just a lot of pressure to move on, so to speak.

Frank eventually yielded to the pressure that existed in the factory to 'move on' and took a voluntary redundancy. After taking up the redundancy, Frank re-entered education. Frank's experience of industry restructuring not only involved disruptions to his employment but also resulted in Frank reconsidering how human bonds inherent in employment contexts connect with changing social arrangements. For Frank his world was changing:

> Between November [1998] and January 1999, I was on the dole. And then I just kept on making more enquiries about the engineering degree and if I had to go through all of that I thought: I'll do something completely different.

Frank pursued what he considered was a 'real education'. As a qualified manual tradesman he went after an education that he thought would provide him with ways of understanding his employment experiences and the changes that impacted on them. He wanted to know what was happening to him and his former fellow workers and to understand why these changes were being foisted upon them. The different people he encountered in his employment at the factory, in the staff side of the factory, provided him with a curiosity about himself and the world. Intellectually, Frank deduced that what he called a real education would provide him with something completely different and set out on just that course of action.

In losing the regularities and certainties of employment, Frank turned to learning in pursuit of a new type of education. For Frank, the pursuit of further education became a series of events that offered him ways to understand, know and address the changes he encountered in his employment circumstances as a tradesman and engineer. Pursuing further education enabled Frank to extend himself as a person by developing his sense of self and understandings of the world. Frank didn't conceive of his previous technical schooling and his apprenticeship learning as an education 'per se'. He believed an education was something that would assist him to make sense of the changes he was enduring: 'I never really had what you would call an education, because it was always in engineering and automotive, and all that kind of stuff at Glenroy Tech . . .'

While Frank recognises himself as technically skilled he was not certain about his broader intellectual abilities. He possessed an intellectual curiosity and sought out an academic training he felt would give him more knowledge.

Frank pursued a liberal arts education in a Technical and Further Education (TAFE) school as the result of a newspaper advertisement. In his words, Frank was spurred by relationships he had initially encountered in the staff part of the factory. Frank explains his reasons for seeking out a liberal arts education as follows:

> I realised when I was at work that there were people that were . . . there were people really smart through education. Does that make sense? . . . It's not that they were any brighter than anybody else, they just seemed to have a lot more knowledge about the world, and why things were happening.

Frank knew they were not any 'brighter' than him but they had what might be referred to as a confidence about themselves and the world. This confidence could be understood as a 'semblance of autonomy'. Frank was seeking from this 'real education' a way to develop and legitimate his views and ideas about his own lived experiences.

Making the transition from technical and trade education to a liberal arts education exposed Frank to worlds of difference. In liberal arts he encountered different people, new ideas, other ways of thinking and, for him, new ways of knowing:

> It was very informal. The types of people were varied. When I say that, I just mean that everyone was the same at trade school. Everyone wanted a job, everyone's working, everyone's doing fitting and machining. They were just the same; everyone was into cars – everyone fixed up their own cars. Whereas at TAFE, it was just all different. People were different.

Frank pursued his liberal arts education because he had a sense that there were other ways of being and other ways of knowing. He pursued this course of study: 'Just to become more knowledgeable. I had great difficulty in writing and I wanted to learn how to write better. And from writing better you speak better.'

Knowing about metal crafts and all that is encompassed in being a certified fitter and machiner had become less valued in the world Frank inhabited. Frank equated being knowledgeable and clever with people who are articulate, worldly and able to express themselves with confidence.

The displacement Frank experienced through the restructuring and the redundancy process fuelled a thirst and hunger for knowing. In his words: 'Not knowing makes you confused about life and the world. But knowing, at least then you have an idea of what's going on and why things are happening, which leaves less confusion.'

Unlike his trade education, there were no certain guarantees of employment or financial return in studying liberal arts. Rather there was recognition on Frank's behalf that clarity and other ways of knowing and being were central to keeping on top of the changes that he had experienced first hand in the factory.

Since completing his Liberal Arts Diploma in TAFE, Frank has completed an honours degree in sociology and politics. On reflection, he maintains that socially and subjectively his world continues to cohere around the same social networks but he nonetheless articulates a difference in himself:

> I still see a lot of my old peers, but it has been . . . I've been able to understand things. Like, I've been able to understand things better now – in politics, for example. I can understand what John Howard wants to do, even though I might not agree with them. It's helped me understand, but it hasn't really changed my opinions. When I read the newspapers for instance, and they talk about structure of society, I know what they're talking about,

whereas before university education, I wouldn't have known what that meant.

Frank forged and renegotiated the multiple identities that make him who he is. His life has persisted through and among the continual changes he has both been the subject of and been subjected to. When asked what he has achieved through his education pursuits Frank is clear that he has developed ways of knowing that he finds particularly useful:

> Well, I am more articulate now. I'm able to write better. I know about history. I know about Australian history – political history, anyway. I know certain classic literatures. I would never have been able to have known before, which all helped me to understand society today.

Frank's family background and the socio-economic positioning of communities and identities change through time and space. The issues of access and equity in education persist in new ways in these times of mass participation in post-secondary education. Frank's experiences reveal this but further highlight the flexible subjectivity now required to accommodate multiple identities and appreciate the external dynamics that render some of those identities redundant. Frank continues to identify himself as working class, Maltese-Australian, a tradesman, and now a thinker and a knower. Frank's employment situation today traverses non-standard engagements as a project engineer, a community development worker and a family carer.

## Learning work in precarious times

It is in a context of precarious employment that the relationships between education and work are being reconfigured. Lifelong learning and the relentless pursuit of skills and capabilities has become an imperative for employability. Credentials and qualifications, as delivered by education providers, are sought out and secured by individuals in order to access employment options and to better understand themselves in relation to a changing world. The labours of learning have become intrinsic to the development of a 'self-hood' for people pursuing labour market participation. It is in this context of self-work that the acquisition of skills, talents and capabilities obtained in the pursuit of education in all its tertiary forms becomes a specific form of work. Participation in post-compulsory education becomes a form of self-work. The changing patterns of employment, careers and occupational identities are bound up with new experiences of employability tied to a new individualism. This new individualism is premised upon a subjectivity that is flexible in a fluid sense, yet remains cohesive in terms of a self that unrelentingly forges and accommodates multiple and changing identities.

Frank undertook an apprenticeship in fitting and machining, then a Diploma in Engineering, followed by a Diploma of Liberal Arts and, more recently, the completion of his honours degree in sociology and politics. The transitions within and between education modes, transitions between trade education, professional technical education, adult and general education and undergraduate academic education, makes Frank's story remarkably compelling, yet not uncommon. The transitions involved in moving between technical and trade education and adult and general education and academic training for Frank impacted on and affected his opportunities for further education and employment. Further to this, these transitions differently position and construct who Frank is and knows himself to be. Frank's learning trajectory could quite easily be read as one person's individual dispositions to particular courses of study. His education is wholly and absolutely a personal matter. Employment is central to understanding and appreciating the pathways, transitions and detours that are inherent to Frank's education trajectory. In moving between trade, vocational, adult and general and academic education spaces, Frank's experience sheds light on a range of conceptual issues that now illuminate what contemporary employability means and how work and learning are being reframed on a subjectivist basis.

Frank's post-secondary education experiences were carried out over a 20-year period and are reflective of the use value and exchange value of educational achievements. Such valuing processes are at once socio-cultural and politically economic. The values attributed to particular types and levels of education are socially and culturally produced through a political economy that differentially awards different types of education achievement. The cash nexus represented by income, wages and consumer participation are the obvious effects of this political economy where high wage, high return courses and credentials represent the pinnacle of education achievement.

Education provision is hierarchically organised in and through the contours of employment patterns that differentially define and value different forms of labour. In this hierarchy, trade certification represents a lower status of educational achievement commensurate with the symbolic values socially attributable to doctors and plumbers or lawyers and hairdressers. The differential valuing of all occupations is historically determined and gendered through outmoded divisions of mental and manual labour.

Frank's education and learning pursuits, while all connected with employment and a drive to develop himself, nonetheless involved purposeful exchanges and productive engagements that were mediated subjectively, together with encounters that were always at once personal and in most instances personable. Education in all its forms requires engagement and is organised around meeting and confronting ideas, practices and people with intent. It is individuals who are rewarded with sustained employment, not groups or classes of workers. So it falls on the individual today to be a fluid, adaptable and receptive team player. Frank's story is an example of an education and learning that attends to these issues of a freedom to move, with capacities to engage and the necessary abilities to perform in a team without coming to unnecessary harm.

## Conclusion

At stake in this discussion is what subjectivities are deemed for inclusion in the employment arrangements of the flexible new capitalism. Those without employment, or the many made redundant or excluded in the new economic arrangements of flexible capitalism, are subjects of, and subject to, economic arrangements that do not recognise or value their particular subjectivities.

Once 'the litmus test of a "good society" was workplaces for all and a productive role for anyone' (Bauman 2004: 11). Contemporary employment, by contrast, hinges on utilising particular sets of personal capital that change at random and without notice. How we deal individually with this depends on our personal resources, mental, manual and material. Narrowly confined curricula or occupationally bound credentialing contributes to institutional forms of power and inequality that reproduce the specific interests of particular groups. The explicit organisation of education along the lines of a mental and manual division of labour is explicitly linked to the reproduction of power patterns based on class, gender and ethnicity. There is now, more than ever, a need to meld the mental and manual learning that characterises the academic and vocational spilt in tertiary education.

Technical and trade education that includes theoretical literacies and an academic education that includes practical and applied literacies is relevant to a world of precarious employment. This results in education and curricula offerings that more directly address, and converse with, the many and varied cultural contexts in which we now find ourselves immersed. Such learnings would necessarily be more comprehensive and immediately relevant to a self with a semblance of autonomy for a 'sociality of precariousness'.

## References

Bauman, Z. (2001) *Liquid Modernity*, Cambridge: Polity.

Bauman, Z. (2004) *Wasted Lives, Modernity and its Outcasts*, Cambridge: Polity.

Blackburn, J. (Chair) (1985) 'Ministerial review of postcompulsory schooling', final report, Melbourne: Ministry of Education.

Brown, P. and Hesketh, A. (2004) *The Mismanagement of Talent*, Oxford: Oxford University Press.

Chappell, C. (2003) *Reconstructing the Lifelong Learner*, London: Routledge.

Hall, S., Held, D. and McGrew, T. (1992) *Modernity and its Futures*, Cambridge: Polity.

Sennett, R. (1998) *The Corrosion of Character: The Personal Consequences of Work in the New Capitalism*, New York: W.W. Norton.

# Chapter 11

# Employers coping with their ageing workforce in Eastern Germany

## Rudolf Husemann

## Introduction

This chapter deals with ageing and employment in small and medium enterprises in Thüringen, a *Bundesland* in the eastern part of Germany. Through a case studies survey we look at the awareness of demographical changes, age-related policies and regional co-operation among owners or representatives of these small to medium sized enterprises. The case studies show that understanding of the issues facing older workers in 'disturbing times' among employers is low and that activities on the level of individual support and external co-operation between enterprises and regional institutions is rather selective but in progress because of regional political activities.

Older workers face not only insecurity, increased occupational risk and uncertainty, but they also face the ambivalence of making efforts to stay in a working environment in which they might be seen as 'disturbers' and in jobs they may not any more feel are any longer their own but that they need to get to a sufficient pension. On the other hand, the employers look with a suspicious eye on the demographical projections and ask themselves how these changes will impact on their enterprises.

## Disturbing work and demographic change

Politicians at all levels, from small town councils to the European Commission, are warning us of the disturbing effects of an ageing society; since they are mainly concerned about the financing of the social security systems, the rise of the average age in the employment system is proclaimed as a political aim, but remains problematic. The theoretical and practical background of this policy goes back to the discussion about 'the third way', initiated by Giddens (1998), who outlined the importance of individual provision for social security and subsistence and the contribution of education to this aim of self-responsibility (Kraus 2004). In the field of adult education this long-lasting process of economic and social change shows features of marketisation and governance (Husemann and Vesala-Husemann 2004). Governance as a concept for social and economic development processes has been transferred to the description of changes in the world of work (Streek and Schmitter 1985; Sol 2005) and to the education system (Ioannidou 2008).

During the 1990s public employment policy, staffing strategies of big companies and trade unions were all in agreement that work-life time should be shortened by promoting possibilities for early retirement. Lowering the average age of employees was considered part of re-shaping the workforce in correspondence with economic restructuring and the gaining of workplace productivity through the introduction of technological innovations and the reduction of the workforce in general. Lowering the average age of the workforce was also seen as making a contribution to the 'humanisation' of working life. In fact, the growing efficiency of labour went together with growing constraints, and early retirement was seen as a condition for restructuring changes in the employment system. However, the working life was highly disturbed by the influence of global capitalism on the business strategies of companies and the growing demands on employees to compete in extending markets. Within companies, the knowledge of how to create working conditions that allowed older workers to stay in employment until the retirement age disappeared. One remarkable effect, still being observed, is that of the low participation of older employees in current or further vocational training (Statistisches Bundesamt 2007).

Current demographic changes in many middle European countries, which can be described as a combination of a rising average age and a declining population, is again leading to higher employment rates for older workers. We have to assume that companies, as well as employees, are having to show some creativity to cope with this challenge. Being aware of these questions the European Commission has launched research projects to look at ways of supporting the employment of older workers. One intention has been to create a better balance between those countries and areas which have already developed solutions and those which have not but are facing significant demographic change (EU Declarations of Stockholm 2001 and Barcelona 2002).

This is the case in Thüringen, a *Bundesland* in the east of Germany with a population of about 2.3 million inhabitants. The loss of population in the present decade is about 5 per cent per year. Two main factors influence this reduction. First, the decline of the birth rate – which will lead to a reduction of school leavers from 30,000 in 1993 to 16,000 per year within the next five years. This also affects the number of entrances to vocational education. Second, young people aged 15 to 25, mainly young women, leave Thüringen for regions in the west of Germany, where they find better chances for education and employment. In the decades up to 2050, the population of Thüringen will decline by 10 per cent per year, while the percentage of older age groups will grow considerably.

The economic structure of Thüringen is dominated by small and medium enterprises, 85 per cent of which have 20 employees or less and a total of approximately 310,000 workers, 70,000 of whom are aged 50 and older. Significant economic growth in this region is not to be expected. Industrial investment has turned to other European Union countries, following the stream of public/European Union financial support.

Case studies have been carried out in several branches of Thüringen enterprises to see how prepared they are for the demographic changes. Staffing strategies, work organisation and personnel development and further vocational training were all considered. Companies' staffing strategies towards older persons were identified as a major focus of our observations. Ilmarinen (2000) describes four dimensions influencing the employment of older workers:

- attitudes towards ageing – reduction of stereotypes;
- patterns of co-operation – possibilities for team work;
- organisation of work according to individual resources – profiting from growing mental power and adaptation of work time regimes to physical needs of older workers; and
- communications culture – possibilities for open communication about technical support at the workplace: more flexibility, compensation for reduced physical abilities, competence and personnel development, career planning, support for continuing vocational training (CVT), including action and experience-based concepts of learning.

## Demographic change and employment of older workers in small and medium enterprises

We concentrated our field research on small and medium enterprises because these companies represent about 90 per cent of all enterprises and employ about 66 per cent of the workforce in Thüringen. Adding to this, small to medium enterprises tend to maintain jobs, while bigger companies constantly reduce them.

We further concentrated on the engineering sector and included the health and care sector in order to get a gender-balanced sample. We assumed that in these sectors it would be possible to work up to the retirement age and avoid early retirement because of health problems. The working conditions and the qualification demands in these vocational fields could be adapted to the needs of older workers. The employees would be interested in, and be able to follow, further qualification and career planning up to the age of 65.

The case studies were carried out in eight companies, the biggest of which had 170 employees. The employment rate of older workers varied between 16 and 61 per cent. In the majority of cases it exceeded the average rate for the region. It should be noted that companies in the study were already experienced in the employment of groups of older workers. We knew little, however, about how this experience was reflected in staffing strategies by those responsible for human resource development in these companies. The field research included partly open interviews with one representative of each company (owner, business manager, staff manager) and a number of employees aged 50 and above. The interviews of the company representatives (seven males, one female) were taken directly at their workplaces or in their breakfast rooms. The interviews with the employees were taken at their workplaces or at coffee corners.

Our study was based on the idea that small and medium enterprises with little formal organisation would need to become sensitive to the conditions of their future labour market if they wanted to ensure the future existence of their company. They would have to develop a framework for their staffing strategy, a set of instruments and means for human resource development, and for continued training. Our assumption was also that these enterprises could benefit from external resources to establish staffing strategies for an ageing workforce if they lacked their own capacities in this field. Based on these assumptions we concentrated our research interests on:

- awareness of the ageing trend;
- support for continuing employment for older workers and their human resource development needs; and
- collaboration with external support structures among employers in small to medium sized enterprises.

## Awareness of the ageing trends

None of the employers' representatives who took part in the study mentioned the current age structure or the ageing of their staff as a substantial problem for their company and a broadly shared assumption was that, in cases of problems with staffing, a solution would be found.

Four interview participants mentioned concerns about finding qualified younger workers and expected this problem to grow in the future. They specified these problems when asked how they would replace older workers who performed certain highly specialised work tasks. They explained that it could become difficult to replace older workers who performed certain, highly specialised, work tasks and who had a high commitment to high quality work. One argument that appeared in this context was the question of salaries and the related assumption that in the eastern part of Germany they could not compete with wage levels in the west. Their assumptions were that young applicants with the required qualifications would have better job chances on the West German labour market where they could expect higher salaries in general. Only one interview partner did not see a problem with the future replacement of qualified staff.

In the metal and plumbing sector, where there were higher rates of older workers, three interview participants underlined the importance of the experience-based knowledge of the older workers as a relevant resource within their staff. This was a far cry from considering them as a problem.

In one case the importance of experience-based knowledge was connected with the age of the machinery. The interview participant argued that older employers were able to handle the machinery on which they had worked for many years and had become experts at keeping them in proper working condition. They maintained and repaired them and, therefore, they were especially valuable workers.

In the social sector we found a corresponding opinion concerning the competences of the older workers. One of the enterprises followed an anthroposophist (Rudolf Steiner) approach of staff integration, which would not allow for exclusion by age.

Seven out of eight interview participants considered that there was no barrier to their staff staying in employment up to the legal retirement age. However, one employer was of the opposite opinion and argued that the type and organisation of the work tasks (outbound work, handling of heavy metal pieces and so on) would justify dismissing an employee at the age of 60. In this company the responsibility for the work conditions seemed to be underdeveloped as the use of assisting tools and gear for heavy work were kept at a low level.

In general, retaining employees up to the age of 65 was appreciated by the employers we talked to because of the human capital investments involved. However, problems were seen with regard to physical strains and the continuous development of qualifications, especially in the IT programming of metal mechanical production and machinery. In most cases our interview participants were of the opinion that it would be possible to reduce the physical strains and that qualification and further training should start at least at the age of 53 or 54 (one company representative thought even earlier) to keep the employees fit and support their handling of new technologies.

However, the interview participants also mentioned that a remarkably high number of older workers wished to take early retirement. This led us to the conclusion that the problem is not only how to improve and adapt the employment conditions to the needs of older workers but also to include their life-course planning and the legal framework in the process of developing support strategies for the employment of older workers.

The employers' representatives generally held positive views on the value of their older workers. When asked to consider a list of 18 positive features of all workers and to say whether each characteristic also applied to older workers, the positive features in the list were identified 35 times as characteristics of older workers. Of the interviewees 33 identified the characteristics as independent of the age of the worker while another 14 identified them as characteristics of young employees. This method corresponded with another regional survey (Institut für Arbeitsmarkt- und Berufsforschung 2002) and the results can be interpreted as a sign that older workers are not discriminated against because of their age and employers do not consider them to be less employable than younger workers.

This positive picture, and the perception of the importance of older workers to their companies, was underlined in the interviews:

- Older workers were seen as the 'backbone of the company', 'carriers of experience' or as 'pillars'.

- Older workers were seen as having high levels of social competence – expressed, for example, in their customer contacts.
- Older workers' flexibility with working time arrangements, in cases of urgent tasks or specialist expertise required at work, was frequently acknowledged.

Apart from these positive aspects, the interviews also brought out a controversial picture about the employment of older workers:

- Work attitudes: older workers were seen to be little interested in innovations, not showing initiative for further education and sticking to their habitual practices in their work processes. On the other hand, they were also seen as reliable, responsible and committed.
- Attitudes towards current vocational training: 'generally' enterprises demanded a high acceptance of continuing vocational training activities from their employees. These demands were often combined with complaints about the (older) employees' lack of interest in new tasks, especially with respect to information and technology and computerised work. Most of the employers' representatives did not see a relation between the ability to learn and the age of the worker. But it was well recognised that continuing vocational training was more often offered to younger or middle-aged employees, since a longer-lasting benefit could be expected for the company. Employees in positions demanding a current update of qualifications were expected to care for their current vocational training self-responsibly and to initiate their continuing vocational training activities by themselves during the course of their working life.
- Sick leave: older workers were seen to be less often on sick leave but if they were it was for a longer duration. Younger workers were seen as being more often on sick leave, but only for shorter times.

In summary: we found older employees were highly valued by the employer representatives who took part in our study because of the older employees' qualifications, experience and reliability. This was seen to make them top performers within their companies. This positive estimation was mostly seen to be due to their level of qualification and the length of their employment. Employers saw remarkable problems in replacing these types of older workers, and some employers made agreements with their older workers to extend their working life by counselling contracts or part-time work arrangements for the period of their early retirement. To some extent employers were afraid that qualifications could be lost 'forever'; they doubted that their very experienced and qualified workers could be replaced by the internal or external labour market.

Aside from these 'functional' arguments, we found more reasons for the appreciation of older staff. Employers were grateful to those who stood by their company during bad times or had been a big support during the period immediately after the company's formation. In one case, the owner said that he would not have started the business without the company of one former colleague. This indicates that a level of social responsibility which is still part of the relationship between representatives of enterprises and their older workers.

## Support for continuing the working life of older workers

Some companies in the study said they used policy instruments to support the work of older staff, especially higher-qualified personnel who could not easily be replaced. These instruments included:

- tandem work, in which there was collaboration in a team of young and old workers. Typically, this was used in those fields of work where physical strain could not be avoided and older workers faced their physical limits more easily;
- younger workers joining work groups 'on demand' if they were needed because of time pressures or other special conditions;
- developing work arrangements that reduced physical strains: for example, switching work activities between sitting and standing or walking;
- avoiding involving older workers in work groups that required high speed and physical strength;
- changing older workers' work patterns from a three-shift system to day-work;
- allowing older workers to change to a different work activity. This allowed the company to continue profiting from the experience and knowledge of the older worker even though that workers might receive a reduction in salary. Quality management, logistics, transport, storage and specialised work in the social health sector were some of the areas in which this was being adopted;
- offering salary increases or additional counselling contracts after retirement in situations where there were problems replacing certain functions; and
- long-term training opportunities if the special competence and long-lasting experience with products, processes or markets was needed by the company.

Discussion of these various initiatives turned attention to the question of the health of older workers. Possible health problems dominated employers' reflections about their ageing workforce. But they also identified individualised solutions companies had adopted. As a general attitude, employers expect the outcome of paid work to be maintained at 100 per cent, and consider this to be a normal duty to be delivered by the employees. The idea of higher or lower periods of work efficiency – during the day as well as during the whole working life – which are more or less to be expected as an ontological fact, did not appear to influence the views of the employers in our study.

The opposite of the support to stay in the enterprise is the support to leave it. In this context we found that offers of part-time work were not often available. Most companies assumed it would be too cost-intensive to put into practice. Other alterations to the worktime, such as reduction or flexibilisation of work hours, were seen as a disturbance in the workflow of the company. In one enter-prise the employees were advised to leave at the age of 60 because of the heavy physical work and the workers were prepared for this early retirement through discussion and mediation well in advance.

The interview participants did not see demographic change as a big problem for their human resource development policies. Nor did it have an influence on their work practice or result in any reduction in their staff numbers. One expla-nation could be that most of the companies had already had some experience with the phenomenon of ageing and could show their expertise in the discussions with the researchers. From their individual perspectives, and the way they indi-vidually approached demographic change in their company, it can be concluded that problems will not lead to crises but will be handled within the range of instruments that have already been shown to work.

Based on early studies, we started our field research with the expectation that participation in, and the relevance of, further vocational training among older workers would be low. In our case studies, however, we found that representa-tives of the companies expected their employees to be active in further vocational education, to participate in 'lifelong learning' activities and to care for planning and participation by themselves in a self-responsible way. They also expected their employees to take part in in-house training activities whenever these were offered – for example, when new production processes were introduced. The employers' qualification demands were, never-the-less, job-specific. They spoke in terms of key qualifications, competence and 'snug-fit qualifications'. They did not see any requirement for higher or various qualifications for functional flexi-bility within the work organisation of their companies. They appreciated high qualifications less than general values such as reliability, loyalty and experience.

Our small-scale research found remarkable deficits concerning the importance of further training activities. Demands for new qualifications were not seen as a reason to have employers prepared, through further training courses, in advance of need. Not even a training programme running parallel with the innovation process was regularly promoted, especially if 'private' qualification activities were recognised instead. To pay for a course in a certain field of current vocational training for older workers would be exceptional for an employer and far from belonging to the set of typical instruments of a company's human resource devel-opment activities.

In our study costs were usually mentioned as a reason, as well as the lack of interest of the workers in further training. It was reported that workers sometimes missed individual activities or were not willing to support the current training activities with their own resources – mainly their time. Another argument against offering further training to older workers was that extra qualification courses would increase workers' mobility and, therefore, also the risk of them leaving the company for better-paid positions.

In relation to the idea of 'lifelong learning', our interview participants held the view that this was a matter of public/policy concern rather than an issue for their particular company. This might be seen as an outcome of the huge, state-funded, public qualification programmes in the 'new Bundesländer' following German reunion. This may have created a culture in which neither companies nor employees understood vocational qualification as a private investment.

Employers were all well aware of one topic. This was the well-publicised rapid decrease in the number of school leavers that will result from the declining birth rates in Eastern Germany in the early 1990s following German reunification. Being aware of the rising competition that this will bring between companies and further education institutions, including technical colleges and universities, our interview participants expected that they would have rather low-qualified applicants for their initial training programmes, if they had any at all. They feared this could result in a drying-up of the main source of staff renewal in their industries given that they had rather high reservations against foreign workers or other ways of coping with the situation.

As a result, we conclude that small and medium enterprises do not lack concepts for personnel development and staffing strategies but – since they know their staff members as individuals – their strategies tend to aim for solutions at the individual level. They are not so much led by the idea of logistics and methods (fixed plans, instruments) but rather by the need for flexibility, direct personal communication and pragmatism. Our discussions with personnel managers and company owners provided evidence of a remarkable interest in questions related to ageing and employment. They said they were willing to test instruments to push solutions in their company. Our impression was that the interview participants knew that their own work day does not leave enough space to think about the special problems of personnel management. Rather, they trusted in their ability to improvise and in lucky coincidents.

## Collaboration with regional support structures

The structural regional frameworks available to support the employment of older workers in the region provided another field for our research. However, the structure of these frameworks does not always say much about their functioning. These frameworks can best be observed in the collaborations, and especially the communications networks, that exist between the different actors at the regional level and between the different levels of actors. One indicator of success is the attitude of enterprises towards the regional institutions; another, the utilisation of their offered support in areas that added to, or enriched, the internal human resource development competence of the companies.

In our study we tried to identify elements of communication that could indicate the utilisation by companies of the existing regional support structures. In practice we tried to investigate the dimensions of collaboration between companies and regional institutions involving labour market processes and qualifications. One line of our analysis looked at the attitudes of enterprises towards the regional institutions in general. Here we found that those regional organisations established to assist the business field of the enterprises were well known, as were the public regional labour market organisations. Institutes of vocational training are known if they belong to the field of economic institutions. If they are situated outside this sphere of influence they are only known by a few enterprises. Labour market and qualification programmes that aim to support the employment of older workers are much less known.

We also wished to find out if employers were willing to draw on external competence to develop an age-related staffing strategy for their companies. Here we met major reservations as the programmes offered at the regional institutes were not seen as appropriate to meet the demands of the enterprises. This reluctance usually seemed to be a result of bad experiences rather than prejudice. One company owner, who was also working as a teacher in a training institute of vocational education, complained about the lack of curricula for the target group of older workers. He generally doubted that the qualifications on offer would count as an essential aspect for a prolongation of work life.

So it was not surprising to find a lack of collaboration and communication between enterprises and training institutions concerned with personnel management. The reasons for employers refusing a collaboration, or for considering it as of little use, partly resulted from cost calculations and partly from doubts about the possibilities of these training programmes transferring something positive into the working life of those who undertook the training. But the strongest reservation might be seen in a rather hegemonic picture of the strategic decisions and development of the enterprise. Where owners see risks about the future as falling on their shoulders they tend to resist external influences.

## Issues arising from the study of employer attitudes to older workers

Our study of German employers in small and medium enterprises supports wider European Union findings that attitudes to older workers remain paternalistic in nature. Although our study was small-scale and case-based – based in one region of Eastern Germany – it indicated that employers' perceptions, attitudes and strategies for supporting their older workers to remain in their jobs remained centred on their perceptions of the needs of their own company and on their own power to manage changing staffing situations as they arose. Wider demographic and other changes that impacted on more long-term planning of personnel management more generally – such as policies that provided access to further education and training opportunities to all workers, irrespective of age and other assistance to prolong the working careers of their older workers – were not matters they gave much thought to.

Decisions about employment or unemployment depend to a large extent on markets, national economic, financial and labour policies. However, policies at the regional or local levels also have considerable influence. At the same time, job decisions still happen at the level of the company. All these 'fields of action' play a role in determining what happens to older workers and to the decisions they are able to make about staying in work or retiring from the workforce. These various levels of policy action can be seen as a communication system, where the employer's and the employee's interests meet and where meaningful solutions are constructed. Our study indicates that the *quality* of this communication process is characterised by the employer's power dominance in relation to questions such as the type of education and training opportunities provided for older workers.

Participation in further education and training among older workers can be seen as one meaningful measure of support for older workers. At the company level it has been shown that participation in courses leading to a formal qualification is minimal among older workers. One reason appears to be cost. Another is the investment in time – a cost to the employer if the education and training is done in worktime, or a cost to the employee's leisure time if done out of work hours. A third reason appears to be doubts over the effectiveness of these investments of time and money. More informal and 'just-in-time' learning is seen by both employers and employees as more relevant to their needs.

The regional support institutions, such as labour market agencies and training institutions or organisations, offer qualifications conceptualised as a market good. However, what companies often want are courses that correspond to the demands of individual enterprises for courses based on existing work tasks. This leads to a mismatch. In situations where regional training institutions use the strategy of offering training courses that correspond to these 'just-in-time' and single company demands of employers, the training demands tend to be short and this places strains on the training institutions and their staff.

Collaboration and communication between companies and regional public support is of growing importance if issues facing older workers are to be tackled in a coordinated way. However, enterprises in our study had high reservations in relation to their regional institutions and collaboration was at a low level – that is, without much continuity and only within a small range of subjects serving special qualification demands. We found that common interests were hardly ever identified between the two groups even though the small and medium sized enterprises recognised that they were not themselves experts in the development, organisation or planning of courses leading to recognised qualifications. Their greatest reservations were towards the labour market agencies – even without knowing much about their programmes. The qualification activities of the tariff organisations were also seen sceptically, except if these organisations had responded to a certain request by an individual company. These findings suggest that greater communication between companies and regional public support agencies is an important area of action that needs further attention.

## Conclusion

This chapter has discussed a small-scale study of employer attitudes to their older workers in a group of small to medium sized enterprises in the East German region of Thüringen. The study shows that employers tend to think in terms of the staffing needs of their own company and few take wider demographic and other labour market factors into account. Decisions relating to hiring, retaining and redeployment of older workers tends to be done in a paternalistic and individualised way. In addition, when it comes to issues such as further education and training opportunities for older workers, there seemed little participation in regionally organised programmes and a widespread lack of collaboration and communication between company managers and regional institutions and agencies.

## References

Giddens, A. (1998) *The Third Way*, Cambridge: Polity Press.

Husemann, R. and Vesala-Husemann, M. (2004) 'Governance as a model of analysis and driving force for vocational and adult education', in R. Husemann and A. Heikkinen (eds) *Governance and Marketisation in Vocational and Continuing Education*, Frankfurt: Peter Lang, 11–29.

Ilmarinen, J. (2000) 'Die Arbeitsfähigkeit kann mit dem Alter steigen', in Ch. v. Rothkirch (ed.) *Altern und Arbeit: Herausforderungen für Wirtschaft und Gesellschaft*, Berlin: Sigma, 88–96.

Institut für Arbeitsmarkt- und Berufsforschung (2002) *Betriebspanel für Thüringen, Ergebnisse der siebten Welle*. Berlin.

Ioannidou, A. (2008) 'Governance – Instrumente im Bildungsbereich im transnationalen Raum', in S. Hartz and J. Schrader (eds) *Steuerung und Organisation in der Weiterbildung*, Bad Heilbrunn: Klinkhardt, 91–110.

Kraus, K. (2004) Education, Social Policy and Governance – An Analysis of the Third Way, in R. Husemann and A. Heikkinen (eds) *Governance and Marketisation in Vocational and Continuing Education*, Frankfurt: Peter Lang, 31–48.

Sol, E. (2005) 'Contracting out of public employment systems from a governance perspective', in T. Bredgaard and F. Larsen (eds) *Employment Policy from Different Angles*, Copenhagen: DJOF Publishing, 155–173.

Statistisches Bundesamt (ed.) (2007) *Continuing Vocational Training Survey 3*, D-Statis Betriebliche Weiterbildung. Wiesbaden.

Streek, W. and Schmitter, P. C. (eds) (1985) *Private Interest Government: Beyond Market and State*, London: Sage.

Walwei, U. (2006) 'Beschäftigung älterer Arbeitnehmer in Deutschland: Probleme am aktuellen Rand und Herausforderung für die Zukunft', in C. Sproß (ed.) *Beschäftigungsförderung älterer Arbeitnehmer in Europa*, Nürnberg: Institut für Arbeitsmarkt- und Berufsforschung, BeitrAB 299, 15–29.

# Chapter 12

# Young adults' career prospects and aspirations in Eastern Germany and the United States

*Antje Barabasch*

## Introduction

Changes in the world of work as well as different approaches towards the institutionalization of the life course have led to tremendous cultural differences in the way young adults view their life and career prospects. Particularly in the phase of the school-to-work transition, future pathways are partially determined by institutions, but the individual mindset that has been shaped through the socialization in families, peer groups and schools also plays a major role in young adults' risk perceptions and planning concepts. This chapter draws on a study of East German and American (US) young adults' views of their life courses and career prospects to explore not only structural conditions in terms of the organization of the school-to-work transition but also young adults' risk perceptions regarding their future prospects of finding gainful employment and stability in labour markets that are increasingly stratified and destabilized in both these countries.

Sennett (1998) talks about a shift away from a linear concept of time. This, he argues, undermines people's ability to predict their futures. They have a growing sense of randomness in which they have lost control over events in time. A meaningful connection between the past, the present and the future is missing. Consequently, the planning of a life course loses its meaning when the future becomes unpredictable (Nilsen 1999). Chisholm and Hurrelmann (1995) label these discontinuities in the process of transition 'structural contradictions' that emphasise that these are fundamental risk factors for young adults.

In the United States the life course is much more flexibilized and less institutionalized than in Germany. The labour market offers a lot of jobs that do not require any formal qualification or only a few weeks on-the-job training with people juggling work and school at the same time. Initial work experiences are mostly unstable and young adults switch jobs many times before making stronger commitments to a company (Arum and Hout 1998). The underlying philosophy in the United States is an emphasis on individual choice (Furstenberg 2003) and equal opportunity (Hochschild 1981). Therefore, access to various educational institutions is generally open to everybody and seldom connected to age norms (Heinz 1992), although certain entry requirements always have to be fulfilled.

Nevertheless, the chances of graduating from college decrease with social status (Bauman 2001; Cook and Furstenberg Jr 2002; Mortimer 1996). The functional perspective in the United States applies to the assumption that markets regulate supply and demand in the workforce, which includes further education (Rosenbaum and Jones 1995).

Regardless of what the situation looks like for a young adult, whether there is a strong formalized institutionalization of the life course or a strong tendency towards individualization, the transition from school to work requires a conscious orientation and navigation and imposes the risk of making wrong choices. The unpredictability of economic developments and new educational requirements generates insecurity and causes scepticism about current decisions and future outcomes. Sennett refers to a loss of control, which is reflected in the narratives outlined in this chapter. Young adults in Eastern Germany who were struggling to find apprenticeships are now concerned about the value of their apprenticeship in the labour market. Their concerns are contrasted with American students in similar technical training programmes who, although their lives are less coupled to formalization, are also less protected by a social welfare state. They still appear to be less concerned about their future. The disturbance that we address in this book is on the side of the East German apprentices, while their counterparts seem to be much less disturbed by economic developments and more trusting in their advancement, based on their individual performance and control.

## The school-to-work transition in Eastern Germany and the United States

In Germany the societal expectations as well as structural conditions determine that young adults need to decide about their vocational training depending on the type of school they are attending at an age between 15 and 19. Between 60 per cent and 70 per cent of one cohort group each year want to start an apprenticeship, but only about 50 per cent are successful in entering one straight after school (Bundesministerium für Wirtschaft und Arbeit 2006). The others end up in full-time vocational schooling, private academies or programmes to prevent unemployment. Some of them try for up to five years after they finished their first school degree to enter an apprenticeship. This indicates not only the high reputation of this step towards gainful employment, but also the difficulties that many young adults face at an early age in transitioning from school to work. Full-time vocational schooling has little value for employers and therefore most of the time serves as a bridging period until landing an apprenticeship.

Those young adults in particular who attended the extended primary school (nine years of schooling) have few chances to enter an apprenticeship (Beicht et al. 2007). There are little employment options for people without qualifications in Germany, and to receive one of the increasingly difficult-to-find apprenticeships puts a lot of pressure on young people. This rigid structure leads to a high subjective risk among young adults (Biggart *et al.* 2002; Evans *et al.* 1999). They are expected to start vocational training directly after finishing school. The underlying philosophy in Germany is a functional approach based on the assumption that a driving competitive export nation needs highly qualified workers who strongly identify with their occupational identity and would become efficient employees, trained to think for themselves and contribute to innovations in the company.

Programmes implemented to facilitate a smoother transition only help a small percentage of the students at risk (Bundesministerium für Wirtschaft und Arbeit 2006; Preiß *et al.* 1999). Every year there is a deficit of apprenticeships in Eastern Germany. By the end of 2005 more than 11,000 young adults had not been placed in an apprenticeship (Sachverständigenrat Wirtschaft 2006). The demand increases with those who have not found an apprenticeship the year before. Nevertheless, what the statistics do not clarify is how many of the young adults who have been channelled into an apprenticeship are not satisfied with the context of their training because it was not their choice. The statistics are also not explicit about placements in full-time vocational school programmes that have little value in the labour market. The situation of supply and demand is complicated. In 2005 only 27 per cent of all companies trained apprentices and 51 per cent of all companies had no permission to train. Of the companies who could train, 22 per cent were not taking any apprentices (Sachverständigenrat Wirtschaft 2006).

Also problematic is the transition into the job market after an apprenticeship has been completed. Only about 40 per cent of the apprentices can stay in their training companies; the others have to seek employment elsewhere (Schäfer and Wahse 2002). Ketzmerick and Terpe (2000) and Lutz (2001) describe the specific human resource situation in the East German labour market as a 'blocked generation exchange', because workers in many companies are very homogeneous in terms of age (Behr 2000; Lippert 2003), so that currently only a few new positions are available for young people. Therefore, young adults need to flexibly re-orient themselves and change their career aspirations depending on the availability of apprenticeships (Granato and Schittenhelm 2004) and jobs. Today it is more common than it used to be that young adults pursue more than one training programme and remain in the educational system for increasingly longer periods of time (Böhnisch *et al.* 2002).

In the United States what is problematic is the low status of vocational education and training (Lewis 2000; Orfield and Paul 1997). Colleges are on an aggressive expansion course even though the labour market does not necessarily need graduates who often undertook a mainly academic training that connected to workplace requirements. At the same time, the low level of standardization of credentials makes it difficult for employers to base hiring decisions on degrees (National Center on Education and the Economy 2006; Rosenbaum and Jones 1995). Schneider and Stevenson (2000) emphasize the importance of aligned ambitions that impact the timeframe for finishing a degree and getting a self-supporting job. The authors point out that approximately 24 per cent of young adults in the United States complete a bachelor degree by five years after high school. Youth without a bachelor degree (42 per cent of those who start at four-year institutions; approximately 85 per cent of those who start at two-year colleges) end up in considerable debt and only a few achieve credentials beyond the high school diploma. There are no reliable statistics about those students who attend technical colleges at some point in their lives in order to ensure their employability and increase their income.

Gray and Herr (2006) write about the widely spread desire of getting a college degree. They argue that this excessive desire for college is not based on academic ability or maturity. It is often not a choice that is even well thought out. While the majority of high school students enter college, a shortage of skilled technicians has evolved, particularly in areas such as information technology, precision manufacturing, electronics production, and building construction. Although most students strive for a college degree, only 24 per cent of all work in the future is estimated to actually require postsecondary education. The authors argue further that the value of degrees in the United States has declined while the value of technical training is underestimated. Many high skill/high wage occupations were actually in the areas of craft/precision, metal/repair and technical support and did not require a bachelor degree. Workers trained in those fields earned more than most people with a college degree apart from those who worked in the managerial/professional ranks. In the above-mentioned professional areas only 133,000 workers are trained yearly, while there are jobs for 455,000 of them. These opportunities are often overlooked by high school students who increasingly think they need a college degree. Jobs that require technical skills are becoming more demanding but higher skill levels are paid with higher wages.

Unemployment in the United States is overall lower than in Germany but cannot be measured exactly because people do not often report their unemployment. The reasons range from avoiding stigmatization to not knowing the potential benefits of contacting the Department of Labour. Especially those who are floundering between jobs and phases of unemployment are little protected and often live on the poverty line. Official rates of unemployment vary between 4 and 7 per cent in most regions of the country. The issue itself is little addressed in the media. Individual workers are mostly left to fend for themselves.

## The organization of vocational or career education and training in Germany and the United States

### Germany

The school system in the German-speaking countries generally follows the European model of free public education and a variety of secondary schools for academic and vocational education. Despite the worldwide acknowledgement of the success the high standardization of the German vocational education system has at a federal level, it contributes to the structural failure in Eastern Germany where training providers are too limited (Furlong *et al.* 2000; Mortimer and Krüger 2000). The completion of an apprenticeship does not offer job security either. Many young adults still leave Eastern Germany and seek employment in the West or other European countries. Additionally, not all apprenticeships provide the same level of job security. Fewer construction jobs, but also a high supply of cheap labour from mainly Eastern European countries and a high number of illegal workers, make it increasingly difficult for young adults to enter long-term employment (Miller-Idriss 2002; Taylor-Gooby *et al.* 1999).

According to a study by Miller-Idriss (2002) weaknesses of the system include the inadequate preparation for the job market in certain apprenticeships. Teachers in some apprenticeship programmes are not familiar with the newest technology and schools may not also be sufficiently equipped with the hardware and software. This hinders young adults from acquiring up-to-date skills for the modern workplace. For students who attended *Hauptschule* (extended primary school until grade 9 or 10) or *Realschule* (secondary school until grade 10) more prestigious apprenticeships are not accessible and their chances of upward mobility are very limited (Pollmann-Schult and Mayer 2004).

### United States

In the United States, vocational education differs in its structural organization, institutionalization and philosophical approaches from the provision of general education (Dewey 1910/1966, 1916). Although vocational qualifications can lead to well-paid jobs and starting salaries – and salaries can even be far above the average salary for bachelor graduates – the field still struggles because of the stigma associated with vocational education and training. In addition, approximately 50 per cent of US high school graduates never acquire a higher degree (Zirkle 2004). New terms such as career education or technical education have had limited success in drawing more students into vocational-oriented classes.

In the United States all students attend high school, but they are often tracked into vocationally oriented classes and classes with lower academic standards or in college prep classes with higher academic standards. Besides the regular high schools, a variety of vocationally oriented schools prepare for occupations. The majority of students are still attending the average high school. A variety of standardized tests are in place to prepare students for entry exams into college.

Students who have attended one of the vocationally oriented schools are inclined to move on to community colleges to earn an associate degree in their respective field. Cooperative agreements between schools and colleges lead to the recognition of prior classes. Students can enter higher institutions of education at any age and stage in their lives. Those who do not fulfil the requested entry requirements can take remedial classes in the core academic courses such as maths and English offered at the intended college or a collaborating institution. Those students who do not move on to college often end up floundering between short-term employments in low-qualified jobs interrupted by phases of unemployment. The youth unemployment rate in the United States in 2006 was 10.5 per cent (Bundesministerium für Wirtschaft und Arbeit 2006). Depending on the availability of vocational programmes in the individual high school, students can acquire an entry degree into a variety of occupations such as car mechanic, cosmetologist or carpenter.

An advantage of the US system is the flexibility of the school-to-work system that supports upward mobility. Students always have chances to move on to another college and pursue higher degrees of education. The average age at community colleges is 29 years. For the most part vocational training is offered in school-based programmes. Only 1 per cent of the students attend apprenticeships which are usually offered by unions.

Overall, the educational system in the United States emphasizes general academic education and offers little incentives to pursue vocational degrees. In order to attract students to attend vocational classes, high starting salaries that exceed starting salaries of bachelor degree students are used as an argument. Workers in their mid-twenties and older who have experienced a variety of workplaces are more inclined to pursue such programmes because they have often acquired an understanding of what is needed in the workplace. At the same time, employers in the United States are more willing to support the education and training of the individual worker once they appear to be more mature and settled so that the investment would pay off at the end.

## The study

This section will outline some of the results of a dissertation project about the comparison of career aspirations and career prospects among young adults in Eastern Germany and the United States (Barabasch 2006). A cross-cultural case study was carried out in which 129 students filled out a questionnaire, nine focus groups met and talked about the topic for up to two hours and 29 individual interviews were conducted. The different methods of data collection led to contradictory or supplementary pieces of information which were cross-validated with each other and the existing literature. The study followed a concurrent triangulation design that combines quantitative and qualitative data and interconnects them in the data analysis (Creswell 2008). The design of the study leads to a parallel analysis of quantitative and qualitative data. Afterwards, a multilevel analysis was performed that was concerned not only with the structural conditions of the school-to-work transition but also with the impact of various institutions on the individual risk perception regarding opportunities in the labour market and individual life planning. This chapter focuses on some of the major differences that occurred between East Germans and Americans, outlines the results of the questionnaire to three of the survey questions and supplements these findings with some of the results of the qualitative part of the study.

This multiple-case study (Stake 1995) follows the life-course approach (Heinz 1991) which is concerned with the construction of meaning and making sense of an individual's life course as well as agency. The life cycle is defined as a sequence of status configurations. The interplay of institutions and policy and how they regulate timing and sequencing of the life course of the individual are analysed. Case studies are located in social time and institutional space, and 'they are constructed at the intersection of biography, institutional regulations, and opportunity structures' (Heinz 2003: 78). Disruptions in the life course, which include the impossibility of finding the apprenticeship of choice or the need to wait in order to retry to enter a placement a year later, as well as the early experience of unemployment or contact with people who are affected by unemployment, leads to disturbances that can best be described in individual narratives. The labour agency (*Arbeitsamt*) as well as the labour market situation regulate access to apprenticeships and jobs and influence the individual life course. In order to pinpoint some of the discovered major differences between the students in the two countries, answers to questions about the following three aspects are outlined here:

- choice in regard to the apprenticeship/technical programme;
- satisfaction with the preparation for future jobs in the apprenticeship/ technical programme; and
- feelings of confidence about future employment prospects.

Between June 2005 and February 2006, I visited two vocational schools in Erfurt, Eastern Germany, and interviewed students of four vocational dual programmes (Drafting, Office Clerk, Accounting, and Heating, Gas and Sanitary Installation). In the United States students attended programmes aimed at similar occupations. The students in Eastern Germany were all in the second half of their training programme. In the United States, programmes of study were highly individualized so that students were not necessarily with the same peers in each of their classes. Students were also at different stages in their programme of study. Their programmes were of shorter duration than those in Germany. US students also often worked in jobs not related to their programmes of study while attending classes. This is very common among US students who often do not pursue linear pathways and start a vocational programme later in their life. Some of the participants have to juggle work, family, voluntary activities and school. In comparison with their German counterparts many of them were more life experienced. It often took them some years to decide about a vocational programme they would like to attend or, because entry requirements are tested, prepare for entry into the programme. If students fail the entry requirements they can take preparatory classes to improve their test results.

## Results

The population demographics in each country differed quite a bit. In the United States many participants who filled out the questionnaire were older than their

German counterparts. The majority of the young adults in both countries had a working-class background.

Satisfaction with education and training could be one indicator for the feeling of security towards a future professional life. This has a lot to do with individual choice, which can be influenced by market mechanisms and also by institutional limitations. This is seen in the responses to the question: 'Is this the apprenticeship of your choice?' The results are remarkable. There were 36 students in Eastern Germany who said 'yes' and 29 who said 'no'. In the United States, 59 students said 'yes' versus four who said 'no'. These figures show that a large proportion of the East German students were not in an apprenticeship they had originally desired, while most of the American students consciously chose to enter theirs. The results indicate how occupational choice is biographically interpreted in different ways in the two societies – in Germany through an external institutional governance structure and in the United States as an individual choice. In Germany companies and public institutions such as the labour agency regulate the apprenticeship provision and direct students. In America the discourse is dominated by the ideology of independent individuals taking their chances in the free market. East German students have often tried to find an apprenticeship in another field without success and, therefore, had to take what was available. Besides the structural condition of an undersupply with apprenticeships, a weak interconnection between the training institution companies may also have supported a tendency to be dissatisfied with the choice.

The students in the United States had the impression that they consciously decided which programme they wanted to enter. They sometimes had to fulfil additional requirements but were able to pursue studies in their desired field. Choice has a great impact on motivation and the way one views his or her situation as well as individual risk perception.

The qualitative results clearly indicate that many of the young East German adults knew which apprenticeship they wanted to pursue but were not successful in entering. Other reasons for not being able to undertake their preferred training were that they had not fulfilled entry requirements for certain apprenticeships, the scarcity of apprenticeships, regional immobility, health issues, bankruptcy of former employers and not knowing what to do. It is the labour agency (*Arbeitsamt*) that channels young adults into unfilled apprenticeships. Almost half of the students in the heating and air conditioning programme had not found an employer for their apprenticeship. The workplace training was provided instead by the chamber of crafts in a specific workshop. Tobias, a participant in the study, explained how he and some of his fellow apprentices ended up in their apprenticeship (Heating, Gas and Sanitary Focus Group, 15 June 2005):

> For some of us as we sit here the labour agency has organized this apprenticeship. It is in fact a non-company-based training, which means from the Chamber of Crafts [*Handwerkskammer*] here in Erfurt. For six weeks we are here in the school in the Chamber of Crafts and after two years we have to

find a company for one and a half years. Some have already found a company; the others have to stay at the Chamber of Crafts. The plan is to help them finish their apprenticeship. They will be trained by the custodian of the building. Sometimes, they will be able to attend a special workshop. Half of us are affected by that. They are put off.

(Tobias, 18)

An apprenticeship in the dual training is the best foundation for a job afterwards because it is well recognized among employers and because there is the chance to be employed by the company after the apprenticeship. Since the students in Tobias' group did not find an employer, the apprenticeship undertaken at the Chamber of Crafts has a pseudo character and might not be very helpful in finding employment later. The institutional intention was to offer these young adults a chance to receive training, preventing them from being unemployed.

While the individual had to make a conscious choice about which programme to start, societal regulations prohibited many from pursuing their chosen career. Instead, many young adults were forced to take the apprenticeship that was available. They knew that they needed to finish the programme in order to have a chance to access skilled employment, a salary and various social benefits. The general expectation in society is to finish an apprenticeship (or a programme of study) as the next step after school. This imposes a lot of pressure and leaves young adults with no other acceptable choices. Choice is, therefore, experienced as the option for a specific vocation – the realization of this vocational choice, however strongly desired, depends on the availability of apprenticeship places. Particularly in Eastern Germany, where the apprenticeship market has virtually collapsed since the reunification of Germany, these structural deficits contribute to a discouraging perception of vocational training as a waiting loop or even as a dead-end road.

In the United States choice is highly emphasized. Taking an active step towards acquiring further education requires more personal agency than in Germany because people can, for example, consciously decide when they would like to pursue another degree. This requires them to be pro-active negotiators in their own life course and decreases their risk perception of future outcomes and employment prospects. For many young adults in this study, it meant consciously seeking a school and a programme that would suit their self-interests and apply for admission. Some students had heard about this technical college in their neighbourhood and had taken advice from the school counsellor about programmes in their area of interest.

Marcus, for example, pointed out that he hoped to have more job security as well as to gain the necessary skills to have his own business and be an independent entrepreneur (Heating and Air Conditioning Focus Group, 8 November 2005):

I chose it because of the future and stability. I don't have to worry about my company closing and being out of work. There is always work available in this field. You can also work for yourself. You don't have to worry about money. You can be independent.

(Marcus, 25)

Another question in the questionnaire was: 'Do you think that you are well prepared with your courses for the professional life?' Although the majority of the participants indicated that they felt well prepared, in Eastern Germany almost a third of the young adults did not feel so. This can be interpreted as high insecurity about their future employment prospects. A total of 43 German students and 56 US students said 'yes'; 22 German and seven US students said 'no'. Most of the German comments again refer to the involuntary choice of their apprenticeship.

The students who responded 'no' also added such comments as:

- 'Poor imparting of context. They just tell us that everything gets worse' (drafting);
- 'I don't think that this occupation has a future because of computer technology developments' (drafting); and
- 'I should learn more in the company. I didn't learn enough there' (office technology).

Sometimes employers would not allow their apprentices to participate in a workshop due to demands in the office (workplace), while at the same time doing little to ensure that apprentices acquired all the skills and knowledge determined in the curriculum (Office Clerk, Individual Interview, 10 June 2005):

> In our class, there are many who learn the occupation of office clerk but what they do in the company has nothing to do with the occupation. Most of the ones in my class have never made a booking or written an admonition or a bill or something. And I don't understand how the Chamber of Industry and Commerce allows that.
>
> (Ilka, 21)

Ilka expressed doubts about the quality of her education and the institutions which are supposed to ensure it. She claimed she was not trained in the full range of required job skills.

Ellinor was more sceptical about the benefits of her theoretical education for her practical work and suggested having more case-oriented learning in the classroom (Assistant Tax Accountant, Individual Interview, 14 June 2005):

> Well, theory and practice are sometimes so divided that it is not nice any more. The training is relatively superficial. You gain a wide general knowledge, a little bit of everything. At the Berufsakademie [college education that is based on a prior apprenticeship] we will probably learn more about specific cases. That is missing here.
>
> (Ellinor, 25)

The majority of East German students in the focus groups expressed dissatisfaction with their apprenticeship and were concerned with the value of their training. A number of students in the drafting programme pointed out that teachers had told them that their skills, which they would acquire during the training programme, were not in demand at the labour market any more. Therefore, these students were highly concerned about their employability after three years of training. The early discouragement in the apprenticeship contributed to their demotivation to learn as well as to feelings of fear, insecurity and desperation.

In the United States, students spoke very positively about both their school, and their programme, and seemed to be satisfied. These students highly valued the applied knowledge of the teachers, and the engagement of teachers to find employment for their students. They spoke positively about the way the school built connections to industry. Concerns about the applicability of the acquired knowledge rarely occurred (Drafting Focus Group, 10 October 2005):

> School has been great. Our teacher is very hard. Not everybody made it in the first year, but if you show ambition and you work a lot, he looks after you. He has a lot of connections to the industry and every one of his student found a job. He told us that he will connect us to companies . . . And he knows such a lot about the field. He has worked in Asia and Latin America. I really learn a lot from him.
>
> (Kevin, 24)

Differences in the perceived risk among East Germans and US students was also represented in the answers to the question: 'How sure are you that you will find a job with your training programme?'

Thirty-three students in the United States were very sure that they would find employment after their graduation, 21 were sure about it, seven indifferent and only three (immigrants) were not sure at all. In Germany, the situation was completely the opposite. Only three students were very sure of finding a job after their apprenticeship, six were sure about it and the majority was either indifferent or unsure. These results are a clear indication of the high risk perception of career prospects in Eastern Germany, while their US counterparts showed no indication of that, except the three immigrants who were in very different situations to those of the other students.

The East German students were sceptical about their prospects of finding a job, particularly long-term appointments. This was intensely analysed in the Office Clerk Focus Group (10 June 2005):

> At the labour agency they also told me that they have the highest unemployment rate among office clerks because there is nothing available. No jobs are there. That's my biggest concern, that I won't find anything.
>
> (Susanne, 21)

An acceptable alternative for many is to leave their home region, advice also given by teachers and career counsellors. Students in the individual interviews pointed out that they were either prepared to move to West Germany or to find employment in their home region, even if it meant they worked in a completely different field.

In the United States the majority of the students were convinced that they would find employment in the region. Atlanta's unemployment rate is around 5 per cent. Additionally, participants referred to the possibility of working in low-skill, low-wage jobs in order to make ends meet if they failed to find a job that required the latest qualification. They showed a high level of flexibility and little concern about being in another field of expertise. Some students pointed out that unemployment should not even be addressed because there is always work for those who want to work. Another student pointed out:

> We say here, you can always find a job, but at a time you can't be picky. I once lost a job when I was young bussing tables. I lost the job and I was more qualified than a busboy. Two days later I had a job in a car wash. I wasn't picky. I needed a job, whatever. So I got a job.
>
> (Matthew, 27)

This indicates that the students often rely on generic skills acquired through school, work and life experiences instead of qualifications and an occupational identity. It could also be argued that their early socialization that emphasized self-reliance, persistent optimism and belief in unlimited opportunities contributes to their positive outlook. The absence of an institutional structuration of the life course after high school might also support the idea of multiple options and the freedom of choice and contribute to a higher level of satisfaction as well as a lower risk perception regarding future career and job prospects.

## Conclusion

My data show that young East German adults differ considerably from their US counterparts in regard to the notion of choice, career prospects and satisfaction with their vocational training, including the feeling of being appropriately prepared for the labour market. The data collected in Eastern Germany support the notion of a high risk perception that reflects the current critical labour market situation in the country. Strong evidence has been found to support the impression that young adults in the United States seem to be less disturbed by the free market mechanisms. The high level of satisfaction is probably based on the conviction that a life path is the life path of choice. In spite of social developments in the United States over the last decades, which have led to an increasing segregation and inequality in society, the patriotic belief in the system and oneself seems to go along with a certain level of ignorance towards possible socio-economic barriers.

Many students in Eastern Germany had little choice regarding their next career step after finishing school. They were confronted with high levels of unemployment and the discouragement of teachers and career counsellors to find gainful employment in their home regions. Additionally, part of their training programmes seemed to be outdated and teachers indicated to them the uselessness of their training. The divide of theory and practice contributes additionally to the feeling of being insufficiently prepared for the labour market. The critique that there is not a strong relationship between classroom learning and practical application at the workplace needs to be reviewed.

In the United States the young adults were little concerned about unemployment. Their technical college even promised that those students who would not find gainful employment after their training could take additional classes free of charge. The main theme was that everybody needed to 'lift themselves up by their bootstraps' – be an agent of their own life course and always be motivated. Some students seemed to emerge from a rather desperate childhood with the desire to change their lifestyle and gain a higher social status in order to live differently than their family members and surroundings. They had little stability in their lives and were accepting different possibilities. Life plans were highly individualized, short term oriented and did not follow linear patterns. Technical programmes were viewed as a step towards stable employment and higher salaries.

Sennett's (1998) critique of the flexibilization of the life course with the negative consequences seems an appropriate description of the situation of young adults in Eastern Germany. In the United States the participants have grown up under conditions of uncertainty and a higher imposed social risk and are not so aware of any alternatives. They seem to have a relative high comfort level, as indicated by a low risk perception and high optimism. Therefore, the concluding questions of this cross-cultural research include:

- Are societal developments that demand a higher flexibilization of the individual more or less disturbing depending on the point of departure?
- Is the disturbance differently perceived by different age groups and cultures?
- Is flexibilization the main contributor to the disturbance or are structural limitations, as existent in the East German context, the real disturbing factor for the further development of young adults?

These questions could be referred to further-clarifying research.

## References

Arum, R. and Hout, M. (1998) 'The early returns: The transition from school to work in the United States', in *From School to Work: A Comparative Study of Educational Qualifications and Occupational Destinations*, Oxford: Clarendon Press, 471–510.

Barabasch, A. (2006) *Risk and the School-to-Work Transition in East Germany and the United States*. Unpublished Dissertation. Dissertation Abstracts International, URN etc 07262006155533.

Bauman, Z. (2001) *The Individualized Society*, Cambridge, UK: Polity Press.

Behr, M. (2000) 'Ostdeutsche Arbeitsspartaner', *Die Politische Meinung*, 369: 27–38.

Beicht, U., Friedrich, M. and Ulrich, J. G. (2007) 'Steiniger Weg in die Berufsausbildung – Werdegang von Jugendlichen nach Beendigung der allgemeinbildenden Schule', *Berufsbildung in Wissenschaft und Praxis*, 36(2): 5–9.

Biggart, A., Walther, A., Stauber, B., du Bois-Reymond, M., Furlong, A., Lopez Blasco, A., Moerch, S. and Pais, J. M. (2002) 'Misleading trajectories between standardization and flexibility – Great Britain, Italy and West-Germany', in B. Stauber and A. Walther (eds) *Misleading Trajectories: Integration Policies for Young Adults in Europe*, Opladen: Leske and Budrich, 44–65.

Böhnisch, L., Blasco, A. L., Morch, M., Morch, S., Rodríguez, J. E. and Seifert, H. (2002) 'Educational plans in segmented societies: Misleading trajectories in Denmark, East Germany and Spain', in B. Stauber and A. Walther (eds) *Misleading Trajectories: Integration Policies for Young Adults in Europe*, Opladen: Leske and Budrich, 66–93.

Bundesministerium für Wirtschaft und Arbeit (2006) *Youth unemployment rate in International Comparison*. Available at: http://www.bmwfj.gv.at/NR/rdonlyres/65227651-A50C-411E-B7F3-339B1EB93629/0/aminteralqjugend interjahren.pdf (accessed 5 August 2007).

Chisholm, L. and Hurrelmann, K. (1995) 'Adolescence in modern Europe: Pluralized transition patterns and their implications for personal and social risks', *Journal of Adolescence*, 18(2): 129–158.

Cook, T. D. and Furstenberg Jr, F. F. (2002) 'Explaining aspects of the transition to adulthood in Italy, Sweden, Germany, and the United States: A cross-disciplinary, case synthesis approach', *The ANNALS of the American Academy of Political and Social Science*, 580(1): 257.

Creswell, J. W. (2008) *Research Design: Qualitative, Quantitative, and Mixed Methods Approaches*, Thousand Oaks, CA: Sage.

Dewey, J. (1910) *How We Think*, Boston, MA: DC Heath.

Dewey, J. (1916/1966) *Democracy and Education: An Introduction to the Philosophy of Education*, New York: Free Press.

Evans, K., Behrens, M. and Kaluza, J. (1999) 'Risky voyages: Navigating changes in the organisation of work and education in Eastern Germany', *Comparative Education*, 35(2): 131–150.

Furlong, A., Stalder, B. and Azzopardi, A. (2000) *European Youth Trends 2000. Vulnerable Youth: Perspectives on Vulnerability in Education, Employment and Leisure in Europe*, International Expert Report. Strasbourg: Council of Europe Publishing.

Furstenberg, F. F. (2003) *Growing Up in American Society. Social Dynamics of the Life Course: Transitions, Institutions, and Interrelations*, New York: De Gruyter.

Granato, M. and Schittenhelm, K. (2004) 'Junge Frauen: Bessere Schulabschlüsse-aber weniger Chancen beim Übergang in die Berufsausbildung', *Politik und Zeitgeschichte B*, 28: 31–39.

Gray, K. C. and Herr, E. L. (2006) *Other Ways to Win: Creating Alternatives for High School Graduates*, Thousand Oaks, CA: Corwin Press.

Heinz, W. R. (1991) *Theoretical Advances in Life Course Research*, Weinheim: Deutscher Studienverlag.

Heinz, W. R. (1992) 'Institutional gatekeeping and biographical agency', in *Institutions and Gatekeeping in the Life Course*, Weinheim: Deutscher Studienverlag, 9–27.

Heinz, W. R. (ed.) (2003). *Social Dynamics of the Life Course: Transitions, Institutionalism and Interrelations*, New York: De Gruyter.

Hochschild, J. L. (1981) *What's Fair? American Beliefs about Distributive Justice*, Cambridge, MA: Harvard University Press.

Ketzmerick, T. and Terpe, S. (2000) 'Die Blockierung der Generationenablösung im ostdeutschen Beschäftigungssystem', in *Generationenaustausch im Unternehmen*, München: Mering, 177–190.

Lewis, M. (2000) 'Vocational education and the dilemma of education', *Journal of Vocational Education Research*, 25(4): 575–584.

Lippert, I. (2003) 'Handlungsfeld: Personal- und Organisationsentwicklung – wichtiges Erfordernis bei der Sicherung der Innovationsfähigkeit Brandenburger Unternehmen', in *BBJ-Consult AG (ed.) Fachkräftebedarf: Problembestimmung und Handlungsanforderungen im Land Brandenburg*, Potsdam.

Lutz, B. (2001) 'Im Osten ist die zweite Schwelle hoch', *Fehlende Arbeitsplätze und Nachwuchsstau vor den Toren des Arbeitsmarktes. Forschungsberichte aus dem zsh*, 1–2.

Miller-Idriss, C. (2002) 'Challenge and change in the German vocational system since 1990', *Oxford Review of Education*, 28(4): 473–490.

Mortimer, J. T. (1996) 'US research on the school-to-work transition', in *Youth in Transition: Perspectives on Research and Policy*, Toronto: Thompson, 32–45.

Mortimer, J. T. and Krüger, H. (2000) 'Pathways from school to work in Germany and the United States', in *Handbook of the Sociology of Education*, New York: Kluwer, 475–498.

National Center on Education and the Economy (NCEE) (2006) *Tough Choices or Hard Times*. The Report on the Skills of American Workforce. Washington, DC: Jossey Bass.

Nilsen, A. (1999) 'Where is the future? Time and space as categories in the analysis of young people's images of the future', *Innovation: The European Journal of Social Science Research*, 12(2): 175–194.

Orfield, G. and Paul, F. G. (1997) 'Going to work: Weak preparation, little help', *Advances in Educational Policy*, 3: 3–32.

Pollmann-Schult, M. and Mayer, K. U. (2004) 'Returns to skills: Vocational training in Germany 1935–2000', *Yale Journal of Sociology*, 4: 73–97.

Preiß, C., Wahler, P., Bertram, B. and Klar, C. (1999) 'Berufliche Integrationsprobleme Jugendlicher in einer ostdeutschen Region'. *Abschlußbericht*, München/Leipzig: Deutsches Jugendinstitut.

Rosenbaum, J. E. and Jones, S. A. (1995) 'Creating linkages in the high school-to-work transition: Vocational teachers' networks', in M. Hallinan (ed.) *Restructuring Schools: Promises, Practices, and Policy*, New York: Plenum, 235–258.

Sachverständigenrat Wirtschaft (2006) *Berufliche Bildung: Chancen für mehr Ausbildungsplätze wahrnehmen* (Ziffern 690 bis 700). Available at: http://www.sachverstaendigenrat-wirtschaft.de/gutacht/themen.php (accessed 2 October 2007).

Schäfer, R. and Wahse, J. (2002) *Aufholprozess in Ostdeutschland kommt nur schleppend voran. Öffentliche Förderung bleibt weiterhin unverzichtbar.* IAB-Betriebspanels Ost 2001, Reihe/Serie: IAB-Werkstattbericht Nr. 07/2002, Nürnberg.

Schneider, B. L. and Stevenson, D. (2000) *The Ambitious Generation: America's Teenagers, Motivated but Directionless,* New Haven: Yale University Press.

Sennett, R. (1998) *The Corrosion of Character: The Personal Consequences of Work in the New Capitalism,* New York: Norton.

Stake, R. E. (1995) *The Art of Case Study Research,* Thousand Oaks, CA: Sage Publications.

Taylor-Gooby, P., Dean, H., Munrom M., and Parker, G. (1999) 'Risk and the welfare state', *The British Journal of Sociology,* 50(2): 177–194.

Zirkle, C. (2004) 'The school-to-work transition process of students in high school in the United States', *Bildung und Erziehung,* 57(2): 195–213.

# Part IV

# Coda

# Chapter 13

# A politics of working life

*Frigga Haug*

> In the end it's finally all a question of the economy of time.
>
> (Karl Marx 1983: 105)

In this Coda, I draw out important themes from the chapters presented in this book and show how they contribute to a platform for practical politics around the regime of time in working life. I develop this position through three steps. First, I underline what seems to be of importance to me. Other readers will find other aspects of this book instructive. Next I add to this overview by reporting on a study that I completed in 2008 in a similar field. This study, like the chapters in this book, was concerned with the question of what kind of politics is possible in our times. Using this study as a bridge, I take this book's themes, which document what is disturbing with education and work, into a question of time regime. I think it is about time for such a turn, but this does not mean the work presented by the researchers here is no longer up-to-date or of importance. Rather, it is embedded within and preserved in the wider framework provided by the time project.

## The transnational book project

The chapters in this book are inspiring because the authors have recreated the global context in the construction of their book project. They are reporting from different points, from different countries, even from different continents, and in doing so they cautiously and unexpectedly build a global context for themselves and their work together. World development has already taken this step, but academic work must follow suit before it is possible to draw conclusions about learning, work and politics of working life today.

Global high-tech capitalism has destroyed traditional ways of working together, with their habits and all their firmly rusted-on relations across occupations. These changes also disrupt the occupation of research. This disruption is particularly clear for those researchers in the field of work and education who continue to value the way humans grow and develop through work and, hence, the importance of maintaining a relationship between work and education. These researchers are puzzled as they confront the broken pieces of their hopes and also of their whole profession. How can someone, who has understood her or his profession as a contribution to human emancipation, do research today when so many established values and practices around education and work seem not to be valid any more?

What is good about the chapters presented in this book is that the authors are honest with their doubts. They question themselves and, once again, start from the beginning. Some impressive lessons are drawn.

If the disturbing insecurity of work, which people experience through the fragmentation of their work-life courses, can no longer be fully grasped by traditional research concepts, does it not require a re-thinking of concepts? Likewise, if the researcher's own life is subject to contemporary disruptions, does not that academic working life become something to research and a means of understanding work and education in global times? And if this research is to be extended, do those researchers not have to relay what they discover about global standpoints, concepts and research methodologies through their work as teachers in educational contexts?

This lesson about researching and learning at the same time enlarges the empirical sample – as it enlarges the imagination of the researchers. If their own life course is subject to the same disruptions as other occupations, then the process of researching working life turns into a first-hand learning process within working life, which one had hardly dared to hope for. As a result, their own way of life, their own habits and, especially, their concepts in use, which were hardly able to capture the changes in train, are now under discussion.

A new intercontinental sensitivity comes into view and the ruptures, which have almost become too familiar already, become visible as central points of fracture where territory might be regained. The replacement of the concepts of work and education, with all their high hopes and pathos, by employment and lifelong learning, illustrates the way neo-liberal patterns of thinking and practice have set in. The loss is not visible immediately but then shows itself to be fundamental. In the concept of lifelong learning it is the continuous 'new' that counts; in the concept of employment it is self-responsibility to find a job, whereas the older concepts captured work and working life in more complicated ways. 'Work' grasped the human ability to appropriate an individual's own life, which first had to pass through the historical stages of alienation to become a human need. 'Education', as an historic development of the dormant human abilities, was a utopia. Both work and education were critique and perspective at the same time and, consequently, difficult to reflect upon.

Both 'work' and 'education' have vanished in the neo-liberal melting pot of daily functioning without reserves. It seems as if development simply jumped over the historical point of time when humanisation could have been possible on a world scale. Instead of reducing hard work and generalising more time for personal development, the contemporary disruptions in working life have mainly produced unemployment and many poor but many immeasurable rich people. Far from encouraging people to take their fate into their own hands, regulations now come with the promise of freedom, while in reality increasing the lack of freedom.

The chapters in this book tell in their different areas how the loss of identity, vocation, traditional apprenticeship into working life and home can be dealt with. Different concepts on offer were tried out. Sennett (1998, 2006) provided a starting place for understanding the decay of work and personality as interrelated processes through his famous example of a baker. Yet this discourse on pauperisation, which was common for the sociology of industry and therefore also fascinated adjacent researchers in the educational corner, proved to be inappropriate because it grasped the ruptures in working life in a way that reduced them to a farewell song to former power.

Here again it is fascinating how the authors proceed as they construct their research process. Their steps are not only determined by the discomfort of daily exclusionary procedures within world society, but also by the discomfort of their own exclusion from the ideals of research design embedded within academic work. In the end not all are male craftsmen. This is possibly not a loss for those who are doing the researching, and may be not an evil in itself, but provides a platform for research, if one is able to grasp it.

The authors recall that the concept of 'education' originally represented the development of all as a social task. It did not aim at the development of the single individual as self-determined director of his or her life course in opposition to all others, but was speaking about the education of humanity overall. The same is true for work.

Understanding the concepts in this social way redefines the research task. Rather than linking the concepts of education and work to the development of individuals, it opens up the possibility of approaching education and work as means of forming collectives. It is therefore important to concentrate on individuals, and hence on the individual researchers as well, precisely because the development of any individual is the prerequisite for the development of all.

The perspective in this book departs from this apparent contradiction: that, in order to research the collective experience of education and work, the researchers had to research the experience of individuals. The contradiction itself is taken as the driving motive in societal development and as an essential element in the research process and the insights gained from it.

Going beyond Sennett, and in accordance with Marx and Haug, the research team realises that such a logic of contradiction needs a different type of research. It is not aiming to look for the average patterns of decay in working life, but to trace and to support the signs of the coming new. Counter-narratives and unexpected collectives become the new issues. It is not the fragmentation that is looked for in the first place but the dissolution of borders – a dissolution that allows for re-building given formative interventions. The researchers define their task as looking for and speaking out about the possibilities of building collectives, forming new groups for collective agency in their respective areas, so that they might become an option for many.

This process of working with individuals as a way of building collectives is something that I am also engaged in. In the next section I describe a German project that is actively engaged in collective-building as a basis for a practical politics in working life.

## The German research study

Ten women had come together. They were all new inventions of the neoliberal German labour market. This is because they were no longer in wage labour, but were directing small projects as self-employed entrepreneurs.

Their work consisted mainly in counselling the shipwrecked – that is, unemployed persons. They arranged 'one-Euro jobs', procured qualification programmes and created places for possible alternative meetings as a part of the neoliberal workfare agenda in Germany. These policy initiatives mean that recipients can increase their welfare or unemployment support by doing an additional job of social importance for one Euro per hour – like picking garbage up from pavements, watering flowers in the parks, cleaning playgrounds, mending school fences and the like. The aim is to keep up their spirit of employability. And, of course, these self-employed women counsellors are incessantly writing proposals. This is because the state pays their socially necessary work only if they prove that they deserve financial support through submitting project applications. In this way they provide their own work. They determine the content, time and place of work by themselves as they have to experience themselves as absolutely free. In a way they are a model for the new neoliberal way of being human.

In reality they chase through their lives. They are constantly under stress. They describe themselves as totally over-challenged. With these symptoms they and I formed a study group looking for reasons that accounted for their experiences. Of course, they had long followed all the advice provided by the multitude of experts who write about counselling. They had recorded time spent on different activities, prioritised work tasks and integrated breaks in their working lives. But nothing had helped. Indeed, it seemed as if this feeling (for which 'over-challenge' or 'overload' is still an empty term) was getting even worse the more carefully they paid attention to their lives.

In the beginning we tried to make sense of these experiences with everyday concept definitions. As expected, this did not take us very far. Over-challenge means you have to give more than you have. That is, there are more competences demanded from you than you can provide, so something is more than bearable. In short, we agreed, 'over-challenge' has to be defined as something that is too much, and less of it would be better.

It worried us that this term, which pretended to be such a secure diagnosis of a feeling, was actually a non-term, not saying anything exactly. We tried the opposite concept, 'under-challenge'. This was rejected immediately for not offering a perspective. The women wanted to be neither over- nor under-challenged, but . . .

We changed our research method and started to write stories from our over-challenged lives. Strangely enough these scenes from different persons, different regions and different occupational areas all had strong similarities. They all talked about too many tasks that were impossible to manage. They all talked about lacking time or self-consuming time without making any ground. And behind all this was a longing that the old times might somehow come back, when we were still baking cookies, singing songs and smelling Christmas. This regression to a utopia left us helpless in the face of monotonous minute-by-minute daily routines.

For a long time we worked through these texts, examining ourselves as both equal and different at the same time. We were unable to find out what exactly was rendering life so vain, what should be neglected, where to head for. We approached the question anew. We analysed where the individuals spent their work lives, where they were escaping to and what they did not do. In this way we tried, as we had learned, to work out a counter-perspective on what we complained about.

Finally the solution came unexpectedly. Over-challenge appeared whenever there was no demand for the dimension of our human nature. For example, we described over-challenge when we were unable to move our learning forward and unfold untried abilities, or actively care for ourselves and others, or to intervene in politics that influence the conditions of our own action.

We boldly put into words our hypothesis, which later became the title for our work report, that has been published as a brochure: *Over-challenge is Under-challenge* (Haug *et al.* 2009). We feel over-challenge whenever we are not demanded as a whole person, but in parts, fragmented. If this feeling of over-challenge lasts for any length of time, we feel exhausted, which usually is described with the empty word 'stress'. We hear this talk about stress as a heartfelt cry for the possibility of being human.

Contemporary disturbances in working life present these women, and all humans, with a crisis of living. They (we) do not want to miss life, by just being functioning parts of an incomprehensible total. They want to live life humanly, but in greedy working relations the question is, how?

## A possible politics: the four-in-one perspective*

Without an idea – however uncertain – of how a different society could be, it is difficult to put an engaging politics into practice. For more than 150 years, the labour movement oriented thoughts of liberation by focusing on the collective challenge

---

\* Reprinted and updated from Haug, Frigga (2009) 'The Four-in-One Perspective: A Manifesto for a More Just Life', *Socialism and Democracy*, 23(1): 119–123. Routledge, Taylor & Francis Ltd, http://www.informaworld.com, reprinted with permission of the publisher.

of overcoming alienated wage labour. These struggles persist in campaigns for better wages, wage agreements and jobs. The women's movement of the twentieth century stood up against this labour politics, insisting that work went beyond the world of wage labour. Home and family work was a place lacking freedom as well as a place of human care – and that recognising home and family work is basic for a kind of thinking which takes the liberation of all human beings as its goal.

Writing in the nineteenth century, Karl Marx had already made explicit that which was not sufficiently clear in these twentieth-century debates within the two movements: that the development of each individual is a necessary prerequisite for the development of all. Translated into our prosaic words, what this meant is that a goal of liberation must be to allow the capacities that lie dormant in each of us to unfold.

Finally, within all of these – in the labour movement, the women's movement, and in the question of individual self-development – there is a precondition that is so basic it seems unnecessary to mention it especially: the liberation of humans can only be taken up by themselves. It cannot be fought for them. It cannot be executed from above. 'When we do not free ourselves it remains without consequence for us,' Weiss (1975: 226) wrote. Politics for a different society means politics from below.

What is the utopia now? More and more people cannot access the realm of labour or no longer earn wages. Tired, weary and discouraged they see all hope for change in demands for wages and workplace security with those who are still 'labouring'. It is against this that I searched for a utopia that does not displace these hopes for change but incorporates the hope of many others in striving towards dignity in life as a human aim. The art of politics, as I learned recently from Rosa Luxemburg, is not about defining the 'right' goal and then implementing it. The art of politics is about building connections and about creating a space of orientation which can re-contextualise fragmented struggles.

### Life is more than labour

I take my consternation seriously when the government promises to create more work – as if we didn't have enough work about us, necessary for the survival of society, which remains undone. It is not about magically coaxing new work out of a hat but about distributing the work that we have in a just manner. That does not mean allocating workplaces equally to all capable of working. It means instead that all of us can conceive of distributing all human activities – employment, reproduction, our own development and politics – proportionally among each of these spheres.

Since according to our framework we have way too much work, we can depart from a concept of a workday entailing 16 hours. In this workday the four dimensions of life, in an ideal-type calculation, are allotted four hours each. This is obviously not conceived of mechanically, something to be carried out with a stopwatch. Rather, it should serve as a compass to steer each of our steps.

In the first part, in the well-known sphere of wage labour, it is immediately clear that to speak of a crisis, because we are running out of labour, departs from a highly restrictive concept of labour and clings on to this concept – no matter at what cost. Yet from the perspective of a more integral concept of life and its human conduct the situation looks radically different. A new guiding principle in labour politics would mean a necessary shortening of every person's labour time to one-fourth of the time spent actively, that is to four hours. Thus, the problem of unemployment including precarious and part-time employment would be obsolete since we would then have fewer people than workplaces. According to this concept, we all pursue part-time employment and the term itself ceases to be meaningful. We can concentrate on the quality of work and on the question of whether each is provided for adequately in the deployment of their capabilities. Thus, it will no longer be necessary to carry out labour involving the same repetitive movements as in Charlie Chaplin's *Modern Times*. But also the modern form of work in front of the computer screen, exerting a unilateral burden on us, should be taken critically and lead to a concept of labour which joins the greatest possible diversification with the development of all human senses.

### Emancipation is for everyone

Reproductive work, the second of the four dimensions, is not only to be conceived of as work around house and family. It brings together all which is necessary for the reconstruction of civil society. It encompasses work on each of ourselves and on others – that which we are used to defining as the human dimension of life. And that which led Marx (1844), following Charles Fourier, to note that

> the degree of women's emancipation is the natural measure of general emancipation . . . [since it is] . . . here, in the relation of women to men, of the weak to the strong, that the victory of human nature over brutality most clearly appears.

When the weaker may develop in the same measure as the strong, what is truly human surfaces. This also encompasses love. According to Marx (1844/1980: 208), it is 'in the relation of man to woman . . . [that is decided] . . . to what extent the needs of humans . . . have become a human need, the extent to which he, in his individual existence, is at the same time a social being'.

This applies also to the elderly, the disabled, the ill and includes even our relationship to nature. In Grimm's fairy tales the relationship of ecology and help among humans is shown with foresight. An old woman kneels on the ground and sews together the torn-up earth. When the youngest son of the king asks her what she is doing, she in turn asks him the same question. This is how she can help him in his search for the fountain of life for his dying father.

For reproductive and family work this means first and foremost its generalisation. Just as no one should be left out of employed labour, the same applies to reproductive work. All humans, men and women, can and should develop their social human capabilities. This resolves the contention surrounding payments for child-rearing without devaluing the quality of the work that is carried out in this area. On the contrary, only then, in its generalisation rather than its being assigned only to women and mothers, is it possible to achieve our demand that reproductive work is skilled work and as such needs to be learned, just as applies to other labour.

The third area is about unfolding lifelong development through learning, about living not only as consumer, but enjoying it actively and herewith to be able to draft a different concept of a good life. Put differently: we should no longer accept that some speak many languages, dance, make music, compose, paint and travel, that they accomplish themselves as fully as Goethe did; while others ought to be happy if they can read and write at all.

All humans possess a development potential which comes to life out of the slumber of the possible. To activate all human senses should no longer be a luxury only accessible to the rich. Rather, each human being should be able to live according to her or his capabilities. In order to accomplish this, space and time is needed.

For the fourth dimension of life, that in which humans are political beings, the following demand is made: constructing a society does not mean specialisation on the basis of labour. No longer should some do politics while others – and these are by far the majority – must carry the burden of their consequences.

## A new time regime

The four dimensions of human life can be woven together in an alternative model: it is an outline for a more comprehensive definition of justice. This definition can be formulated by women and men today. It takes as its point of departure the division of labour and the time dedicated to each. In other words, it seeks to alter our society's time regime in a fundamental way.

One could decide to work on each of the four areas of labour individually: wage, reproductive, political and individual development. This would, however, lead to forms of reactionary political action. It could, for example, result in a division of labour in which certain groups take up one of the four areas in isolation as their individual hallmark. Some, led by their class consciousness, might take up labour politics which would be effective for those employed. Others would search for a perspective of the past, a backwards utopia for mothers which nails us lively women to the cross of history, as the philosopher Ernst Bloch put it.

A third group might work towards the development of an elite, which could show with Olympic talent what human capabilities can be like. A fourth group might take participatory politics to insignificant areas: they would make television a model institution for the wishes of viewers; they would incorporate the employees into the preparation of Christmas festivities; or they would seek the participation of the population in recycling activities. In all of these cases we can see that each area, taken as the sole focus point of politics, can become downright reactionary.

The art of politics lies in the weaving together of all four areas. No one area should be followed without the others, since what is sought is a political constitution of life which, when carried out, would be enjoyed as truly lively, meaningful, engaging, relishing. This is not an immediate goal; it is not capable of being implemented here and now. But it can serve as a compass for our demands, as the basis of our critique, as hope, as a concrete utopia which incorporates all human beings; and in which, finally, the development of each and every one may become the precondition for the development of all.

## References

Marx, K. (1844/1980) *Ökonomisch-philosophische Manuskripte*, Marx-Engels-Werke 42, Berlin/DDR: Dietz-Verlag. Translation available at: http://www.marx.org/archive/marx/works/1844/manuscripts/comm.htm (accessed 6 August 2008).

Marx, K. (1983) *Grundrisse der Kritik der politischen Ökonomie*, Marx-Engels-Werke 42, Berlin/DDR: Dietz-Verlag.

pro:fem Autorinnengruppe (2009) *Überforderung ist Unterforderung (Over-challenge is Under-challenge). Auf der Suche nach der vergeudeten Zeit*, Hamburg: Argument-Verlag.

Sennett, R. (1998) *The Corrosion of Character: The Personal Consequences of Work in the New Capitalism*, New York: W.W. Norton.

Sennett, R. (2006) *The Culture of the New Capitalism*, New Haven: Yale University Press.

Weiss, P. (1975) *Die Ästhetik des Widerstands: Vol. I*, Frankfurt: Suhrkamp.

# Index

Abel, E. K. 93
adult literacy teaching (Australia) 12,
157–68; changes in occupational
knowledge 158–62, 163; developing
applications for credit within
university programme 164–5;
diminishing of in universities 162;
evolvement of 158–60; future of
167–8; introduction of vocational
qualifications for 160–1, 162, 164;
struggle of teachers to hold open a
space for occupational knowledge
164–7
ageing workforce (Eastern Germany)
13, 186–97; collaboration with
regional support structures 194–5,
196; dimensions influencing
employment of 188; health issues
192; high employment rates of 187;
importance of experience-based
knowledge 189–90; and lifelong
learning 193–4; positive view of and
seen as valuable 190–2; supporting
working life of 192–5; and
vocational and further education
193, 196
agency 9, 27; building of through
learning 134–6, 137
Andrews, M. 65
apprenticeships: Germany 199, 200,
202, 205–6
'art of politics' 13, 222, 225
articulation 163
Australia 10–11, 12–13, 69–82; adult
literacy teaching in see adult literacy
teaching; economic and social
reforms 71, 173; education reforms
72, 174–5; industrial relations

reforms 71; industry restructuring
173, 180; mainstreaming of
secondary technical schooling 175,
178; 'National Training Reform
Agenda' 176; use of education to
effect labour market participation
176; vocational education and
training (VET) sector 72–3, 157,
160, 175–6; and work-related
learning 72; workplace regulation
see workplace regulation
Australian Language and Literacy Policy
159
Australian Qualifications Framework
176
Australian Way 71–2
Australian Workplace Agreements
(AWAs) 70
Ayers, D. F. 89

Barabasch, Antje 13
Barker, K. 93
Bateson, G. 138
Bauman, Z. 51, 177, 178–9
Billet, S. 127
Blackburn report 175, 176
Bloch, Ernst 224
Boyer, E. L. 101
Britain: paraproffesional development
see paraprofessionals; radical redesign
of health and social sector 125
Brown, P. 176–7

car industry: and 'Virtual Workspace
Project' 8, 69, 75–7
care workers 42, 126, 128, 132 see also
paraprofessionals
Casey, C. 59–60, 65

Vehviläinen, J. 53
'Virtual Workspace Project' 69, 75–7, 81
virtual workspaces 74, 76–7
visibility: and paraprofessionals 131, 136
Vocational Education and Culture (VET) 142
vocational education and training: Australia 72–3, 157, 160, 175–6; Finland 51, 52–3, 60–1, 143; Germany 11–12, 109–10, 201–2; and older people 193, 196; United States 202–3
vocational teachers (Finland): and reforms 53; use of ironical counter-narratives 10, 51–66

Wagner, P. 142
Wagoner, Richard L. 11, 87
women: and division of labour 22; Nordic welfare states and collective agency of 42
women academics: mentoring and self-improvement 79–81
women's movement 222

work 218–19; collective organisation of 4; globalisation of 13; sociology of 4–5; and tecnology 74
'Work Choices' legislation (Australia) 69, 70–3
workday 222
work-life narratives: creation of in US community colleges 97–8, 99
workplace: incorporation of virtual into 74, 76–7
workplace regulation (Australia) 11, 69–82; mentoring programmes 69, 77–81; and self-regulation 81; and 'Virtual Workspace Project' 69, 75–7, 81; and 'Work Choices' legislation 69, 70–3
Wosket, V. 136
Wyatt, D. et al. 160

Yeatman, A. 161, 168
young adults' study 203–10; and choice of apprenticeship/programme 205; courses and preparation for professional life 207–8; future employment prospects 208–9